DAT

BRAZIL

Map of Brazil showing the country's five regions. From E. Bradford Burns, *A History of Brazil,* 3rd ed. (New York: Columbia University Press, 1993), p. 11. Copyright © 1993 Columbia University Press. Reprinted with the permission of the publisher.

BRAZIL

Politics in a Patrimonial Society

Fifth Edition

Riordan Roett

PRAEGER

Westport, Connecticut
London

Library of Congress Cataloging-in-Publication Data

Roett, Riordan, 1938–
    Brazil : politics in a patrimonial society / Riordan Roett.—5th
ed.
      p. cm.
    Includes bibliographical references and index.
    ISBN 0–275–95899–X (alk. paper).—ISBN 0–275–95900–7 (pbk. :
alk. paper)
    1. Brazil—Politics and government. 2. Brazil—Economic
conditions. 3. Brazil—Social conditions. 4. Brazil—Armed Forces—
Political activity. I. Title.
    JL2431.R63   1999
    320.981—dc21   99–21593

British Library Cataloguing in Publication Data is available.

Library of Congress Catalog Card Number: 99–21593
ISBN: 0–275–95899–X
      0–275–95900–7 (pbk.)

First published in 1999

Praeger Publishers, 88 Post Road West, Westport, CT 06881
An imprint of Greenwood Publishing Group, Inc.
www.praeger.com

Printed in the United States of America

The paper used in this book complies with the
Permanent Paper Standard issued by the National
Information Standards Organization (Z39.48–1984).

10 9 8 7 6 5 4 3 2 1

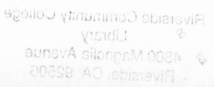

Contents

Tables

Preface

The fifth edition of *Brazil: Politics in a Patrimonial Society* ends with the re-election of President Fernando Henrique Cardoso in October 1998 and the dramatic devaluation of the Brazilian currency, the *real*, in January 1999. The instability in world financial markets finally reached Brazil. Cardoso's place in history will reflect his government's response to the devaluation and the efforts to address long-pending fiscal adjustment issues.

This edition raises as many questions as it answers as Brazil enters the twenty-first century. Will the impressive beginnings of economic restructuring proceed? Will the essential elements of the "patrimonial society" be more susceptible to change or evolution, given those economic changes? Will Brazil finally address the social issues that cast an appalling shadow over the country's national development? There are no certain answers to these questions, but they need to be considered in light of the progress that began with Cardoso's election in 1994 and the introduction of the *Plano Real*.

In contrast to previous editions, the armed forces are a benign presence at century's end. The progressive privatization of the exaggerated state sector in Brazil raises a number of questions and issues about the role of the state bureaucracy in the maintenance of the patrimonial society. And the inability to institute minimal electoral and political reforms indicates that many of the obstacles to introducing meaningful reform remain securely in place.

The key issue for Brazil's elite in the next century is how to reconcile substantial economic progress with an unfair political system and an unjust society. These are important and critical questions for the country's leadership. How they respond to these challenges in the next few years will determine, to a large degree, the development trajectory of Brazil in the twenty-first century.

Acknowledgments

I owe my deepest gratitude to Russell Crandall, who has been a conscientious and imaginative assistant in preparing this fifth edition of *Brazil: Politics in a Patrimonial Society*. His research and assistance were invaluable. I also am indebted to Guadalupe Paz for her assistance in completing the manuscript.

Introduction

As Brazil enters the twenty-first century, one is struck by two sharp contrasts. The first is the impressive program of economic reform that has been implemented in the last decade. While a good deal remains to be done, the Brazilian government has moved quickly to join countries such as Chile and Argentina in modernizing its economy. State corporations have been privatized; tariffs have been reduced; regional economic integration has moved forward; new legislation reforming the public administration has been approved; and foreign capital has flowed into Brazil in response to these positive "fundamentals." But in spite of the best of intentions, the reform program did not address the fiscal imbalances in Brazil. By late 1998, international investors were increasingly nervous about the failure of the Cardoso administration to deal with fiscal reform. The International Monetary Fund (IMF), strongly supported by the U.S. government, cobbled together a major financial support package in late 1998 with the expectation that the Brazilian Congress would move quickly to approve budget reduction measures. They failed to do so. In mid-January 1999, the government was forced to devalue the currency and allow it to float. Fearful of being blamed for the economic collapse of the currency, the Congress finally approved the fiscal adjustment package in early 1999. Nevertheless, Brazil will spend the remainder of the year in an economic recession.

The second contrast is more ominous. While committed to introducing fundamental social reform, the Cardoso government has been unable to do much of substance in this area. Income distribution remains among the most unequal in the developing world. Health care and basic education are still inefficient and beyond the reach of many Brazilians. Land reform has been slow and contentious. What explains the new and relatively vibrant economic future of Brazil—and the sharp contrast to the high levels of social inequality?

In large part, as it will be argued in this book, it is the unwillingness of the political elite to cooperate with reformers such as President Fernando Henrique Cardoso in completing the process of fundamental reforms that will give the government the financial resources to address the social agenda. But equally important, the current structure of political power—what I call the "patrimonial state"—acts as an invisible barrier to the introduction of fundamental reforms. The key players in this drama today are a reform-oriented presidency and a set of political actors at the regional and state levels, working closely with their delegates in the national congress in Brasília, the capital, to weaken or water down reform efforts. They do so because the current system of power favors their interests. And they do so because it is a system that has served to weaken popular participation and the involvement of the ordinary citizen in the affairs of the state. It has been a comfortable situation for the political elite—both during military governments and civilian regimes. The elite is self-perpetuating in that it recruits its own substitutes. It is flexible and very pragmatic. And it survives.

The challenge for the Cardoso government is to find ways to both continue with the needed economic and financial reforms and to address the outdated political structures that protect and serve the interests of the country's political leadership. This will be the principal goal of this book—to comprehend the dynamics of political decision making in Brazil. It is important to understand at the outset that the attitudes and demeanor of the political elite do not mean that change is impossible; rather, it is that change often takes place on its terms. Or, if it is not in its favor, it is often able to delay or dilute those changes.

The political game in Brazil is a subtle one. For instance, those who most oppose change often profess to be democrats. But there is little that is "democratic" in their unwillingness to support fiscal reform, which is the sine qua non for a progressive set of social changes that should benefit the majority of Brazilians. This remains a controversial argument, of course. Much of the opposition to the government's privatization program—to transfer state companies to the private sector—is based on the argument that the process benefits the wealthy (domestic and foreign) and not the poor. It is a replay of the old populist argument that only the state can protect the poor. While there is much to question in the market reform model, the Cardoso government appears to understand that the role of the state, redefined, in the next century will be to reconcile economic market changes with social equity. If it can do so, it will be the first government in Brazilian history to be committed to social development.

There also is little that is "democratic" in a political class that refuses to consider any changes in the electoral system when it remains one of the most confusing—and unrepresentative—in the developing world. These themes are discussed throughout this book.

BRAZIL

Chapter 1

Brazil: A Framework for Analysis

There are certain basic concepts that underlie our study of the Brazilian political system. These are "givens" in that they have been dominant over time and relatively immune to change from outside the system. The purpose of this chapter is to explore the most important of these concepts and to illustrate historically their significance, as they provide a framework within which we can assess the roles of institutions and socioeconomic groups in a broader political context. Among the most important of these are: (1) the concept of elite rule; (2) the maintenance of a bureaucratic state that traditionally has been at the service of the patrimonial order; and (3) the persistence of a social dualism—a gap between the standard of living of the richest and the poorest Brazilians that is as pernicious as it is endemic. I will argue that this intolerable "gap" must now be seen as a deliberate strategy to retain power by the elites as they are confronted with the probability of a reduction in the power of the bureaucratic state that has for so long protected and furthered their interests. The following historical sketch of Brazil is followed by an analysis, in greater detail, of the significance of these variables and their relevance to contemporary politics.

THE HISTORICAL SETTING

The Colonial Period

Discovered in 1500 by the Portuguese, Brazil was ignored for the ensuing 30 years (see Table 1.1 for a chronology of the main phases of Brazilian political development). In 1530, a colonizing expedition, financed by the Crown, set out for the new colony and established São Vicente (near modern-day São Paulo) in 1532. The Portuguese monarch divided the Brazilian coastline into 15

Table 1.1
Historical Phases of the Brazilian Patrimonial Regime

I. Colonial Period, 1500–1822

1. Rule from Lisbon, 1500–1808
2. Rule from Rio de Janeiro, 1808–1822

II. Empire, 1822–1889

1. Pedro I, 1822–1831
2. Regency, 1831–1840
3. Pedro II, 1840–1889

III. Old Republic, 1889–1930

1. Military/civilian oligarchy, 1889–1898
2. São Paulo–Minas Gerais hegemony, 1898–1930

IV. Transitional Republic (The Vargas Era), 1930–1945

1. Provisional government, 1930–1934
2. Constitutional government, 1934–1937
3. Estado Novo (dictatorship), 1937–1945

V. 1946 Republic, 1946–1964

1. Presidential government, 1946–1961
2. Parliamentary government, 1961–1963
3. Presidential government, 1963–1964

VI. The Military Republic, 1964–1985

1. Controlled government, 1964–1968
2. Authoritarian government, 1968–1979
3. Liberalizing authoritarian government, 1979–1985

VII. The New Republic, 1985–present

1. Transitional government, 1985–1995
2. Modernizing democracy, 1995–present

---

hereditary captaincies that extended inland from the coast as far as the colonial boundaries. Within each captaincy, the *donatário*, the individual who had received the captaincy from the king, assumed responsibility for colonization and financial underwriting in exchange for broad powers of governance and profit-making possibilities. The only captaincies that were relatively successful were São Vicente in the Center-South and Pernambuco in the Northeast. In 1549, the

Crown determined to establish a central government at Bahia, and the first governor-general arrived to assume direction of Brazil.

As agents of the Crown, the *donatários* were the first instruments of state capitalism in Brazil. Their land was assigned by the royal government, their rights and prerogatives were defined by the king, and their economic and social functions were seen as complementary to and supportive of the interests of the monarch. The Crown attempted to assert its right to regulate and stimulate, for its own advantage, the development of the Brazilian colony.

With the arrival of the governor-general, the patrimonial regime received its symbolic head. While the governor-general represented the power of the Portuguese throne, 250 years of conflict between the mother country and colony ensued before the patrimonial state became permanently ensconced in Brazil. During the first 100 years, roughly from 1550 to 1650, the magisterial bureaucracy represented the Crown's claim to authority. It attempted to represent the interest of the central government without stifling the vital initiative of the settlers. This magisterial bureaucracy was the historical antecedent of contemporary Brazil's administrative bureaucracy.

By 1640, when Portugal had regained its independence from Spain, with which it was forcibly united in 1580, the Crown began to cancel all concessions given to individuals. The fiscal interests of the Crown became the paramount determinant of public policy toward Brazil. Stimulated earlier in the settlement period by Brazil wood and sugar, the Crown's determination to impose its rule on the colony increased with the discovery of gold in Minas Gerais in 1695. The period of unbridled hegemony in public affairs enjoyed by *os poderosos* (the influential) was curtailed with the assertion of royal prerogative. While the autonomy of the landowners survived—as it does today in the Northeast and Center-West—it increasingly did so because their interests began to coincide with the goals of the monarchy. Profit became the greatest single force in Portugal's colonial policy and came to overshadow disputes about jurisdiction and administrative influence.

The society that emerged in the seventeenth and eighteenth centuries was divided between the coast and the interior. The coast, dominated by the bourgeois merchants (the commercial class), aligned with the public bureaucracy (the agents of the monarchy) to direct public affairs. The interior, the reserve of the patriarchal figures, remained under the jurisdiction of the local oligarchy.

Local and private initiative played an essential role in exploring the far reaches of Brazil; the *bandeirantes* (pioneers), who used São Vicente as their headquarters, opened the interior of the country. Although the royal government was never far behind and often served to guide the initial ventures,[1] the local elite was the final determining factor in the success or failure of such ventures in the vast, sprawling colony. The Portuguese Crown was aware of the rival forces at work in the colony: increasing bureaucratic centralization, on the one hand, and the drive for autonomy at the regional and local levels, on the other hand. This theme survived the colonial period and structured the political process throughout the Empire and the Old Republic.

As part of its claim to preeminence in policy making, the Crown co-opted the local landowners into the colonial system through the bureaucracy. Public positions were utilized by the royal government to begin to gain the adherence of the great families of the interior as well as the bourgeois class of the coast. Sons and nephews were incorporated into the state apparatus in exchange for the loyalty and support of the landowning families. As the agricultural producers became more and more dependent on the commercial bankers and traders of the coast, their reliance on the state grew. The Crown supported the coastal groups against the pretensions of the interior. The period until 1822 and independence saw a continuing rivalry among landowners, bureaucrats, and commercial interests.

During this early period, there was little demonstration of nationalism in Brazil. Ironically, the Portuguese Crown viewed the colony as an integrated unit, while its inhabitants continued to identify with their region or province. The effort by the Crown to centralize authority while allowing local and regional variation produced a flexible situation that allowed for continuing local autonomy and the assertion of the royal position, in contrast to the rigidity and formalism of Spanish rule.

By 1780, the formal centralization of royal rule began to prove successful. In 1759, Sebastião Pombal expelled the Jesuits from the Portuguese Empire; with their departure, the traditional Church, an arm of the Portuguese settlement process, returned to a supportive but nonparticipant role. With the transfer of the colonial capital to Rio de Janeiro in 1763, the early regional predominance of the Northeast declined and the center of gravity in the colony began to shift, permanently, to the Center-South.

At the end of the colonial period, church and state were united. Two high courts, one at Rio de Janeiro and the other at Bahia, provided a rudimentary judicial system. Major towns had circuit judges for local justice, and each captaincy had a treasury commission to oversee the fiscal income of the Crown. Local town councils, indirectly elected, were with rare exceptions dependent on the whim of the local governor or the governor-general.

By independence, the regional variety that had emerged during the early years remained strong. Different economies and corresponding social stratification co-existed. The plantation system of the Northeast had been followed by the emergence of a mining industry in gold and precious stones in Minas Gerais. A cattle-raising economy appeared in the Center-South and South. The social and economic orders of the coast and the interior remained separate but complementary.

Independence and the Empire

The Portuguese court, driven from Lisbon by Napoleon's armies in 1808, settled in Rio de Janeiro. Prince João, acting as regent on behalf of his incapacitated mother, opened Brazilian ports to world trade for the first time and allowed manufacturing and commercial enterprises to flourish without severe restriction. The Portuguese patrimonial state was carried to Brazil, and its bureaucracy merged with the colony's. The rivalry among the three predominant social groups in Brazil—landed aristocracy, merchants, and *lusos transmigrados* (Portuguese immigrants) who manned the state bureaucracy—pitted the landed group against the other two. The Republican Revolution in Pernambuco in 1817 was the climax of this tug-of-war among the competing groups. The revolt was suppressed by the Crown with the help of the British fleet.

With the return of King João VI to Lisbon in 1821—he had become king in 1816 upon the death of his mother—his son Pedro became regent. After the Lisbon Assembly attempted to curtail the autonomy of Brazil, in the same year the landed aristocracy in Brazil endorsed the regent's decision to oppose Lisbon. When the king ordered Pedro to return to Portugal, he refused; in September 1822, he dramatically declared Brazil's independence from Portugal, and the Brazilian Empire came into existence.

The succeeding decade was one of uneasy compromise among three groups; a liberal faction that favored a loose federation under the emperor; a conservative group supporting centralization and unitary government; and the remains of the Republican movement, totally at odds with the continuation of royal rule. In general, the remaining Portuguese at court and the commercial barons favored a strong central government; the landed aristocracy, the voice of regional autonomy, clamored for federation and decentralization. Emperor Pedro I opted for centralization, he said, to avoid anarchy and the dissolution of the Empire when, in 1824, he dissolved the Constituent Assembly and promulgated his own constitution.

The 1824 Constitution provided for a two-chamber legislature: a Senate with life members and an elected Chamber of Deputies. The emperor possessed the *poder moderador* (moderating power), which gave him the authority to approve legislation, make appointments, and select members of the Senate. Each province had an elected assembly, possessing only a consultative role, and an executive appointed by the central government. From 1824 to 1831, the lower chamber of the legislature opposed the emperor's centralizing tendencies. Growing dissatisfaction with Pedro's reliance on his Portuguese advisors and his arbitrary decisions forced him to abdicate in 1831 in favor of his infant son.

Brazil was governed by a series of regents from 1831 to 1840, a crucial decade in the country's development. Revolts broke out during the decade in many of the provinces; some were republican in intent, others were in protest over local issues.

Raymundo Faoro identifies two institutions that provided a modicum of stability during the 1830s as the regency struggled to keep the nation together.[2] The first was A Sociedade Defensora de Liberdade e Independência Nacional (The Society in Defense of Liberty and National Independence), created in May 1831, which fought against the federalist clubs. It came to play the role of an unofficial council of state favoring the retention of the monarchy and a strong central government. The other was the Guarda Nacional (National Guard), also created in 1831, which gave the government an armed force that was apolitical, loyal, and able to defend the interests of the Crown—against the traditional armed forces, if necessary. The regency downgraded the army in favor of the National Guard, which was much more its creature. Fernando Uricoechea's study of patrimonialism in the nineteenth century emphasizes the key role of the Guarda, "a private militia made up of freemen."[3] He notes that although the organization was bureaucratically controlled and supervised by administrative agencies of the central state, it remained a patrimonially administered corporation.[4] Indeed, the Guarda was able to mobilize 200,000 freemen during its early years of activity; the professional army of the Empire numbered only about 5,000 men at the time.

It became apparent by 1840 that the regency had not functioned very well; the unofficial experiment with republican rule had failed. The Interpretive Law of 1840 ended the experiment with federalism, which had begun in 1834 with the series of constitutional amendments comprising the Additional Act. Pedro II's majority was declared, although he was not yet 18, and he assumed the throne. He ruled Brazil until 1889 and the advent of the Old Republic.

The political rivalries of the Empire were played out by two amorphous political parties, the Liberals and the Conservatives, both drawing their members from the same social and economic class. Under the strong tutelage of the Crown, the patrimonial state asserted itself in Brazil. The honors and appointments of the monarchy ensured continued support for the center from the periphery. The imperial court, acting through the national bureaucracy, determined policy with little more than formal consultation with the landed oligarchy and with no concern for the wishes of the rest of the population. The center continued to structure and dominate Brazilian society through the nineteenth century.

In one of the Empire's few foreign adventures, the 1865–1870 War of the Triple Alliance (Brazil, Argentina, and Uruguay) against Paraguay, the armed forces became politicized. From 1870 until the military coup that ended the Empire in 1889, the military was increasingly involved in public affairs. The two political parties competed for the support of military officers; the military buildup for the war against Paraguay provided an organizational structure ready and able, for the first time, to fight for the institutional prerogatives of the armed forces.

In addition to disaffection among the officer corps, the emperor, by the last decade of the Empire, had lost the support of the landed aristocracy over the issue of slavery. The first slaves had been brought to Brazil in the mid-sixteenth century. They provided the labor for the flourishing sugar plantations of the Northeast coast. By 1800, slaves represented nearly 50 percent of the population. Abolition gained strong support in the eighteenth century from the British, who, because of their influence in trade and commerce, were able to lobby effectively for an end to slavery.[5] The movement toward emancipation had proceeded slowly in Brazil. The slave trade was abolished formally in 1850; in 1871, the

Law of the Free Womb freed all children born to slaves; and in 1885, a law freed all slaves at age 60. With the Crown supporting these reforms, the land-owning aristocracy felt betrayed as its economic and social eminence decreased. The Golden Law of 1888, which abolished all slavery without compensation, was the final break between the emperor and the landed and commercial elites.[6]

The Crown lost the support of some elements of the Church over the issue of Freemasonry. It had taken the position against the demands of the Vatican and the Brazilian bishops that the movement be stamped out. While Church support eroded at the end of the Empire, the Church itself was a relatively weak institution in Brazil. By 1889, there were only 12 dioceses, 13 bishops, and about 700 priests in a country of 14 million people. In contrast, at about the same time, the United States, with a much smaller Roman Catholic population, had 84 bishops and some 8,000 priests.[7]

In response to growing discontent with the Empire, viewed by some as an anachronism, a Republican Club was organized in Rio de Janeiro in 1870, and the first Republican Manifesto was issued. The Republican Party took part in elections thereafter, achieving modest success at the polls. Many of the future generation of political leaders received their earliest experience in public life as members of this party, which provided a structured way of discussing an alternative political model for Brazil.

Thus, by the 1880s, the traditional sources of support for the monarchy were seriously weakened. Many members of the aristocratic oligarchy were less than enthusiastic about the accession to the throne of Pedro II's daughter, Isabel, and her unpopular French husband. In addition, the emperor had lost much of his personal prestige by his seeming inability to direct national affairs with more acumen; there were rumors that he had become senile. The Empire fell in a bloodless coup on November 15, 1889. Marshal Deodoro da Fonseca, an army hero, headed the provisional government. The overthrow of the monarchy was almost exclusively the work of the military.

The Old Republic (1889–1930)

The armed forces, aware of their corporate strength after 1870, acted in 1889 to assert their institutional influence. The break with the patrimonial regime of the Empire signified the creation of a new force, related to and supportive of the central government but able and willing to challenge and control it when deemed necessary. While from one perspective the Old Republic represented a victory for decentralization and the landed aristocracy, it also signified, more meaningfully, the continuation of oligarchical rule. The levels of popular participation did not increase. The groups that had occupied prominent positions in the Empire did so during the Old Republic. The patrimonial state remained the dominant influence in the development of Brazil.

The two most influential groups from 1889 to 1930 were the military and the state governors. The armed forces dominated the Old Republic from 1889 to

1894, when the first civilian was elected president. The military was never far from politics and power in the Old Republic. Marshal Hermes da Fonseca, with the backing of the political machinery of Rio Grande do Sul, served as president from 1910 to 1914.

The national leadership came primarily from the powerful states of Minas Gerais and São Paulo in the framework of the Republican Party, the only national party organization. The *política dos governadores* (politics of the governors) was an agreement among state leaders that granted the São Paulo and Minas Gerais axis preeminence in national, particularly economic, affairs in exchange for a guarantee to the smaller states that the central government would not interfere in internal state affairs. The co-optation of recalcitrant political leaders continued. The sons of the establishment were given public employment in the bureaucracy as part of the tacit understanding between political center and periphery. The Republican Party was, in fact, a loose network of provincial organizations that served to funnel patronage to the states and provided candidates for the bureaucracy of the patrimonial state.

Civilian and military factions in the Old Republic competed for the privilege of exercising the prerogatives of the bureaucratic state. Regional and local leaders vied for favors from the central government. The economy remained firmly based on coffee, a commodity heavily subsidized by the government. Social stratification continued to be rigidly hierarchical. Representative government, the supposed core of the 1891 Constitution, was a fiction, and politics remained the game of the few in the service of the patrimonial state.

The Constitution of the Republic mirrored the Western liberal democratic model of government without the substance. It provided for 20 states, coterminous with the provinces of the Empire, and a federal district in Rio de Janeiro. Significant prerogatives were reserved to the states, allowing them to construct their own administrative and tax structures in conformity with their regional differences. The federal government had three branches. The legislature contained two houses; a Senate representing the states and a Chamber of Deputies elected on the basis of population. The executive consisted of a powerful presidency with cabinet ministers responsible to the chief executive. The judicial branch was made up of a Supreme Court and lower courts. It was a constitutional structure ideally suited to the Old Republic, in which the franchise was limited, voting remained low, literacy encompassed a small percentage of the population, and social mobility was rare. The national population remained passive, object of the political machinations of the few. An individual's loyalty was given to a patron or a state or region before the nation.

The Transitional Republic: The Vargas Era (1930–1945)

The Old Republic fell when the bargain among the state governors over the presidential succession collapsed in 1930.[8] President Washington Luís Pereira de Souza of São Paulo refused to endorse the presidential candidacy of the governor of Minas Gerais and instead supported a fellow Paulista as his successor. The opposition candidate, Getúlio Vargas of Rio Grande do Sul, was backed by many young military officers, the *tenentes* (lieutenants), who had launched a series of unsuccessful rebellions against the Old Republic throughout the 1920s; the small states (Vargas's vice-presidential candidate came from Paraíba in the Northeast) and Minas Gerais. After losing the election, and with the assassination of opposition vice-presidential candidate João Pessoa, the forces behind Vargas's Liberal Alliance revolted in October 1930. Weakened by the 1929 economic crash and repudiated by its former political supporters, the Republican regime acceded to the counsel of the armed forces and the Church, and resigned. Vargas became provisional president in November 1930.

The Transitional Republic, dominated by Vargas, is divisible into three distinct periods. The first encompasses the provisional government from 1930 to 1934. During this time, Vargas moved to revise and modernize the economy. He put down revolts against the centralization of state power in Pernambuco and São Paulo in 1932. Delegates elected in 1933 wrote a new constitution in 1934 and elected Vargas to his first presidential term.

During the second period, from 1934 to 1937, Vargas ruled within the 1934 Constitution. He successfully manipulated and defeated all potential political opponents. A Communist uprising in 1935 gave him justification to suppress the party and its leader, Luis Carlos Prestes. The only other organized political movement, the fascist Integralistas, led by Plínio Salgado, was suppressed in 1937. Under the pretext of maintaining law and order, Vargas decided to ignore the 1934 constitutional ban on his succeeding himself. He abolished all political parties, canceled the 1938 presidential elections, and promulgated, with the 1937 Constitution, the Estado Novo (New State). The third phase of Vargas's rule included the years from 1937 to 1945.

Executive authority was greatly expanded under the New State. The president was empowered to rule by decree, and Vargas chose not to convene the legislative assembly, thus avoiding any potential check on his unlimited power. He intervened in the states, replacing recalcitrant governors with men who would do his bidding. The central bureaucracy, in the absence of any check by an elected parliament, assumed its traditional role of creator and implementor of public policy. Extensive nationalization of economic institutions and natural resources increased the power of the patrimonial state. The ban on all organized political activity and strict censorship allowed the government to monitor public affairs with relative ease.

An opportunist rather than a totalitarian ideologue, Vargas did not organize a party to inculcate Brazilians with a particular set of beliefs. His paternalistic interpretation of his role led him to use his position to consolidate his influence with the urban working class. An extensive welfare system, the first labor unions for the privileged urban working class, elementary education programs, and public health programs were gifts from the state to the people. In return, the state expected compliance and no popular expectations of political involvement in decision making. This represented the purest patrimonial tradition in Brazil.

In 1943, the secret but widely circulated *Manifesto mineiro*, written by politicians in the state of Minas Gerais, called for a return to democratic government. The Brazilian Expeditionary Force, sent to Europe in 1944, returned home in 1945. The military officers supported presidential elections; their interest in reopening the political system coincided with a growing demand by the political elites for an end to the authoritarian New State.

The election that Vargas scheduled for December 1945 initiated a period of intense political debate. When it appeared that Vargas might subvert the election, as he had in 1937, the military issued an ultimatum. In October 1945, the dictator left for his home in Rio Grande do Sul after his unceremonious ouster by the armed forces.

The 1946 Republic

The elections took place as scheduled, with General Eurico Gaspar Dutra, Vargas's minister of war, defeating a former *tenente*, Brigadier Eduardo Gomes, for the presidency. Dutra was the candidate of the Social Democratic Party (PSD) and received the endorsement of the Brazilian Labor Party (PTB). Both parties had been organized by Vargas before his abrupt withdrawal from politics. The National Democratic Union (UDN) endorsed Gomes. While the political system of the 1946 Republic expanded to 13 parties, these three remained preeminent.

Of the four presidential elections held from 1946 to 1964, the PSD-PTB coalition triumphed in three: with Dutra in 1945, Vargas in 1950, and Juscelino Kubitschek in 1955. Jânio Quadros, the victor in 1960, backed by the UDN, resigned in 1961, and PTB leader João Goulart, then vice president, became chief executive. Thus the PSD-PTB system of co-optation and cooperation dominated national politics after 1946. While the number of people voting increased substantially, their relationship to the political system changed very little.

Francisco C. Weffort and others have termed this period one of populist politics.[9] Characterized by an emphasis on the urban electorate, with little if any tendency to institutionalize linkages between voter and government, concerned not about programmatic but about pragmatic interests, the populist politician sought votes only to gain public office. Once successful, the populist used his position of influence not in the service of the electorate or "public good" but in the narrow, parochial sense of satisfying his "clientele" or political following. A populist politician represents clients who are able to "deliver" the popular vote needed for election. To maintain this arrangement, the politician must have access to payoffs: jobs, contracts, rewards, and so on, which only the bureaucracy and central government can provide. In return, it is tacitly understood that he will not attempt to introduce real structural changes or disturb the equilibrium of power between the central government's preeminence in policy making and its clients on the national level. The system functions as long as each participant understands and accepts the rules of the game. Anyone who does not is either co-opted into the system, and his challenge is rendered futile, or is defeated, ignored, or belittled.

The principal power contender during this period was the armed forces. Given the tentativeness of the fragile electoral system and its unrepresentative nature, the military became constant participants in politics. Their involvement was due to a number of factors, which included an interpretation of their constitutional duty as calling for political intervention when civilian politicians failed to govern properly; institutional security, which appeared to be challenged in the 1961–1964 era; and the personal ambition of individual officers. In every presidential election of the 1946 Republic, at least one military man ran as a candidate.

Equally important as the military presence in presidential elections was their intervention in national politics. There were military coups in 1954 and 1964, an attempted coup in 1961, and the beginnings of a coup in 1955 that brought about a countercoup by another military faction in defense of the constitutional regime. As we will see in Chapter 4, these military interventions were accomplished by growing dissent among the military over the appropriate role of the patrimonial state in the modernization of Brazilian society. The segment of the military and civilian political elite favoring radical reform was clearly defeated with the coup d'état of 1964 that sent President Goulart into exile.

The 1946 Republic was characterized by high rates of social mobilization, an expanding urban electorate, populist politics, a weak multiparty system, growing military politicization, and a continuation of the guiding hand of the patrimonial state in preventing reforms that would unbalance the carefully structured distribution of power that favored the continuing preeminence of the public sector in policy formation.

The Military Republic (1964–1985)

The fragmented, drifting 1946 Republic fell before a military coup, as had the Empire, the Old Republic, and the Transitional Republic of Getúlio Vargas. Once again, very limited civilian political participation facilitated the determination of the military to oust the incumbent constitutional regime. The Military Republic, initiated in 1964, can be divided into three segments: the first encompassed the years from 1964 to 1969, the era of General Humberto Castello Branco's government and that of General Arthur da Costa e Silva. During this time, the 1946 Constitution was modified by a series of Institutional Acts issued by the military high command. A number of former politicians and public servants were declared ineligible to hold public office; many had their political rights suspended for 10 years.

The political party system was completely reorganized, and the electoral procedures and standards of the 1946 Republic were severely modified. After direct gubernatorial elections were held in October 1965, and two candidates identified as opposed to the regime had won, the electoral laws were rewritten to provide for the indirect election of state governors. Two new parties, the National Renovating Alliance (ARENA) and the Brazilian Democratic Movement (MDB), emerged as the parties of the Military Republic. ARENA attracted the bulk of the UDN and conservative PSD members; MDB, the opposition party, appealed to the PTB, the left wing of the PSD, and members of the leftist-leaning smaller parties. The Second Institutional Act of October 1965 further centralized administrative and political power in the hands of the military president. In 1966, the minister of war in Castello Branco's cabinet, General Arthur da Costa e Silva, emerged as the military's candidate for the presidency.

Costa e Silva assumed office in March 1967, at the same time a new constitution was promulgated after being rubber-stamped by Congress. The new government retained the broad policy outlines of its predecessor. Congress was allowed a ceremonial role in policy, but even that was foreclosed with the congressional crisis of December 1968.

When Congress refused to remove the immunity of one of its members who stood accused of defaming the integrity of the armed forces, the government recessed Congress indefinitely, and it did not meet again until March 1970. During the congressional recess, President Costa e Silva governed by decree. The bureaucracy of the central government continued to make and to implement policy with little need for concern over popular opinion or legislative monitoring.

After the incapacitation of the president in August 1969, the Military Republic moved into its second phase, one of increased authoritarianism. With the publication of a series of Institutional Acts and a constitutional amendment, the military further gathered political power in the central government and gave the military regime the means to dominate society totally. When it became clear that President Costa e Silva would not recover his health, the military commanders bypassed the civilian vice president, declared the presidency vacant, and proceeded to select another army officer. Congress ratified the military selection, General Emílio Garrastazú Médici, on October 25, 1969.

The Médici government was the most popular—and the most repressive—of all governments that have held power since 1964. Médici was an appealing figure to the public, although his style of governance was authoritarian. His administration saw the tremendous takeoff of the Brazilian economy, often referred to as a ''miracle,'' which strengthened the economic position of the middle class. New directions in foreign policy found support among the intellectuals and professionals in the regime.

General Ernesto Geisel succeeded Médici. The origins of the political liberalization process (*abertura*) are to be found in the Geisel government. Selecting as his chief political adviser General Golbery do Couto e Silva, the founder of the National Intelligence Service (SNI), Geisel was determined to begin a slow but deliberate process of redemocratization. Both the president and Golbery were identified with former president Castello Branco and with the more moderate intellectual wing of the army. Although strong defenders of the 1964 Revolution, both believed military rule to be transitional. Geisel lifted press censorship and eased television and radio censorship. In December 1977, he dramatically announced to the government party, ARENA, that the political party structure would be reorganized and the Fifth Institutional Act, the most repressive, would be abolished. Other liberalization plans would be initiated during the remaining years of his presidency and completed by his successor.

Geisel chose the incumbent head of the SNI, General João Figueiredo, to become the fifth military president of the 1964 Republic. Figueiredo presided over the third phase of the Military Republic, the process of *abertura*. Habeas corpus was reestablished, a political amnesty was promulgated, press freedom was maintained, and direct elections were held in late 1982 for municipal, state, and national offices.

The military regime's hope of selecting another general as president in 1985 collapsed soon after Figueiredo took office. The president proved to be an inept politician. His health deteriorated, and he demonstrated little interest in governing. The economy, long overheated and overborrowed, was negatively impacted by the debt crisis of 1982. Rampant inflation, budget deficits, and soaring prices led to demonstrations and fueled the nationwide campaign to hold direct presidential elections in 1985. Congress considered an amendment to the constitution to restore direct balloting in 1984, but it was defeated because of strong pressure from the armed forces and the government. But the opposition forces regrouped and were determined to defeat the patrimonial order at its own game. Tancredo Neves, an impeccable representative of the establishment, was chosen as the opposition presidential candidate in the 1985 electoral college voting. He easily defeated former São Paulo governor Paulo Maluf, the candidate of the government party.

The New Republic

While the political opposition won a major victory in 1985, it almost lost the war. Tancredo Neves was incapacitated on the eve of his inauguration on March 15, 1985. After hasty consultations, the political elite decided to swear in, as acting president, Senator José Sarney of Maranhão, Neves's running mate in the electoral college election. Sarney had been an integral member of the military regime's team until late in the transition process. His shift to the opposition earned him the opprobrium of his former colleagues and the suspicion of many of his new colleagues.

Following a tortured illness, Neves died in April. Sarney, unprepared for the presidency and quite disinterested in it, assumed office with great trepidation. The Sarney years were lamentable. "I told anyone who would listen that all I wanted was to wait for Tancredo Neves to recover so that I could begin to serve as his second-in-command," he wrote.[10] The new president appeared interested in only one thing—retaining the office for a period of five years and peacefully transferring the presidential sash to a civilian successor in 1990.

The economy was subjected to a heterodox shock program called the Cruzado Plan in 1986. It almost worked—but almost was not good enough. The tough price and wage controls were maintained too long. The Sarney government hoped that the euphoria over winning the war against inflation would result in a large majority for the government coalition. It did. But the plan exploded days after the election results were counted. The government never recovered from the disaster of the Cruzado Plan.

In 1987, the government unilaterally declared a moratorium on its foreign debt. That decision was not followed by other Latin American or Third World debtors. It merely isolated Brazil, resulted in reduced lines of credit for trade from the private commercial banks, and proved costly in a number of ways to the economy and financial system.

The Sarney years witnessed the convocation of a Constituent Assembly to prepare a new document to replace the discredited 1967 Constitution, which had been heavily amended by the armed forces in 1969. Those elected to Congress in November 1986 served both as legislators and members of the assembly mandated to draft the new constitution. The process was confusing to most Brazilians, with many elements of the populist-nationalist position written into the document. The final product, by the most objective standards, not only is cumbersome but also severely constrains rational decision making. Almost as soon as it was promulgated, calls began for a reform of the document. Efforts in 1993 failed; the Cardoso administration initiated a reform process in 1995, which continues today.

The Constituent Assembly grudgingly granted Sarney his five-year term of office. Without a working majority in Congress, the president initiated little new legislation. The system drifted. The national election campaign of 1989 was long and drawn out as Brazilians prepared to vote directly for a chief executive for the first time since 1960. All except two candidates were eliminated in the first round of voting in November 1989. In the second round, one month later, the voters were given a clear choice. On the one side stood Fernando Collor de Mello, the scion of a wealthy, provincial political clan from Alagoas, in the impoverished Northeast. On the other side stood Luis Inácio da Silva, known as Lula, a famous union leader from the 1970s. Lula argued for a socialist program of government, Collor de Mello for a liberal model, which was then becoming the vogue in the region. After a bitter second-round campaign, Collor de Mello was chosen in December 1989. He was inaugurated on March 15, 1990.

During his first year in office, Collor de Mello attempted to implement a far-reaching economic reform program. By the middle of 1991, the program had indeed reduced inflation, but it had also infuriated many Brazilians because of price and wage freezes, confiscated savings, and the deindexation of the economy, with a resulting sharp drop in real income. Collor's commitment to a liberal and an open market economy was rhetorically impressive. Whether he had the right economic team to put it into place remains a matter of debate. The president did not have a working majority in Congress and implemented much of his program by decree. When the first phase of his reform began to falter, the president launched a revised version, known as "Collor II." It held promise, but it remained a paper proposal as the Congress elected in late 1990 (taking office in early 1991) was unwilling to support the broad outlines of the new program. The efforts at economic reform stopped with the eruption of a series of campaign-financing scandals in mid-1992. The Chamber of Deputies voted to remove Collor from office on September 29. On October 2, Vice President Itamar Franco was sworn in as Acting President. Franco was a traditional politician from Minas Gerais with little grasp of the intricacies of economic policy. The Brazilian Senate then voted for the impeachment of Collor on December 29, 1992; the president resigned from his office as the final impeachment debate began, but the Senate nevertheless proceeded to vote for impeachment. Vice President Franco assumed permanent office immediately thereafter.

While deemed a political failure, the Collor government must be given relatively high marks for the general direction of its economic policies. Collor had the courage to undertake fundamental reforms—the liberalization of the trade regime, privatization of state-owned companies, and so on—that set the stage for the 1994 Real Plan and for Brazil's expanded role in today's globalized economy. The tragedy of the Collor government was that the president failed to distinguish between his private interests and his public responsibilities. The former poisoned his efforts to build political support for the latter. But his term of office, 1990–1992, remains a pivotal turning point in the ways in which Brazilians think about the economy and the role of the state in the economic process.

Franco was a little-known, idiosyncratic, regional politician. Seeking to distinguish his presidency from that of his predecessors, he cast about for a new team. Through cabinet changes in 1993, he finally appointed São Paulo Senator Fernando Henrique Cardoso as finance minister; Cardoso had served briefly as Franco's foreign minister. Cardoso quickly assembled an economic team of young, highly professional economists—"technocrats"—who would remain with him through his period as finance minister, as presidential candidate in 1994, and as president (1995–1999). Cardoso and his team created the "Real Plan," which was fully implemented by July 1994. Its hallmark was a highly successful reduction in inflation, a serious fiscal adjustment, and a balanced budget. The new currency, called the *real*, was quickly accepted by the Brazilian population. Cardoso, as a presidential candidate, used the anti-inflationary platform to defeat his principal opponent, Luis Inácio da Silva, "Lula," of the Workers' Party (PT), in the first round of presidential voting in late 1994. Cardoso was inaugurated for a four-year term of office on January 1, 1995. In October 1998, the president was reelected, easily defeating his competitors.

As the first "modern" chief executive of postmilitary Brazil, Cardoso had initiated a series of economic reforms that dominated his first administration. But by the end of his first term of office, one issue stood out—the lack of fiscal reform. A relatively weak central government had little influence over the spending of the states and municipalities. The state corporations were often deeply in debt. The 1988 Constitution mandated that the federal government automatically transfer to the states and cities a significant share of federal revenues—but without the local entities accepting responsibility for previous federal programs such as health and education.

In late 1998, the Brazilian currency caught the "contagion" from the instability in world financial markets that began in 1997. Brazil was viewed as vulnerable by currency speculators precisely because of the undisciplined management of fiscal policy. To combat this the IMF offered Brazil financial support in an effort to protect the currency. In exchange, the Cardoso administration promised to move rapidly to have the Congress approve an austere set of budget reduction measures.

But the Congress refused to cooperate. Motivated by personal concerns and local political loyalties, a stalemate developed. The president argued the urgency of the need for decisive, rapid response from the legislature. The Congress, then a lame-duck institution, had little interest in supporting the president—or in making painful decisions that might impact on their future political career at home. The international financial community took note and began to panic.

By early 1999, the situation was untenable and the Central Bank was forced to devalue the currency, and its value quickly plummeted by more than 40 percent. Under intense international scrutiny, Cardoso named a new Central Bank president and the administration confronted the Congress. Fearful of being blamed for the fiscal fiasco, the Congress finally approved the reform package in early 1999. But the second administration began under a very dark cloud with Brazil moving into recession, high unemployment, and sharply reduced flows of capital from international investors.

POLITICAL GIVENS

We return now to the political givens introduced at the beginning of this chapter, the independent variables that have constituted the continuity of the Brazilian political system. We discuss in turn the concept of elite rule, the existence over time of a patrimonial regime, and the concept of social dualism as it relates to Brazil. The current social agenda generated by that dualism is discussed at length in Chapter 7.

Elites of Brazil

One of the leading attributes of the Brazilian political system is its elitist nature. Regardless of the time period, politics in Brazil has been dominated by a relatively small group of individuals that has been able to manipulate the mass of the population and define the goals of the state in its own terms. Until 1964, most members of the elite were drawn from groups such as the landowning oligarchy, the public bureaucracy, the traditional export-oriented and commercial interests, the military, and the family-oriented industrial and banking groups. With the onset of the Military Republic in 1964, the regime favored new groups in its effort to reform the Brazilian economy. A new industrial class emerged; agro-industry became a significant foreign exchange earner, for example. A new generation of younger, better-educated entrepreneurs assumed leadership positions. That trend has continued since 1985, but it is clear that the concentration of power remains a constant in Brazilian politics. There has yet to be a broadening of participation in critical decision making—other than on a token basis— to include the middle class and the more marginal social actors.

The elite nature of the political system has been reinforced by the traditional and hierarchical nature of Brazilian political culture. Throughout history, there has been a high degree of similarity and congruence in the political ideas, attitudes, and action patterns of the elites. Similarly, there has been a notable lack of organized opposition by other groups and classes in Brazil. Emerging social groups have chosen to emulate existing elites and their codes of political conduct rather than challenge or confront them.

Elite domination is further aided by the often noted propensity for compromise and the peaceful settlement of disputes among elite members, and the expectation among the masses that accommodation and bargaining are sufficient to settle disputes. As Bolivar Lamounier commented about the transition to civilian government in the mid- and late-1980s:

both sides, government and opposition, found enough space to redefine their respective roles through several stages, since each perceived what it stood to gain from the continuity of the process. The opposition was capable of extracting important concessions while at the same time organizing itself as a powerful electoral force. The government also benefitted in many ways. Most importantly, it saw a gradual reduction in the costs of coercion. Decompression helped it to contain the growing autonomy of the repressive apparatus, which had seriously compromised, as is well known, the country's image abroad. In short, the government could capitalize on the political benefits of an atmosphere of progressive "normalcy," as if exchanging losses of legitimacy arising from discontent with its past for gains based on the increasing credibility of its intentions as to the future.[11]

What has emerged in Brazil is a pattern of elite interaction that assigns great value to pragmatism (cynics would say opportunism) in policy making, displays little ideological fervor, endorses flexibility in interpersonal relationships, and stresses highly personal or charismatic forms of leadership. As the transition to civilian government was underway, a leading member of the PT, who would later join the administration of President Fernando Henrique Cardoso in an effort to broaden the government's base of support, bitterly commented that the truth is that in 160 years of our history as an independent country, Brazil has never had the opportunity to test the hypothesis of democracy as a form of bourgeois domination. With its origins in the aristocracy and oligarchy, the instrumental conception of democracy runs through our history like a curse. . . . The political tradition molded by the oligarches and the dictatorships is still with us.[12]

The Brazilian elite, historically, could be divided into a "ruling class" and a "political elite." The power of a ruling class stems from its ownership of property. It is composed of a group of families that remains at its core from generation to generation. The most distinctive members of the ruling class in Brazil were the sugar plantation owners and cattle ranchers of the Northeast, the coffee entrepreneurs in São Paulo, and the cattle ranchers of Minas Gerais and Rio Grande do Sul.

The ruling class in Brazil has been in a process of sharp decline and decadence since 1930. While the *latifundiários* (large landowners) retain significant power in the rural areas, their capacity to influence national decisions is limited. The absence of serious agrarian reform and the historical impotence of rural unionization efforts have permitted the landowners to continue to enjoy local supremacy. But the continual flow of the rural population to the coastal cities and the growing industrialization of agriculture, which requires fewer workers, have further reduced the actual power of the traditional landowning class.

Two factors are at work today in Brazil that "update" this analysis. The first is the emergence in the national legislature of a *bancada rural*, or group of rural congressmen. Many of these are young and entrepreneurial. They have benefitted from the efforts of previous governments to subsidize the formation of large landholdings for agro-industrial purposes. They have become, and remain, an influential minority in Congress with which the president must deal. The *bancada* is more than willing to trade its votes for parts of the president's reform program, which they view as "urban oriented." In return, they expect the administration to avoid any extreme measures to introduce radical land legislation or strengthen the rural unions.

Another "new" player—actually an updated version of the weak efforts at rural unionization prior to the Military Republic—is the "Movement of People Without Land" (MST). Originally a movement based in the south of Brazil, the MST formally organized in 1984. It now operates in a majority of the states in the Brazilian federation. Its original tactics in the fight for land reform were encampments and the invasion of unused lands. Recently, the MST has occupied public buildings and roads, staged public protests, and in mid-1998, organized a six-week-long national march to Brasília to press for reform and to protest against the increase in rural violence. The MST has learned to use the national media for its own purposes and has skillfully used its platform for land reform and rural justice to begin to build sympathy among the urban sector. It remains to be seen whether the MST will decide to become a national political movement or political party or will choose to remain an increasingly well-organized pressure group.

While not a replica of the old "ruling class," the new, aggressive landed power brokers in the *bancada rural* do represent a "traditional" set of values that has been "updated" to the twenty-first century. Do they represent a return to the past? No, but they do indicate the strong role that land ownership can play in a country where meaningful agrarian reform has been impossible to achieve. In that sense, they support—and are protected by—the general goals of the patrimonial state. The MST, in contrast, is yet another attempt to radically restructure Brazilian society from the bottom up. But will it have any greater chance of surviving than its predecessors, in other historical periods? While the evidence is not yet conclusive, the weight of history is against the MST, although the movement has gained widespread sympathy in the media and among the urban middle class and intellectual circles. It also has been able to organize and mobilize nationwide. But does its have the fundamental strength to confront the most regressive elements of the patrimonial order and win? That is an issue of some significance for the twenty-first century.

Power in Brazil, today, is exercised by the political elite, whose influence is built on its control of the institutions of the patrimonial state, of which the bureaucracy and the military were the most important before 1985. The armed forces are no longer viewed as the arbiter of public authority in Brazil, as they were for more than a century. Now, the base of support, with the restoration of civilian government, is dominated by the state bureaucracy. But the wave of privatizations—selling off state-owned companies—will sharply reduce that influence. Today, the principal heirs of the long-standing patrimonial regime are the local and regional political actors, highly diverse but brought together by two goals. The first is to retain influence within the federal power structure. The second, more pernicious, is to use their influence to stop efforts at social reform, which will increase the capacity of the average Brazilian to find his or her voice in national life.

While there was a certain amount of social cohesion that characterized the old ruling class, this is not true of the political elite. The driving force behind the political elite today is its desire for public power. The two groups cooperated effectively for generations; their goals were complementary. For the ruling class, the primary objective was to prevent any reorganization of land tenure, the basis of its wealth and influence. It also opposed all efforts to organize the workers to introduce the benefits of modern society into rural areas. The political elite, concerned primarily with gaining public office and with access to the patronage benefits of political power, cares little about real reform. Its interest is in holding power, whether appointive or elective.

First and foremost, the elite is permeable, susceptible to infiltration by new members as long as the aspirants are willing to accept and defend the rules and prerogatives of the patrimonial state. (Thus, Presidents Vargas and Kubitschek were acceptable; Presidents Quadros, Goulart, and Collor de Mello and perennial presidential candidate Lula were not.) These rules are, principally, to avoid the political mobilization of the masses, especially in the countryside; to manipulate the vote of the illiterates (in support of the first objective); to leave land tenure and land utilization patterns untouched; to neutralize destabilizing activism in the labor movement; and to foster a more advanced industrial model of economic diversification by importing advanced technology, expanding exports, and attracting foreign investment. This list is suggestive, not definitive; it seeks to provide, in general terms, the scheme of action of the Brazilian political system.

The national elite is self-perpetuating. Its members serve less as individuals and more as representatives of the social and institutional interests from which they come. The national elite tolerates personal dishonesty if the individual accepts the rules of the game (this is the cynical lesson learned by many in the impeachment of Fernando Collor de Mello in 1992). It is widely believed that many members of Congress who were responsible for his impeachment were themselves guilty of mendacity and corruption. Indeed, a major financial scandal broke out in Congress the following year, and to the surprise of many, a few members lost their positions. The elite mercilessly undercuts and isolates individuals who are personally honest but who are perceived as being threatening to the patrimonial order (it is fair to say that Lula fits this description). Personal integrity is less important than personal loyalty.

The national elite succeeds because it is united; it survives because it is flexible and adaptive; it serves the interests of the patrimonial state, while it serves its own through unalterable but muted opposition to potentially disruptive systemic inputs as "basic reforms" (João Goulart) and personal power exercised independently of the framework of the authoritarian state (Getúlio Vargas in 1945). Its subtle presence is often overlooked because it is so pervasive; its power becomes readily apparent when we examine the crisis leading to changes of regime in Brazil.

Over time, the national elite has co-opted and absorbed new members (technocrats and planners in the 1950s and 1960s, for example), and it has successfully marginalized contentious members, or those who have deliberately broken the understood procedures for permissible criticism of the patrimonial system (Rui Barbosa between 1900 and 1920; Dom Helder Camara, Archbishop of Recife and Olinda; former Governor Carlos Lacerda of Guanabara in the 1960s and early 1970s; MDB congressional leader Alencar Furtado in 1977; Luis Inácio "Lula" da Silva in his three bids for the presidency). It has survived serious crises, both interregime (the 1930 revolution and the 1945 Vargas deposition) and intraregime (the November 1955 attempted coup d'état to prevent President-elect Kubitschek's assuming power; the August–September 1961 military intervention to prevent Vice President Goulart's succeeding Jânio Quadros; the 1969 succession crisis after the incapacitation of President Costa e Silva; the return to civilian rule in 1985; and the populist-statist campaigns of Lula and the PT). It has moved quickly and, on the whole, effectively, from its point of view, to incapacitate any political movement possessing the potential for political mobilization or disruption (fascists and Communists in the mid-1930s and the Peasant Leagues, the Rural Labor Union Movement in the Northeast in the 1960s, and the PT coalition in the 1989, 1994, and 1998 presidential election campaigns).

This is not a "conspiracy theory" explanation of political power. It is an attempt to cut through the meaningless rhetoric that surrounds the discussion of politics in Latin America, particularly in Brazil. What is important here is to grasp the concept of elite control without serious opposition, elite domination without serious dislocations within the political system.

A useful evaluation of the Brazilian elite is that of Peter McDonough's, whose study supports the general argument elaborated here. He stresses the survival instinct in the elites during the 1970s and 1980s, when the authoritarian state appeared to be moving toward domination by a few elements of the national elite—the military, the technocrats, and the multinational corporations. Fissures quickly appeared between the elites, who perceived that they were excluded from the benefits of the system and those who held the formal positions of power. McDonough indicates clearly that the "elites, even the conservatives, want the power of the mightiest among them . . . curtailed."[13] The inherent instinct for self-preservation led the Geisel government to respond to these disaffected elite groups and to begin a process of internal reorganization and restructuring of power, which ultimately resulted in the peaceful transfer of power to a civilian government in 1985. McDonough comments: "It is not surprising that the elites who welcomed the suppression of mass politics in 1964 should, almost a decade later, became disillusioned with the perpetuation of restrictions on their own power."[14] This theme is repeated by Francisco Weffort as the transition to civilian rule took place. Rather than celebrating the return of the political elite to public power, Weffort commented that

Brazilian conservatism bequeathed to us an authoritarian conception of democracy . . . it is composed of all the ideas we inherited from the past about society and the State, about power and freedom . . . the most important part of the conservative tradition is the equivocation by which many can be, or pretend to be, both authoritarians and democrats at the same time.[15]

The Patrimonial State

The interpretation of Brazilian political development in *Os donos do poder*, by Raymundo Faoro, emphasizes the power of the state in Brazilian society from the colonial period in the twentieth century. Faoro stresses the role of the central government bureaucracy in managing the interventionist policies of the patrimonial regime. Unlimited by popular influence, the *patronato político* (patronal political authority of the public sector) established the parameters within which the social and economic structures of Brazilian society evolved. State capitalism provided the major impetus for economic growth; the limited franchise and the elitist domination of public policy making by the public functionaries, the clergy, the military, and the landowners ensured a hierarchical social system that, over time, stratified society into two groups: upper and lower.

The bureaucratic state has rarely, if ever, yielded its domination to the power of the majority—thus, "minority power," the power of the few, has characterized Brazilian society from its founding (with due allowance for different actors in different historical periods). In periods when the concept of representative government has emerged in the political process, the constitution and the rhetoric of representative democracy have been a superficial cover for the continuing influence of the patrimonial regime.

Brazilian literature is replete with many concepts and terms that attempt to capture the style and content of the Brazilian political system. The term *patrimonial state*, as used by Raymundo Faoro (and updated in this book), is more appropriate, I believe, because it conveys a more comprehensive image of politics and society as they are found in Brazil today. The term has the advantage of focusing on the national political system and its continuation over time, regardless of the changing composition of the several political elites that fill the chief decision-making roles. The concept emphasizes the qualities of centralization and authority. It summarizes the difficulty of mobilization in the political system and the consensus among the elites on limiting popular participation. The patrimonial state may be "modernizing," as it attempted to be in the early 1990s under President Fernando Collor de Mello, or it may be "preservatory," as with President José Sarney in the late 1980s. An important question that we will consider in this book is whether the government of President Fernando Henrique Cardoso, clearly committed to modernization and development, will be able to neutralize, or even to overcome, the traditional role of the political elite and the long-enduring aspects of the patrimonial order.

If the Cardoso administration is successful in doing so, the early twenty-first century will be the turning point in Brazilian history that observers have been hoping for throughout Brazil's modern history. If not, the Cardoso administration will be viewed as another valiant but failed effort to uproot many of the deep structural reasons why Brazil remains an unjust society, although it prospers at the macro-economic level, expands its trade ties, and is recognized as one of the 10 largest economies in the world. The crucial change must take place at the sociopolitical level, and that is the greatest challenge for Brazil's modernizing leaders.

In the few instances in Brazilian history when a major segment of the national elite was eliminated—in 1930, when Vargas assumed power, and in 1964, when the armed forces seized control of the government—the basic structure of the patrimonial order was not disturbed. The coming to power of Vargas or the military merely meant that different members of the elite were to occupy key decision-making positions. The administrative bureaucracy continued to function, as did the spoils bureaucracy; both were merely in different hands. In both instances, the new figures were drawn from both the military and civilian sectors of the elite. The new holders of power had been members of the national elite but without primary responsibility for governance within the system. With the change at the top, one subset of leaders was replaced by another. Although they might differ on specific policies, they did not disagree on the basically elitist nature of the political system and the necessity of retaining the patrimonial order as a means of preserving their own status.

Simon Schwartzman, building on Faoro's interpretation, has identified two different political systems emerging in Brazil over time.[16] One, representative and "democratic," appeared in the relatively developed Center-South region, primarily in and around the state of São Paulo. The other, a system of political co-optation, characterizes the states in the North and Northeast. As Brazil has developed in the twentieth century, the two political systems coexisted uneasily; the most apparent period of rivalry between the two was during the short-lived 1946 Republic. That republic provided the framework within which the two systems battled for supremacy. With the prolonged crisis during 1961–1964 and the military coup on March 31, 1964, the limited representative system foundered and then collapsed. It was restored with the transition of 1985, but to many observers it functions quite like the 1946 Republic. Indeed, the military regime deliberately created a group of new states on the Brazilian "frontier" in the North and Northwest, poorly populated but with a significant representation in the national Congress—and these elected officials are among the most ardent supporters of the prerogatives of the patrimonial state from which they benefit handsomely.

The patrimonial state, whether as a populist state (e.g., pre-1964) or a rigorously authoritarian manifestation, as during the Military Republic, relies on corporatist forms of organization to ensure the dominant position of the state over society. It has been defined as:

a system of interest representation in which the constituent units are organized into a limited number of singular, compulsory, noncompetitive, hierarchically ordered, and functionally differentiated categories, recognized or licensed (if not created) by the state and granted a deliberate representational monopoly within their respected categories in exchange for observing certain controls on their selection or leaders and articulation of demands and supports.[17]

As we will see later in this book, corporatism was a major means by which the patrimonial state penetrated and manipulated organized labor for many decades, and strong remnants are still in place today in Brazil.

Spontaneous interest group activity is strongly discouraged in regimes employing a corporatist strategy. Instead, the regime imposes an enforced limited pluralism system. The government, representing the patrimonial state, establishes the terms on which recognized groups are permitted to interact with the public authorities. Hierarchical relations predominate in such a system, and designated leaders understand their assigned role and function as serving the interests of the patrimonial regime.[18]

Control and domination are essential ingredients of the actions of the patrimonial regime. During populist or competitive political periods, the controls are more muted and more prone to manipulation by the political class for self-serving purposes. Under bureaucratic-authoritarian governments, the controls are direct, and their objective is to exclude the popular sectors of the society from political participation. The relations of the bureaucratic authoritarian government with the dominant or productive classes are still characterized by a desire to control, but the linkages are more complex, given the importance of the industrial bourgeoisie in the overall modernization strategy of the state.

The concept of the patrimonial state works on two levels of importance for our understanding of Brazilian politics. The first is the practical level. Here successive regimes, and the governments of those regimes, structure and rule Brazil as guardians of the power (coercive and noncoercive) of the state. In this sense, the state is often synonymous with the regime or the government. The latter, when exercising authority in relation to its subjects, is the state. The second level is one of abstraction. At this level, the state provides a general framework for political action by regimes and their governments. In so providing, the state appears as the embodiment of the historical and social processes that have most influenced the formation of the nation or the society. In this role, the state is greater than the sum of its regimes over time. Once created, the state assumes a vitality and meaning of its own that is not easily altered. It provides the general parameters within which the society functions. Its political system must work within these confines or run the risk of losing its authority—for, in the last analysis, it is how faithful a regime is to the image of the state—constructed through the centuries and accepted by a majority of the population, especially the political elite—that establishes its credibility or legitimacy.

In Brazil, the concept of the state is one of a predominance of public over private power. From the early years of colonization and settlement, the state has intervened in all spheres of societal activity. It has assumed primary responsibility for economic and social development, which often is left to private-sector initiative in other societies. The Brazilian state has been an interventionist, paternalistic, and an authoritarian one. It did not replicate the Western liberal and democratic model, although the institutions of that model would later be implanted in Brazil, providing a confusing and misleading sense of change. Nor did it approximate a totalitarian state in which every facet of societal existence is closely regulated by the coercive power of the central authority.

Through custom as well as usage, the preeminence of the patrimonial order is accepted and safeguarded. To accomplish its purposes in Brazil, the state was—and is—willing to allow limited political activity as long as the actors adhere to the established rules. This provides for a flexible and resourceful system of control. It allows for diversity—social and economic—which is a dominant characteristic of Brazil. In exchange for political support from the dominant social factors, the patrimonial state confirms and supports their local socioeconomic hegemony.

The concern of this type of state is its authority and the unfettered exercise of that authority. It possesses the capacity to control society coercively, but it prefers to utilize the techniques of persuasion, tradition, and co-optation. While it is insistent on dominating, it is not insistent on regulating, and this is a decisive difference from totalitarian states. Regulation of many issues is left to local initiative, with the understanding that local initiative, regardless of its diversity, will be supportive of the general system of power previously established.

What is to be stressed is that the state is not monolithic, nor is the national elite that manipulates its political system. The key characteristics, in addition to survival, are adaptability and resiliency in "guiding" society. Working through and with the complicity of the political elite, the state penetrates and dominates the nation. But the consolidation and extension of its power are explicable in terms of its own interest, which may or may not coincide with the interests and needs of the citizenry.

A critical issue that we will need to address in this analysis of Brazilian politics is whether the dynamic economic changes underway in Brazil, and the election in 1994 of the first "modern" government after the Military Republic, will undermine the long-standing structure of the patrimonial order. There is evidence that supports both a progressive, reformist trajectory; and there is support for the argument that much remains in place, with a superficial adaption in order to preserve the power of the traditional order.

There is no question that the size of the public bureaucracy will be significantly reduced with the measures approved by Congress in 1998 to downsize the public sector and to privatize a number of state companies. Those changes will reduce the number of public servants at the federal and state levels of Brazilian society. But will it reduce the "mentality" that seeks to transfer resources from the center of the system in Brasília to the constituent parts in the states and municipalities? As long as the revenue transfer mechanism put into place by the Constitution of 1988 is sacrosanct, the financing of the patrimonial order at the regional and state levels will remain secure. But some sort of change is inevitable. There will be accommodation and flexibility, as is traditional with the established political order in Brazil. The sophistication of the political elite is manifest in the long, drawn-out battle for constitutional reform from 1995 to 1998 during the first Cardoso administration. Few rational analysts can disagree with the modern, if modest, reform agenda proposed by the new president in early 1995. But the Cardoso government spent four long years attempting to convince the political elite in Congress that those reforms were needed, imperative, and critical to the future of Brazil. The task remains unfinished and will occupy much of the president's new term of office (1999–2003). And the task will be immeasurably more difficult following the failure of the Congress to approve a package of fiscal reforms in late 1998 and the devaluation of the currency which followed in January 1999. The principal reason for the reluctance of the legislative authorities to support the president is simple—they stand to lose for themselves and/or their powerful supporters many of the prerogatives established by the patrimonial state.

It can be argued that a final refuge of the country's political elite will be the continued neglect of social policy—that is, a deliberate effort to ignore the glaring inequalities in Brazilian society. As the defenses of the traditional patrimonial state are weakened, a second "line of defense" for the elite will take on greater relevance. This will be a strategic withdrawal from the elite's traditional argument in favor of the "big" state; it will have to bend to the reforms reluctantly approved by Congress, under growing presidential, public, and international pressures. It is controversial to argue, but I believe it is true, that the second line of defense will be the continued resistance of the elite to meaningful social reform. The elite will refuse to implement substantive changes in the educational and health systems. Income distribution will remain highly uneven and prejudicial to the poor. In a "democratic" system, where votes are the key factor in distributing political power, the local elites in Brazil will do all in their power to avoid "modernizing" society. They benefit from the social duality of Brazilian society. It is easier and more profitable to manipulate poor and marginal citizens than those with an education, access to health care, and salaried jobs. One cynical example—perhaps Machiavellian—was the decision in writing the 1988 Constitution to give the franchise to illiterates and to lower the minimum voting age. In this case, after having achieved their meaningless populist goal, the elites then coldly refused to concern themselves with preparing citizens to vote. It is well known that illiterate, malnutritioned individuals are either ill prepared to make judicious decisions or are highly susceptible to manipulation.

As always, the elites will never admit that this is a deliberate strategy. They will find others to blame for their failure over the centuries to address the basic social needs of their country. But as they cast about for ways of surviving the economic downsizing of the patrimonial state, they will retreat to protecting the patrimonial society from progressive change. How long they will be able to maintain this strategy is critical to Brazil's future.

Will we be able in 2003 (at the end of Cardoso's second term of office) to state that the subtle manifestations of the traditional order have been rooted out and destroyed? It is doubtful. The power of the new generation of rural landowners demonstrates the capacity for evolution of traditional forces. The inability to introduce significant changes in the electoral system, to make representation a reality through greater accountability for elected officials, the fecklessness of political parties—will these elements of the traditional order change in the foreseeable future? As we will consider briefly but return to in greater detail, Brazil's social dualism plays into the hands of the political elite, who must now find a new line of defense against the dangers of modernization and the decrease in the role of the patrimonial state. These important issues will be addressed in the following chapters.

Social Dualism

Brazilian society is characterized by a sharp, social duality, an enduring social framework in which the majority are systematically excluded from the majority of political and economic benefits generated by the system. As Hélio Jaguaribe argues:

The fundamental characteristic of Brazilian society is its profound dualism. On the one hand, as revealed by economic indicators, one finds a modern industrial society, which is the eighth largest economy in the western world and demonstrates an extraordinary dynamism, in the course of the last forty years, although its economic growth has sharply declined since the beginning of the 1980s. On the other hand, as revealed by social indicators, one finds a primitive society, living at subsistence level, in the rural world, or on the margins in conditions of urban misery, facing standards of poverty and ignorance comparable to those of the most backward Afro-Asian societies. The first society is but a fraction of the population, while the second constitutes nearly 60 percent of total population.[19]

And, writing a decade later—at the end of the century—Amaury de Souza comments that

poverty and social uprooting have fractured families, sending hordes of children into the streets to survive by their wits alone. An urban underclass has emerged, and with it has come drug addiction and crime. The changing nature of poverty inevitably changed the way in which the poor are seen. The image of the favela [shanty-town] dweller, enduring year-round hardship to be able to savor one night at the Carnival parade, has been replaced in the public eye by the no less stereotypical AK-47 automatic rifle-toting favela drug lord.[20]

This continued duality, whether deliberately maintained or the legacy of a past that is easily ignored by the national elite, has served the political interests of the patrimonial society. A large, marginal population has lent itself to manipulation. It has demanded little from state or society. The dualistic nature of Brazil has favored short- and medium-term control; it has precluded long-term social development and modernization. But are terms of reference changing? As de Souza also says, ''What started as a vague presentment that things were taking a turn for the worse blossomed in the early 1990s into a premonition of impending social disaster.''[21] But will this turn for the worse force the political elite to act—or react—to preserve what it has? Or will indifference lead to further polarization and eventual breakdown with unforeseen outcomes for the political elite?

While it is difficult to predict the reactions of the elites, Brazilian politics can still be understood in terms of a political class that has effectively been able to dominate national politics, regardless of changes in government. Elite domination has been accompanied by the growth of a powerful centralized government that has effectively bypassed the federal representative structure of the contemporary political system. Low rates of social mobilization precluded unmanageable demands until the late 1950s; and the slow rate of industrialization, in addition to the way in which Brazil industrialized, prevented the growth of autonomous interest groups with an identifiable political role. The social agenda and the dual nature of society preclude informed and sustained participation in national affairs for a large majority of Brazilians. They further ensure the continuation of the patrimonial state and the small political elite. But the fears of the 1990s may or may not generate pressures for reform—from below—or for preservation—from above. The second Cardoso administration faces a complicated set of choices, as it must work within the traditional power structure while fully understanding the impending social crisis. It is evident that Cardoso realizes the tremendous need to reallocate resources and respond with public policies that will begin to address the vast social inequalities and inequities that characterize Brazil at century's end. But to do so will threaten the established rules of the game, and Cardoso and his team will need to be mindful of the consequences for society by moving forward with their agenda of reform.

IMPLICATIONS OF THE POLITICAL GIVENS IN BRAZIL

It is a general thesis of this book that the Brazilian political system can best be understood in terms of a powerful patrimonial state directed by a national political elite. Federalism has been the form of organization adopted to meet the political and administrative needs of the state, and not those of the provinces or states. Regionalism has been, and remains, an important factor in political life. It has been reinforced by the Constitution of 1988, which returned to the states and municipalities many of the revenues that had been centralized in Brasília after 1964. These resources are allocated locally by the elites. Equally important, the monies transferred did not carry programmatic responsibilities for education, health, or housing. These remain the formal responsibility of the federal government. The bureaucracy at the center continues, but now the bulk of the revenues resides with the states and municipalities. Moreover, the bulk of the money has gone to raising the salaries and expanding the prerequisites of local politicians. The implications of this new way of disbursing funds are clear: health care and education remain woefully inadequate, and income distribution remains cruelly unequal.

In part, because of this generous "revenue sharing," we have seen a resurgence of regional elites—particularly state governors—in national politics in the 1990s. They are the logical power brokers between the central authorities and the state and municipal influential. The governors, in the patrimonial order, remain more powerful than the congressional delegations from the states. It is instructive that in the 1990s, many members of Congress have returned to their states to run for governor or mayor. The local and state bases of power remain dominant, even with the restoration of civilian government and the writing of the 1988 Constitution—which, theoretically, strengthened the federal legislative branch of government.

The disorder found in the political party system explains, to a large degree, the continuing ineffectiveness of the national legislature. That state of affairs serves the needs of the national elite.

A well-structured and coherent political party system would offer a more modern, more legitimate mechanism for the aggregation of interests and the distribution of resources in favor of the nation. But as one analyst has observed, "compared to parties in the other more developed countries of Latin America, Brazilian parties are singularly fragile. In fact, relative to the country's level of economic development, Brazil may be a unique case of party underdevelopment in the world."[22]

The combined effect of powerful state and local power brokers, a disorganized political party system that serves the interests of the latter, and the self-serving nature of Congress sustain the patrimonial order. The irony is that any change in the structure of the political system will need to be approved by the parties that sit in Brasília as the country's legislative authority. Self-interest indicates that such institutional changes will be very difficult to achieve. But without those changes, the social duality of Brazil grows. And that should be seen as a deliberate decision by a majority of the country's political leadership.

While the traditional order survives, can it flourish in a new urban order and in the context of a highly competitive, globalized economy in which Brazil must compete? To do so successfully will require new mentalities and modalities of behavior by the political elite. That group has been highly successful in survival; can it learn to adapt quickly enough to preserve its veto power over change—or is it possible that it will be either swept away or greatly reduced in scope and significance in the twenty-first century? If the elites can no longer rely on the automatic intervention of the military, have they lost a critical line of defense? Can the aggressive militancy of the rural landowners movement, which has appeared in the last decade, successfully force change? And when the support of another pillar of the patrimonial order, the Catholic Church, has, in some part, turned to support social justice in a meaningful way, how long can the old ways survive?

If we are correct in our analysis, the next century will see a sophisticated counterplay by the elites as they absorb the meaning of the new economic reform program and the changing role of traditional sources of institutional support. They will be unable, for the first time in centuries, to hide behind the bureaucratic state. What they most likely will do is continue the marginal position of the majority in the patrimonial society. This will be a different sort of challenge for the elites. Their orderly retreat will consist of finding excuses for the retention of the social duality of society, which excludes a large proportion of the population from acquiring the education, health, and skills needed to become critical participants—and not manipulated objects. And they will be strengthened by the rise of a "new" landed oligarchy, intent on retaining their vast holdings for both profit and prestige. The new rural power group is supported by local police and official authorities. Once again, the prominence of local and state institutions and political tradition and culture will be critical to Brazil's future, as it has been in the past.

In this fifth edition of *Brazil: Politics in a Patrimonial Society*, we are at an important turning point in Brazilian history. For the first time, economic and financial reforms that represent modernization are under way. A well-meaning and competent national government has been in power since 1995. Institutional roles are changing in the patrimonial society. Old allegiances are being revisited. A new set of actors—or actors who have redefined themselves—is beginning to appear. What is needed is strong and resourceful political leadership to bring together the elements in society that favor responsible change. Easily said. But that is the principal challenge for the Cardoso administration. Can the president, in his second term, overcome the inbuilt resistance to social change? He has accomplished a great deal in the economic and financial arena. But his task in the final four years of his administration will be more difficult as he copes with the fallout from the January 1999 devaluation of the *real*. He must now confront the most difficult and meaningful challenge—the advocacy of social justice and better income distribution. Only when there are visible advances in these areas will the many unfortunate Brazilians move from passive observers to informed and prepared citizens.

NOTES

1. Richard M. Morse, *The Bandeirantes* (New York: Alfred A. Knopf, 1965); Vianna Moog, *Bandeirantes and Pioneers* (New York: George Braziller, 1964).

2. Raymundo Faoro, *Os donos do poder*, 3rd ed., rev. (Rio de Janeiro: Editora Globo, 1976), pp. 301–303.

3. Fernando Uricoechea, *The Patrimonial Foundations of the Brazilian Bureaucratic State* (Berkeley: University of California Press, 1980), p. 64.

4. Ibid.

5. Richard Graham, *Britain and the Onset of Modernization in Brazil 1850–1914* (Cambridge: Cambridge University Press, 1968), Chapter 6.

6. An interesting alternative interpretation of the role of the landowners in the overthrow of the Empire is that of Richard Graham's. He argues that many landowners favored a republic not out of anger with the Empire but to prevent agrarian reform, which appeared to be the next step in the abolitionist movement. The Republicans had demonstrated little interest in the reform issue, and the landowners believed that they would be in a better position to defend their interests in a republic, given the weakness of imperial institutions. See Richard Graham, "Landowners and the Overthrow of the Empire," *Luso Brazilian Review* 7, no. 2 (Winter 1970): 44–45.

7. Thomas C. Bruneau, *The Political Transformation of the Brazilian Catholic Church* (New York: Cambridge University Press, 1974), p. 25.

8. There are various interpretations of the causes of the overthrow of the Old Republic. An explanation that does not contradict the political-electoral interpretation here

is that the economic interests of the early industrial elite in São Paulo were increasingly divergent from those of the planter class in the Northeast and elsewhere in the Southeast. Washington Luís's insistence on a successor from São Paulo responded to those interests in his state and sought to secure central government support for industrialization in São Paulo with a Paulista president.

9. Francisco Weffort, *O populismo na política brasileira* (Rio de Janeiro: Editora Paz e Terra, 1978). For a study of the origins of populism, see Michael L. Conniff, *Urban Politics in Brazil: The Rise of Populism, 1925–1945* (Pittsburgh: University of Pittsburgh Press, 1981).

10. José Sarney, "Brazil: A President's Story," *Foreign Affairs* (Fall 1986): 105.

11. Bolivar Lamounier, "Brazil: Inequality Against Democracy," in Larry Diamond, Juan J. Linz, and Seymour Martin Lipset, eds., *Democracy in Developing Countries*, Vol. 4 (Boulder, Colo.: Lynne Rienner, 1989), p. 113.

12. Franciso Weffort, "Why Democracy?", in Alfred Stepan, ed., *Democratizing Brazil: Problems of Transition and Consolidation* (Oxford: Oxford University Press, 1989), p. 334.

13. Peter McDonough, *Power and Ideology in Brazil* (Princeton, N.J.: Princeton University Press, 1981), p. 231.

14. Ibid.

15. Weffort, "Why Democracy?", p. 332.

16. Simon Schwartzman, "Representação e cooptação política no Brasil," *Dados* (Rio de Janeiro) 7 (1970): 9–41.

17. Phillipe C. Schmitter, "Still the Century of Corporatism?" *Review of Politics* 36, no. 1 (January 1974): 93–94, reprint, in Frederick B. Pike and Samuel Stritch, eds., *The New Corporatism* (Notre Dame, Ind.: University of Notre Dame Press, 1974).

18. James M. Malloy, in James Malloy, ed., *Authoritarianism and Corporatism* (Pittsburgh: University of Pittsburgh Press, 1977), p. 4.

19. Hélio Jaguaribe et al., *Brasil: Reforma ou caos*, 5th ed. (Rio de Janeiro: Editora Paz e Terra, 1990).

20. Amaury de Souza, "Redressing Inequalities: Brazil's Social Agenda at Century's End," in Riordan Roett and Susan Kaufman Purcell, eds., *Brazil Under Cardoso* (Boulder, Colo.: Lynne Rienner, 1997), p. 64.

21. Ibid.

22. Scott Mainwaring, "Brazil: Weak Parties, Feckless Democracy," in Scott Mainwaring and Timothy R. Scully, eds., *Building Democratic Institutions: Political Party Systems in Latin America* (Stanford, Calif.: Stanford University Press, 1995), p. 354.

Chapter 2

Political Parties and Elections

Among the major countries in Latin America, parties probably have played the smallest role in the development of the Brazilian political system. Mexico's Partido Revolucionario Institucional (PRI), the Radicals in Argentina and Chile, Alianza Popular Revolucionaria Americana (APRA) in Peru, and the Conservatives and Liberals in Colombia are all examples of parties having a relatively long period of growth and impact on their respective national political systems. In contrast, Brazilian parties' principal characteristics are "their fragility, their ephemeral character, their weak roots in society, and the autonomy politicians of the catch-all parties enjoy with respect to their parties."[1]

Parties in Brazil have been subservient to the "givens" that we have identified in the Brazilian political process. They have played a marginal role in exercising decision-making power; they have demonstrated little continuity in organization at the national or the local level; and they have evidenced only minimal interest in seeking popular support for reasons other than immediate electoral goals. The party system has not been viewed as a legitimate means of resolving disputes in Brazil in any phase of national development. It has done little to further national integration or reduce and resolve political cleavages. In fact, parties in Brazil, particularly in the 1946 Republic, exacerbated social and political conflicts rather than helped "manage" them. Parties have not been a means of socializing people into the political system, nor have they been able to fulfill vital input functions in the political system—articulating and aggregating interests, which certainly has been true since the return of civilian government in 1985.

The following historical sketch provides a setting for considering parties during the 1946 Republic, the only period of open, competitive party politics in Brazilian history until the political *abertura* process that began in the late 1970s and ended on March 15, 1985. An analysis of Brazilian parties is instructive because it demonstrates the impact of the patrimonial regime on all aspects of political life and enables us to trace the development and decay of the 1946 Republic. The party system of that period, when contrasted with the Military Republic, will give us an enhanced view of politics in Brazil. The final section of this chapter will review the reorganization of the party system in the early 1980s and the current party system of the 1990s.

PARTIES UNTIL 1946

During the Empire (1822–1889), the Liberal and Conservative parties were divided less by policy differences than by individual and regional rivalries and loyalties. The Liberals, formed in 1831, and the Conservatives, organized in 1837, were rotated in power at the whim of the emperor. The predominant political figures of the Empire were not known as "party men" but as individuals who rendered exceptional and loyal service to the monarch.

Save for the short-lived Progressive Party, formed in the 1860s by the left wings of the two parties, the only new attempt at organized political activity was the Republican Party, created in 1870. The Manifesto of 1870, the founding document of the party, advocated well-known reform measures previously proposed by the Liberal Party. The first state Republican organization was formed in São Paulo in 1873. Not until 1885 did the party succeed in electing its first candidates to parliament. While the party supported abolition of slavery, it did not do so fervently; while the Republicans favored reform, they did not endorse radical change; and while they favored a republic, most were wealthy, comfortable Conservatives. It can be said that the Brazilian Republican movement gained adherents in spite of, and not because of, the Republican Party.

With the creation of the Old Republic (1889–1930) under military aegis, the Liberal and the Conservative parties disintegrated. The state Republican Party units became the political nucleus of the old Republican Party. The patrimonial regime from 1889 to 1930 utilized the Republican Party to run the country with the cooperation of its regional and state units; the latter normally functioned only at election time. Only twice did the Republican Party not succeed in imposing its official candidates on the country. In 1910, Marshal Hermes da Fonseca, with military and partial party endorsement, gained the presidency. In 1918, with a split in the political elite, Epitácio Pessoa was chosen to succeed a president who had died in office. Opposition candidates had little, if any, chance of victory, given the careful understanding between state and federal governments. Only in 1910 and 1914 did an opposition candidate, without an organized party structure, stand against the establishment. In both elections, Rui Barbosa, a statesman of the Empire, was defeated.

One of the few attempts to organize an opposition to the Republican Party was the Democratic Party of São Paulo. Formed in 1926 by middle-class urban groups in the city of São Paulo, the party had little success in challenging the political elite. The Democratic Party supported the candidacy of Vargas in 1930. Participation in elections was limited for a number of reasons. In a predominantly rural and agrarian nation, the constitutional restriction against illiterates voting excluded the vast majority of the potential electorate. Regional and state political and social controls, exercised by the elites, precluded deviant or active political activity by literate citizens. Thus, in the election of 1910, in which there was competition for president, only 1.64 percent of the total population voted. In 1914, 2.14 percent voted; and in 1930, the only other election year during the Old Republic with more than one presidential candidate, 5.10 percent of the total population cast their ballots. In terms of numbers of votes, Júlio Prestes in 1930 was the first presidential candidate to receive more than 1 million votes. He defeated Getúlio Vargas but was kept from taking office by the Revolution of 1930.

From the successful revolution in October 1930 to the promulgation of the 1934 Constitution, the political party scene remained fluid. The Republican and Democratic parties in São Paulo joined forces; both groups feared that Vargas and his entourage were determined to break the national political influence of that state. The friction over Vargas's interventors, economic policy, and the future place of the state in national affairs led to the revolt of July 9, 1932. The other states of the federation did not come to São Paulo's assistance, and the rebels surrendered on September 29, 1932.

The Partido de Lavoura (Labor Party), organized by Varga's intervenor in São Paulo, never received widespread support. It slowly withered away and, with the revolt of 1932, disappeared for all practical purposes.

The national political party system remained confused until 1934. In some states, the old Republican Party merged with new groups; in other states, the Republican Party disintegrated and was replaced by an amorphous organization that represented the immediate interests of those whom the revolutionary government recognized and had appointed to positions of influence; and in São Paulo and Minas Gerais, the Republican Party maintained its autonomy.

The young *tenentes*, who had helped bring Vargas to power, organized a number of clubs, none of which was sufficiently structured and coherent to be mistaken for a political party. The 5th of October Club, named after the date of the successful 1930 Revolution, was the best known. Others were the 5th of July Club and the Agrarian Party. All of these organizational attempts were in support of the vague and idealistic reform program that the *tenentes* hoped to see implemented after Vargas assumed power. By the period 1932–1933, the *tenentes* had fragmented; their program had been co-opted by the regime or sidetracked by other concerns.

The election in May 1933 for a constituent assembly to write a new constitution was confused from the political party perspective. The ballots of the states included hundreds of parties and organizations, none of which were national and few, if any, of which had a mass following. With the proclamation of the

1934 Constitution, two new political movements came into prominence, while the old parties declined in influence.

The Integralists (Brazilian Integralist Association) and the Communists became the dominant political movements from 1934 to 1937. Both were the first ideologically based parties in Brazil. *Integralismo* had come into existence in October 1932 with a "Manifesto to the Brazilian Nation" by their leader Plínio Salgado, a writer from São Paulo. Influenced by the dictators of Europe, particularly Mussolini in Italy and Salazar in Portugal, the movement was conservative, nationalist, traditionalist, and Roman Catholic.

The Communist Party, led by Luís Carlos Prestes, a former *tenente*, continued to grow in popular appeal after 1930. Prestes had been a well-known opposition figure during the Old Republic. The appeal of the party to the masses captured the imagination of segments of the Brazilian population as the first signs of an urban proletariat emerged. In 1935, the National Liberation Alliance was created, with Prestes as honorary president. Publicized as a popular-front type of organization, it was clear that the Communist Party was the principal member and instigator of its activities. Vargas maintained formal and informal contacts with Salgado and Prestes throughout the early and mid-1930s.[2] As the old political parties seemed unable to claim widespread popular support, Vargas saw the two opposing movements as possible alternatives to support for his program. He played one against the other and allowed them to organize freely. The clashes between the two groups increased during 1934 and 1935. Bloody street fighting erupted in the major cities. The growing tension culminated in Communist uprisings in the Northeast states of Pernambuco and Rio Grande do Norte. In November 1935, a raid on a federal military garrison in Rio de Janeiro resulted in a number of officers being murdered. The uprising was put down by the government, the Communist Party was outlawed, and Prestes was jailed.

The suppression of the Communists coincided with the growing tension surrounding the presidential election of 1937; Vargas's term of office, under the 1934 Constitution, ended in 1938. Two candidates emerged: former *tenente* José Américo de Almeida, the government candidate, and the governor of São Paulo, Armando Sales, who spoke of antiregime forces. The campaign progressed bitterly. The nation seemed hopelessly polarized. Rumors of a government coup began to circulate.

Vaguely promising a preferred position for the Integralists in the political order if they supported his coup, Vargas decreed the New State on November 10, 1937. On December 3, 1937, the president dissolved all political parties. Not even the Integralists were allowed to survive organizationally. Slowly, Vargas had outwitted or defeated all organized political opposition. The old Republican units had been discredited or relegated to a marginal position in national politics; the feeble organizational efforts of the *tenentes* and their idealistic supporters had been allowed to wither; the few semiorganized opposition parties of the Old Republic, such as the Democratic Party of São Paulo, were found wanting and allowed to decay; and the Communists and Integralists, used and manipulated by Vargas, were dealt swift, effective blows when they no longer served the needs of the patrimonial state. In May 1938, the last gasp of the Integralists—an attempt to invade the Presidential Palace in Rio and murder the president—was a failure.

Vargas's tactics undermined and destroyed the political party organizations of the 1930–1937 period. No parties were allowed to function between 1937 and 1945. The patrimonial regime, presided over by Vargas, assumed all responsibility for decision making.

THE 1946 REPUBLIC

With the abrupt overthrow of Vargas, the Brazilian political system encountered a mass electorate for the first time. The 1946 Republic paid more than lip service to the principles of liberal democracy that had been superficially adhered to in the previous regime. But the long tradition of the patrimonial state had not provided the institutions and mechanisms that a mass electorate required. Brazil, from 1946 to 1964, became a "praetorian society," in Samuel Huntington's conceptualization of political development.[3] That is, the political system manifested low levels of institutionalization and relatively high levels of participation.

Prior to 1945, the only institutions that had real value in terms of political power were those of the patrimonial state: the executive, the bureaucracy, and those administrative agencies of the state that served to structure the central government's relations with its subordinate units. Suddenly, other institutions and procedures, such as political parties and interest groups, were allowed to act autonomously. As they attempted to fulfill their defined roles in an open, competitive political system, they ran into the intractability of the patrimonial state.

The prolonged constitutional crisis of 1961–1964 was the inevitable outcome of the clash between the operating political realities of Brazilian society and the imagined political changes that the 1946 Constitution represented. Once it became clear to those groups aligned with the patrimonial regime and the status quo—the bureaucrats, administrators, landowners, and urban middle class—that the challenge posed by the newly mobilized groups might succeed in breaking the power of the patrimonial state and give real meaning to the ideals of the 1946 Constitution, the military acted on behalf of the establishment and overthrew João Goulart, thus restoring "order" to public affairs in Brazil.

Throughout the 1946 Republic, the parties remained loose coalitions of state and local units. Little discipline existed within the party structures. An individual or a small group tended to dominate party policy making. Little attempt was made to create a mass base, particularly in the rural areas. Beset by personalism, unable to carve out a constructive role in the decision-making process, and subject to the patronage largess of the state, the parties soon became a group of competing cabals without long-range goals or ideological purpose. The parties confused the voters as much as they represented and guided them. As one party failed to fulfill its campaign promises, the frustrated voters would turn to another party, and then another. When the parties appeared bankrupt, electoral alliances emerged in the competition for votes.

Out of this confusing and hopeless welter of organizations and individuals emerged a mélange of political brokers or go-betweens who played an important role in the politics of the era. Their job was to make the populist political system function by rounding up the votes required by the bosses or candidates by whom they were retained. The classic figure of the *coronel* (colonel), the wealthy and prestigious landowner of the interior, gained new importance as he delivered the votes of his employees and dependents to the party that had arranged to buy them. The *cabo eleitoral* (election chief) arranged for a few hundred or a few thousand votes in exchange for patronage or cash; his interest in his following was based on his need for their votes and, in turn, on their need to have someone intercede with the bureaucratic state for favors.

The classic study of the role and function of the *coronel* remains that of Victor Nunes Leal's.[4] Other studies have described in detail the process of rounding up the vote on Election Day,[5] the control of a state's politics by four men over a 40-year period[6] and the colorful and powerful lifestyle of four *coronels* of the interior of Pernambuco.[7]

The *coronel* and the *cabo eleitoral* were accompanied by political phenomena such as the *cabide de emprego* (employment hanger), *panelinha* (little sauce-pan), and *igrejinha* (little church), all identified by Anthony Leeds in his study of Brazilian society. The *panelinha* is "a relatively closed, completely informal primary group, held together in common interest by personal ties and including a roster of all key sociopoliticoeconomic positions."[8] Typically, a *panelinha* might consist of a customs official, one or two lawyers, a well-placed business-man, an accountant, a banker, and an assortment of local, state, and federal officials (both appointed and elected). Each would make his expertise and range of contacts available to the group, and in exchange his interests would be pro-tected and advanced.

The *igrejinha* is somewhat more hierarchical than a *panelinha*, which is a collaborative effort of equals. There normally is a dominant figure in the *igre-jinha* who promotes and protects the careers of his followers; in return, they supply him with information, support, and a wide range of contacts who can "get things done." These linkage phenomena played a vital role in the disjointed politics of 1946–1964. To survive and prosper politically, an individual required informal, transitory alliances with like-minded citizens. The personalism and informality of politics are well illustrated by these relationships, which had more meaning than formal parties or interest groups in furthering careers.

In an analysis of party politics and elections in Brazil from 1946 to 1964, Gláucio Ary Dillon Soares demonstrated that "the conservative parties have a much stronger position in the Northeast, where they account for almost 70 per-cent of all representatives elected for the Congress, whereas in the Southeast they account for only 45 percent."[9] He concludes that while party politics in the South had become more ideological and class oriented, "politics in the Northeast is the politics of backwardness—the politics of tradition."[10]

THE MAJOR PARTIES: THE "BIG THREE"

Getúlio Vargas organized two parties in 1945 in preparation for his postwar political role in Brazilian politics. The Social Democratic Party (PSD) came about through the efforts of the New State intervenors in the various states. Many of the Old Republic political bosses at the local level, still alive and active, became PSD stalwarts. The party attracted the bureaucrats, landowners, bankers, and industrialists who benefited from the state-directed economic programs of Vargas and that of PSD presidents during the 1946 Republic.

The PSD elected Vargas's minister of war, General Eurico Gaspar Dutra, to the presidency in 1945 and Juscelino Kubitschek, former governor of Minas Gerais, in 1955. It supported Vargas after his reelection on the PTB (Brazilian Labor Party) ticket in 1950 and collaborated with the Goulart administration from 1961 to 1964. The only period during the 1946 Republic when the PSD was out of favor was during the brief Quadros incumbency in 1961. It dominated the national Congress and state legislatures. Of all the postwar parties, it had the strongest organizational base in the states and regions. Moderately conservative but nonideological, the PSD favored centralization of power, state participation in economic development, and the continuation and elaboration of the Vargas welfare system. Throughout the 1946 Republic, it represented par excellence the amorphous party of the patrimonial state: pliant, adaptive, nonreformist, and uninterested in social or political mobilization. For many years, the president of the party was Amaral Peixoto, Vargas's son-in-law.

The second party Vargas created, and the "partner" of the PSD throughout the post-1946 era, was the PTB. Its purpose was to capitalize on Vargas's following among the urban masses and organized labor. Vargas utilized the PTB to return to power in 1950. Predominantly urban in orientation, the PTB was most susceptible to Communist influence in the 1946 Republic. It had strong rural support in the states of the Amazonas and Rio Grande do Sul. Its platform was one of active nationalism, state intervention in the economy, and extended welfare benefits for the working class. The PTB was the most heterogeneous of the major parties. It attracted wealthy landowners like João Goulart, middle-level government employees, artisans, members of the new urban upper class who hoped to use the party for their advantage, and leftist intellectuals. Goulart, as minister of labor under Vargas and the successor to Vargas as party leader, attempted to use the party to control organized labor for the government's advantage. But only a minority of organized labor actively backed the party, and there was widespread resentment of government control of the workers' movement and the paternalistic and corrupt policies of the Labor Ministry.

The PTB was the junior member of the PSD-PTB coalition until 1961, when Goulart succeeded Quadros as president. With the rapid urbanization of Brazil after 1946, the party grew quickly in popularity. The 1962 state and congressional elections indicated a growing electoral challenge by the PTB to the leadership of the PSD. By 1963, defections from other parties had made PTB the largest party in the Chamber of Deputies. The left wing of the party, represented by men like Leonel Brizola, Goulart's brother-in-law and former governor of Rio Grande do Sul, pushed for greater independence from the centrist-PSD position that Goulart occupied and advocated radical economic and social reform. In the federal Senate, the PTB stood second, with 18 of 66 seats (3 per state) in 1963; the PSD was first with 21, and the UDN was third with 15.

The third major political party of the 1946 Republic, the National Democratic Union (UDN), attracted the anti-Vargas forces in 1945. Except for the 1960 victory of Quadros, whom the party had endorsed, it was the principal opposition party from 1946 to 1964. Without access to the vast patronage and financial support of the federal government, it survived by keeping alive the antipathy of its members to the political populism of Vargas and his heirs. With the 1964 coup d'état, the UDN became the "government party" in that its principal leaders staffed many of the cabinet posts of the military regime. A moderate, conservative party, it drew heavily on the liberal professions and urban intellectuals.

THE MINOR PARTIES

The 11 minor parties of the 1946 Republic were a mixed bag. Some, such as the Liberation Party and the Republican Party, were throwbacks to the Old Republic. Others represented offshoots of the major parties. The Labor Reform Movement was organized in 1960 by PTB leader Fernando Ferrari to support his candidacy for vice president. Another PTB offshoot, the Social Labor Party, barely survived between 1946 and 1964.

The Brazilian Socialist Party was originally the democratic Left of the UDN. It represented socialist intellectuals and professional groups, and it was one of the few ideologically oriented parties of the period. Peasant League leader Francisco Julião was a prominent member.

The Christian Democratic Party was another party with a strong ideological orientation. Created to represent Roman Catholic social doctrine with a special emphasis on human dignity and justice, it supported a non-Marxist socialism. It frequently allied with the UDN in elections; its strength rested in São Paulo and Paraná.

The Popular Representation Party, a truly ideological party, was the postwar successor to Plínio Salgado's Integralist Party. It claimed to be the first nationalist movement in postwar Brazil. In 1955, Salgado's candidacy for president drew 700,000 votes.

The Socialist Progressive Party became the fourth largest party in the Chamber of Deputies in 1962. Dominated by its personalist leader, Adhemar de Barros, it was a center party, appealing to the urban lower class in the populist tradition of Vargas. Barros, elected governor of São Paulo in 1947, was reelected in 1962, defeating former president Quadros. He ran for president in 1955 and 1960.

A fourteenth political party, registered in mid-1965, never had time to organize. It was the Goodwill Party (Partido da Boa Vontade), which had some support among housewives and lower-class groups in and around the city of Rio de Janeiro.

THE COMMUNIST PARTY

Founded in 1922, the Brazilian Communist Party (PCB) was led from 1935 to 1980 by Luís Carlos Prestes. Forced underground after the 1935 revolt, the party surfaced in 1945 and sought to keep Vargas in power. The presidential candidate of the party ran third, with about 10 percent of the vote, in 1945. Prestes was elected to the Senate, and 14 deputies were chosen. Four more deputies were added in the 1947 election. The Supreme Electoral Tribunal canceled the party's registration in 1947, when a set of statutes was discovered that espoused Marxist–Leninist principles.

After 1947, the PCB ran candidates on other party tickets; it was allowed to propagandize and work fairly openly before 1964. From 1961 to 1964, the party campaigned to regain legal recognition. Candidates of the Left supported the party's position because they felt its votes would favor them; moderate and conservative leaders spoke out in favor of legalization in order to make the party operate openly. The party was forced underground again in 1964.[11]

The party split into two in 1961 with the formation of a dissident wing favoring violent tactics to overthrow the existing order. The splinter group was known as the Communist Party of Brazil (PC do B). The new group claimed to favor Beijing in the Moscow–Beijing division of the world Communist movement and sought to arouse a following among the Northeast Peasant Leagues, students, and intellectuals. The party reemerged in the early 1980s and was legalized after the restoration of civilian rule in 1985.

THE CONGRESS: PARLIAMENTARY FRONTS, ELECTORAL ALLIANCES, AND UBIQUITOUS POPULISM

From 1946 to 1964, an increasing number of people were mobilized to participate in the political system. Although illiterates still could not vote, more people were available, with different kinds of demands, for politicization by populist politicians.

Brazil became increasingly urban and literate in the 1950s. Although it lagged behind other large countries of Latin America, the movement to the cities and the appearance of a competitive party system created a new political reality: populism. The name of the game was to win elections by promising one's new constituents public services and using rhetorical appeals for the reform of a highly structured, hierarchical society. In order to win elections, and thus gain access to the spoils and patronage available to victors, many candidates and parties formed alliances. Created by any number of the 13 political parties active after 1946, the alliances existed only for the purpose of electing candidates to office under the proportional representation system employed from 1946 to 1964. The alliances offered no true representation, since candidates elected on an alliance ticket entered Congress as party members—Congress was organized along party, not alliance, lines, and it in no way heeded the ephemeral affiliation the alliance indicated. The parties quickly lost coherence and autonomy.

The electoral alliance system reflected the populist tendencies of the post-1946 political system. It indicated the fragility and impermanence of the political party system, the one mechanism that might have overcome the vertical patterns of authority and domination, and the continuing political influence of the traditional social and economic elites. The alliance allowed candidates to appeal for votes on the basis of a nebulous promise to improve the lot of the voter, without any need to worry about specific commitments or returns once office had been gained. The voter, having only the electoral system to turn to in the search for leadership and representation, chose among poorly qualified candidates, bewildered by the "national" political party structure between elections and the sudden emergence of alliances when it came time to vote.

In the five congressional elections of the 1946 Republic, the percentage of votes cast for alliances rose from zero in 1945 to 16.7 in 1950, 25.7 in 1954, 33.3 in 1958, and 41.0 in 1962. In some states in 1962, the vote on the alliance tickets went as high as 86.2 percent (Espírito Santo) and 89.1 percent (Rio Grande no Norte). The disintegration of the national political party system seemed imminent. The movement away from party candidates toward alliance choices and the willingness of the parties to subordinate their identity to an ephemeral alliance indicated the shallowness of both the programmatic content and the ideological dedication of Brazilian parties.

Another manifestation of the weakness of the party system was the emergence in Congress of parliamentary fronts. Since the parties were unrepresentative of public opinion and cut across class and ideological lines, the political polarization of the 1946 Republic was reflected in the organization of ad hoc groupings in the early 1960s. For example, the National Parliamentary Front attempted to galvanize support for "basic reforms" in Congress. An ultranationalist radical reform unit, it often accused President Goulart of timidity.

A conservative group, the Parliamentary Democratic Action, drew its support predominantly from the UDN and attempted to counter the leftist groups. Former finance and foreign minister San Tiago Dantas attempted in 1963–1964 to create a Front for Basic Reforms to lobby for giving the vote to illiterates, legalizing the Communist Party, and reforming labor legislation. It, too, had little success in overcoming the apathy and deep personal divisions that characterized Congress.

THE ELECTORAL SYSTEM

The weak position of the parties in Brazilian politics was further undermined by the electoral system. The Chamber of Deputies had 409 seats, and deputies were elected for four years by popular vote. By the system of proportional representation, each state received a deputy for every 150,000 inhabitants, up to 20 deputies, and an additional deputy for each additional 250,000 inhabitants. Each territory was guaranteed one deputy, the states and federal district, a minimum of seven. Alternates were selected from the unsuccessful candidates of each party in the order of the vote received.

There were no congressional districts in the states. All candidates for the Chamber of Deputies ran at large, on a party-ticket system. Votes were cast for one candidate only. The total of votes cast for each party's candidates was the party's share of the total vote. Each party was assigned a number of seats equal to its share of the vote. Once the number of seats for each party in the state was decided, the individual candidates received those seats in the order of the number of votes they had won.

This system of voting for the Chamber of Deputies—gubernatorial, senatorial, and presidential elections were direct—led to overrepresentation of the smaller states. By basing representation on the number of inhabitants rather than on the number of voters, the backward states with high rates of illiteracy and low rates of electoral participation received the same representation as the more heavily populated, urban, participant states in the Center-South.

Parties contributed little to the political life of the 1946 Republic. There was no tradition in Brazil of a strong party system in either the Old or the Transitional Republic. The organizations from 1946 to 1964 were parties in name only. Poorly organized and susceptible to personal and governmental pressure, they were unable to identify an independent policy-making position in the context of the federal Congress.

Unable to participate effectively in public policy making, and prevented from adequately representing what was, at best, an amorphous constituency, the parties became dependent creatures, the victims of decisions made by others who valued little their existence and, even less, mourned their disappearance. Without purpose and legitimacy, the party system was easily sacrificed by the Military Republic after 1964.

POLITICAL PARTIES FROM 1964 TO 1977

The fate of the political party system was unclear following the overthrow of the Goulart regime. Important segments of the armed forces favored a continuation and an eventual restoration of the traditional party system—after it had been purged of undesirable elements. Others preferred the abolition of parties, and some remained indifferent as long as the centralization of decision making excluded civilian politicians from power. The strong antiradical position of the

UDN in the period preceding the downfall of Goulart led to a predisposition toward its leadership among many military officers.

During the first months of the Military Republic, a number of major political party figures lost their political rights for 10 years, among them former Presidents Goulart (PTB) and Quadros (UDN). The Institutional Act of April 9, 1964, had stipulated that during a two-month period, members of Congress, state legislators, and municipal councillors were liable to lose their political rights if they were found to be Communist sympathizers or to be guilty of corruption. The government was given the power, during a six-month period, to remove from office government officials, such as members of the armed forces, judges, and professors, for the same reasons.

During the two-month purge period, 337 individuals were denied the right to vote or to hold public office. In addition to the 2 former presidents, 6 state governors, 56 members of Congress, and dozens of former ministers of state, military officers, state legislators, public officials, diplomats, and labor leaders were expelled from political life. At the end of the six-month period, approximately 3,500 individuals had been removed from political life, the majority on charges of corruption.

The ambiguity toward civilian politicians and political parties continued into 1965. A stalwart of the PSD from Minas Gerais and a former finance minister, José Maria Alkmin, had been elected vice president by Congress in April 1964. That election confirmed the willingness of the regime to tolerate proven supporters of the Revolution in high political office. But in March 1965, in the first important electoral contest since March 31, 1964, Air Force Brigadier José Vicente Faria Lima won the mayoral election in São Paulo. Faria Lima had been endorsed by former President Quadros, and his election was viewed with suspicion by the hard-line military. A July 1965 decree limited political statements on radio and television, and on July 9, Congress, by a vote of 210 to 115, approved a controversial "law of ineligibilities," aimed at preventing the return to power of the Goulart forces and other counterrevolutionary elements.

On July 15, 1965, President Humberto Castello Branco signed the Political Parties Statute that set out procedures for forming and registering political parties, the conditions under which registration might be canceled, and new rules governing party finances. For recognition, parties needed at least 3 percent of the total vote in the most recent general election for the Chamber of Deputies, distributed among at least 11 states; at least 12 seats in the Chamber from at least 7 states; and an organization reaching down to local-level membership in at least 11 states. The statute was not to apply to the October 1965 gubernatorial elections but would become law before the 1966 presidential election. Its clear intent was to reduce the number of parties that had proliferated during the 1946 Republic and to concentrate political representation in a limited number of parties.

On October 3, 1965, gubernatorial elections were held in 11 states. Candidates backed by the opposition PSD and PTB parties were victorious in Guanabara,

Minas Gerais, Mato Grosso, Rio Grande do Norte, and Santa Catarina. In Alagoas and Maranhão, no candidate received an absolute majority, and a vote of the state assembly was to decide the outcome. The pro-government UDN won only three gubernatorial seats.

Widespread military discontent surfaced over both the holding of direct elections and the results. War Minister Arthur Costa e Silva announced that all winning candidates would be allowed to take office without interference. The hard-line military officers, determined to eradicate subversive elements from Brazilian society and to get on with the modernization of Brazil, pressured the government for a drastic restructuring of the political system to prevent another defeat at the polls. Bending to political and military realities, President Castello Branco decreed Institutional Act No. 2 on October 27, 1965. Among other reforms, the political parties of the 1946 Republic were abolished; new parties were to be formed within the rules stipulated in the Political Parties Statute of July 1965.

After much debate, two new parties were organized in December 1965. The National Renovating Alliance (ARENA) emerged out of the UDN and the more moderate members of the PSD. The opposition Brazilian Democratic Movement (MDB) evolved from the remains of the PTB, the progressive wing of the PSD, and the smaller radical parties of the pre-1946 period. After 1966, ARENA was divided between UDN and PSD elites in some states. While the UDN dominated the party machinery in Alagoas, Sergipe, and Guanabara, leadership was shared with the PSD in Minas Gerais, Goiás, Santa Catarina, and Piauf. In Bahia, São Paulo, Pernambuco, Ceará, and Pará, the UDN had to share control with both the PSD and the PTB. The PSD dominated ARENA in Maranhão and Rio Grande do Sul.

In a further effort to restrict the role of political parties, President Castello Branco, on February 5, 1966, decreed Institutional Act No. 3, which provided that the next president, governors of 11 states, and the mayors of state capitals were to be chosen indirectly by legislative bodies. In July, the president ordered the removal from office of 32 state and local elected officials who had been agitating for direct, popular presidential elections. Members of the group lost their political rights for 10 years.

In August 1966, the MDB announced that it would boycott the indirect elections for state governors and president to protest the absence of political freedom. On September 3, ARENA majorities in 12 states elected government candidates as governor. And on October 3, former Minister Arthur Costa e Silva, the ARENA candidate, was chosen president in an indirect election at a joint session of Congress boycotted by the MDB.

Another purge of ''radical'' elements in October 1966 led to the dismissal of six federal deputies and other state and local officials. The president of the Chamber of Deputies announced that the deputies could be removed from office only by the action of Congress. On October 17, without governmental permission, a session of the Chamber of Deputies was held in which the government was severely criticized by the MDB and five of the six dismissed deputies. On October 20, the president issued a decree recessing the Congress until one week following the congressional elections, and he announced that he would govern by decree in the interim.

The November 1966 congressional elections gave ARENA 260 seats out of 409 in the Chamber of Deputies, a majority of 63 percent, and 44 out of 66 in the Senate, a majority of 67 percent. The opposition party's strength came principally in the large cities; more than 30 percent of all votes cast in Rio de Janeiro of the old PSD took six seats; former UDN representatives won four, and minor parties won the other two.

On January 22, 1967, Congress, by a vote of 221 to 110, approved a new constitution to go into effect on March 15. This document further restricted the power of Congress and concentrated decision making in the hands of the chief executive. In a further move to restrict open politics, the Municipal Security Law was passed by Congress on May 23, 1968. Almost 700 towns were declared areas of national security and were denied the right to hold local elections; mayors and other officials were to be appointed by the central government.

As a result of the growing domination of the party system by the government, the November 15, 1968, elections for mayors and municipal councillors in 1,479 municipalities resulted in a clear-cut victory for ARENA, which won about 80 percent of the seats. The growing resentment among civilian politicians against restrictions on party activity culminated on December 12, 1968, when the Chamber of Deputies, by a vote of 216 to 141, with 15 present and not voting and 37 absences, decided against permitting the trial of opposition deputy Márcio Moreira Alves on charges of having offended the army in a September 7 speech to Congress. In quick retaliation, the government issued Institutional Act No. 5, which gave the president the right to suspend Congress and the state legislatures for an indefinite period (among a series of new powers).

With the closing of Congress, the regime moved against remaining political opponents. Former Guanabara governor Carlos Lacerda and 12 other prominent politicians lost their political rights on December 30. On January 16, 1969, the president deprived 40 federal deputies of their political rights and purged the Supreme Court of three members. On April 29, the government deprived 107 individuals of their political rights and removed from office 15 federal deputies, 59 state deputies, and 9 mayors. With that action, 93 deputies, almost 25 percent of the federal Congress, had been purged.

The 1968 closing of Congress and the promulgation of Institutional Act No. 5 confirmed the diminishing influence of political parties in an increasingly authoritarian regime. The parties were again ignored in the succession crisis of 1969, when the incapacitation of President Costa e Silva led the military high command to bypass the civilian vice president and drastically amend the 1967 Constitution to further centralize decision making in the hands of the president. No congressional participation or approval was sought by the armed forces. The act reduced the number of members of Congress and further limited its power.

Members of Congress were no longer immune from criminal prosecution, and their freedom to vote and speak on political issues did not include matters involving national honor or security. Provisions were included to allow for expulsion from Congress for opposing the institutions of the Military Republic or for disregarding directives of party authorities.

The November 15, 1970, general elections for Congress, state legislatures, and municipal councils demonstrated public apathy and represented the nadir of party autonomy during the Military Republic. ARENA won 41 of the 46 seats in the Senate, bringing its total to 59 of the 66 seats and 224 of the 310 seats in the Chamber of Deputies. The government party won every state legislature except Guanabara (Rio de Janeiro).

The hold of the government over the political party system was again confirmed in April 1972, when incumbent President Emílio Médici canceled the 1974 direct elections for state governors, substituting indirect election by state legislative assemblies. Given ARENA's commanding control in almost all of the state legislatures, it was a foregone conclusion that the government party would control the gubernatorial posts across the country. The government chose candidates for governor in each state, without regard for their membership in ARENA, although all were nominal members of the official party. The qualifications sought were administrative experience, nonpartisanship, and willing acceptance of the economic policies of the central government.

The municipal elections of November 15, 1972, gave ARENA majorities in mayoral and city council elections in some 4,000 municipalities. While the MDB won majorities in Manaus, Natal, and Pôrto Alegre, ARENA carried the remaining 21 state capitals. Mayors were not elected in state capitals or in those towns previously declared national security areas.

President Médici announced in June 1973 that ARENA's presidential candidate in the forthcoming election would be General Ernesto Geisel. The election was carried out by an electoral college composed of 502 members: 66 senators, 310 deputies, and 126 members of state assemblies. The MDB nominated candidates for president and vice president for the first time since 1964. In the balloting on January 15, 1974, Geisel won with a vote of 400 to 76, with 26 abstentions. The inauguration took place on March 15.

The presidential election of 1974 marked a turning point in political party activity in Brazil. In part, as a result of the economic downturn caused by world petroleum price increases, the Geisel government did not possess the popularity of its predecessor. The strong tradition in Brazilian history of liberal constitutional government, as represented by the protest against Getúlio Vargas that erupted in 1943, began to reassert itself. The MDB attracted, for the first time, dynamic, younger candidates who were a sharp contrast to the aged, compromised figures of ARENA. The result of this trend was a strong showing, for the first time, in the November 15, 1974, popular elections for Congress, state legislatures, and municipal councils. The MDB won 16 of the contested 22 seats in the Senate, raising its total from 7 to 18, and increased its membership in the

Chamber of Deputies from 86 to 160 of the 364 members. The opposition also won majorities in seven state assemblies. ARENA still maintained majorities in both houses of Congress, with 48 senators and 204 deputies.[12]

The MDB had taken advantage of popular discontent with the government. More than 80 percent of Brazilians eligible to vote turned out at the polls. The election results began a process of evaluation of ARENA and its electoral base by the government. The president issued stark warnings to the country about hasty efforts to restore competitive elections and representative government. To emphasize the regimen's determination to preclude destabilizing political activity, two MDB deputies were deprived of their posts in Congress and lost their political rights for 10 years following speeches in which they had attacked the regime as corrupt and dominated by a "uniformed aristocracy."

At the government's initiative, Congress further reduced political party campaign activity in June 1976 by passing a bill that prohibited both parties from using radio and television for election campaigning and allowing only presentations of a candidate's name, photograph, and ballot number in the November 1976 municipal elections. Despite governmental efforts, the MDB again drew a heavy vote. The city councils in eight important cities were won by the MDB. While ARENA made gains in the interior, the coastal cities voted strongly for the opposition party. Overall, ARENA carried about 55 percent of the popular vote, against the MDB's 45 percent, nationwide.[13]

The MDB surge at the polls initiated another period of debate within the armed forces about the necessity for and utility of open elections.[14] Throughout early 1977, rumors circulated that further restrictions would be placed on the electoral system in order to preclude further MDB gains. The growing sense of crisis peaked on April 1, 1977. President Geisel suspended Congress for an indefinite period of time, allegedly in response to the unwillingness of that body to accept a judicial reform bill of the regime. On April 14, the president announced a series of reforms that became known as the "April package." The highlights of that reform package, from the perspective of the political parties, reconfirmed indirect elections for the president and state governors and instituted an indirect selection process for one senator from each side. Each state was assigned three senators, two elected directly and one indirectly (quickly labeled the "bionic senator" by public opinion); all were to hold office for eight years. The size of the Chamber of Deputies was fixed at 280 (formerly 310), distributed according to population, and not the number of registered voters. Each state was allowed a minimum of seven deputies (one from each territory) for a term of four years. The indirect electoral college system was retained to elect the president and state governors.

In July 1977, the leader of the MDB in the Chamber of Deputies, José Alencar Furtado, appeared on a government-sponsored television program with other MDB and ARENA party leaders to discuss the political situation in the country. His criticisms were taken to be offensive to the regime, and under the authority of Institutional Act No. 5, Furtado lost his political rights for 10 years.

A NEW POLITICAL PARTY SYSTEM

Responding to the growing pressure for liberalization from Brazilian society, President Geisel announced on December 1, 1977, that the political party system would be reorganized. The restrictions of Institutional Act No. 5 would be substantially eliminated, and the call for a return to a state of law, begun in earnest following the issuance of the "April package," would be respected. Both ARENA and the MDB were slated to disappear, and new parties would be formed; the jockeying for position began immediately among the old factions of the pre-1964 parties that had remained the core of the political dynamics of Brazil, despite the regimen's efforts to establish a two-party system.

The November 1978 congressional elections, held under the population criterion that favored the more traditional states in which the government normally held the lead, produced a reasonable majority in the Chamber of Deputies in January 1979 for ARENA: 231 deputies against 189 for the MDB. In the Senate, ARENA held 42 seats and the MDB held 25.

The government's strategy, masterminded by General Golbery and coordinated in the Congress by Senator Petrônio Portella (ARENA-Piauí), was to divide the opposition forces among three or four parties, if possible, leaving the Center and the Right to coalesce into an acceptable government majority. The indirect election in late 1978 of General João Figueiredo as Geisel's successor and his inauguration in March 1979 set the stage for the new alignments. Golbery continued as the principal political adviser of the new chief executive; Senator Portella became justice minister, the traditional cabinet set for supervising state and local politics. In June 1979, the government sent Congress draft legislation for a general amnesty. After the bill was approved by Congress in September, the vast majority of political exiles returned to Brazil. The government hoped that the return of many of the traditional leaders of the Left would stimulate new party organizations, but by October, no new parties had been formed.

The government pressed for "auto-dissolution" of the parties to clean the slate for ARENA and the MDB and to force the politicians to act. To hasten the process, the government introduced legislation in October 1979 dissolving the two parties, maintaining the *sublegenda* (cumulative party sublists), reducing the number of deputies and senators needed to form a new entity, and allowing the creation of temporary "blocks" of legislators in each house. The latter provision was aimed at those which were not able to meet the 10 percent minimum membership, drawn from any combination of deputies and senators, but were reasonably able to expect that they would meet the registration criteria before the 1982 elections; the next step would then be the election of a minimum quota of legislators and full legal status as a recognized political party. The government's legislation was approved without the *sublegenda* provision, which was subsequently restored by a presidential item veto.

In 1980, a frantic period of maneuvering among the state and local factions of ARENA and the MDB shaped a new multiparty system. Once the government had decided to permit only one "establishment" party (against the initial advice of Justice Minister Portella), those in the opposition began to position themselves. The earliest squabble involved those political leaders attempting to claim the mantle of João Goulart and the populist heritage of Getúlio Vargas. Two irreconcilable factions of the old PTB, led by Goulart's brother-in-law, Leonel Brizola, and Vargas's grandniece, Ivete Vargas, conducted a raucous public struggle to be recognized as the legal heir. The two groups filed registry petitions with the Supreme Electoral Tribunal. Although Brizola's faction claimed the loyalty of more deputies in Congress, and Brizola himself was recognized as the logical successor to Goulart, the tribunal awarded the acronym PTB to Vargas in May 1980. Brizola moved immediately to register another name, the Democractic Labor Party (PDT). The tribunal's decision, it was argued, was due less to the merits of the case and more to the maneuvering in the Presidential Palace of chief political advisor Golbery, who wanted the labor groups divided.

The main bloc of the opposition transformed the MDB into the Brazilian Democractic Movement Party (PMDB), with substantial loss of membership. The PMDB remained the largest opposition party but had only 94 deputies and 17 senators. Some of those who defected—24 deputies and a senator, initially—joined the new government party, the Party of Social Democracy (PDS, formerly the PSD). Others joined either the Popular Party (PP), the Workers Party (PT), or the PTB.

The PP was viewed as an "independent" party that drew the loyalty of ARENA dissidents and MDB moderates. Its leaders included a mixture of new faces, such as Olavo Setubal, the former mayor of São Paulo and president of a prominent bank, and old warhorses of Brazilian politics such as José Magalhães Pinto, former governor of Minas Gerais, cabinet minister, and legislator, and Tancredo Neves, prime minister under João Goulart. It became known as the bankers' and businessmen's party, given its strong base in São Paulo and among private-sector leaders.

The PT organized around the charismatic figure of "Lula," Luis Inácio da Silva, a metallurgical workers' leader in São Paulo, and Jacó Bittar, of the petroleum workers' union. The PT was an effort to avoid cooperation with or absorption by Leonel Brizola and his pre-1964 forces. The PT gained strong support in São Paulo from the unions, students, intellectuals, and the Roman Catholic Church.

A crucial consideration in determining which party to join, for a vast majority of the legislators, was state and regional rivalries. The competition among factions of the PDS, UDN, and PTB and the small pre-1964 parties determined which of the new parties appeared to offer the best electoral possibilities. If a principal contender for Congress or the governorship joined one party, his major rival joined one of the other units, disregarding ideology, party platform, or accountability to one's constituents.

The government was deeply involved in the maneuvering. It was vital that it retain a majority in Congress to guarantee the passage of key legislation. With the death of Justice Minister Petronio Portella in January 1980, General Golbery became both strategist and coordinator of the government's planning. The original scheme of dividing the opposition had succeeded; the government retained a slim majority in both houses of Congress. That majority would dwindle precipitously in 1981 and 1982, as dissidents and opportunists saw stronger electoral possibilities in one of the other parties, or as the internecine warfare within the government party loosened loyalties and required quick tactical decisions at the state level. As the national, state, and municipal elections of November 1982 approached, the government found itself having to cajole and threaten its PDS supporters to guarantee a majority for government legislation. On a series of important issues, the government lost to the opposition, but the retribution remained rhetorical.

Portella's death was followed by the sudden and momentarily shocking resignation of Golbery in August 1981. For a number of reasons, it was at first interpreted as a setback for the *abertura* process that he strongly supported. His successor, João Leitão de Abreu, a seasoned jurist and government supporter who had served in the Médici government, immediately reconfirmed the regimen's intention to proceed with the elections and to respect the new party system.

While the general promise was maintained, the government, in late 1981, became increasingly nervous about its poor showing in the public opinion polls, the ongoing bickering among PDS politicians, and the poor state of the economy, which, the opposition argued, demonstrated the incompetence of the government. In October, Congress refused to endorse a government proposal for *sublegendas* in the November 1982 elections. The government wanted to allow each party to run three candidates in the gubernatorial races. This innovation would have allowed rival PDS chiefs, primarily, to run against each other within the PDS and (it was hoped) prevent them from transferring to another party. The party candidate receiving the highest plurality would have been declared the winner; the honor and political fortunes of the other candidates would have been respected. The opposition, with defectors from the PDS, chose not to give the government an easy way out of embarrassing rivalries at the state level and defeated the measure.

The government decided to act. Reform packages were sent to the Congress, and the PDS was ordered to support them. The first appeared in November 1981. The proposal became law in January 1982 over vociferous criticism by the other political parties. It required parties to nominate candidates for all offices at the municipal level; failure to comply would result in the party's being dropped from the ballot in the November 1982 election in that municipality. The law required voters to choose party slates rather than individual candidates, thus preventing opposition parties from picking and choosing the seats they would contest. Political coalitions were banned.

The opposition reacted immediately. In February 1982, the PP and the PMDB

joined forces in a new grouping that retained the PMDB label. Ulysses Guimarães remained president of the party; former PP party chief Tancredo Neves
accepted the vice presidency. The merger required the approval of the Supreme
Electoral Tribunal. Amid considerable governmental anxiety and pressure, the
tribunal voted four to two in favor of the merger in March. In retaliation, an
April package of electoral reforms extended the time period for changing party
affiliation; the government expected a number of politicians, unhappy with the
merger or concerned about the electoral viability of the small parties, to switch
affiliation. It was correct, and by mid-1982, the PDS had attracted a number of
deputies and senators at the national level and a wide variety of state and municipal adherents.

The April package also required voters to write in the number or the name
of each candidate for each office listed on the ballot. The government party
thought that this requirement would increase the number of opposition votes
disqualified because of voter error and increase the total number of ballots for
the PDS. Also, many in the PDS thought the government's party grassroots
structure would give it an advantage in gaining voter preference. Neither assumption proved true in November. Brazilian voters were careful in preparing
to cast their ballots and learn the name or number of the candidate of their
choice. The opposition parties also were able to challenge the government party
at the local level, except in the Northeast, where the traditional strength of the
regime held firm.

Determined to do everything within its power to aid the PDS, the government
acted again in May 1982. Requiring the government party adherents in Congress
to support the measure, it increased the number of federal deputies from 420 to
479 and extended to six years the term of office of mayors and local councillors,
elected in November, to stagger voting in the future. In the elections of 1986,
the new legislation called for a mixed district voting system to be instituted.

After a campaign marked by high enthusiasm and relatively little violence,
approximately 55 million Brazilians voted on November 15, 1982. At stake were
22 state houses (out of 23), one-third of the federal Senate (23 seats), 479
positions in the Chamber of Deputies, 947 state assembly posts, 3,857 mayoral
races, and more than 60,000 city council spots. It took more than two weeks to
obtain definitive information, but the results were surprising. The opposition did
better than expected, but the government did not do so poorly as to generate a
backlash. The PDS won 12 of the 22 governors' races; the major opposition
party, the PMDB, took 9 and the PDT took 1.

The opposition parties carried 10 states that accounted for 90 percent of the
gross domestic product of Brazil and produced 89 percent of its cotton, 93
percent of its coffee, and 67 percent of its sugar. The PMDB won in the state
of São Paulo, the industrial heartland of Brazil and its most important state in
terms of the number of voters.

The elections provided an important political platform for a number of key
leaders. In Minas Gerais, Tancredo Neves, a veteran survivor of Brazilian pol-

itics, won the governor's mansion for the PMDB. Within a few years, he would become the consensus presidential candidate of the opposition in the 1985 elections. Leonel Brizola, who had returned from exile in 1979, won easily in the state of Rio de Janeiro. His election was seen, at the time, as an important litmus test for the Military Republic. Brizola was deeply disliked by many in the military and in conservative circles. He had been a firebrand mayor of Pôrto Alegre and governor of Rio Grande do Sul in the 1950s. Following his election to Congress in 1962, he had symbolized "negative" populism for many as he goaded his brother-in-law, President João Goulart, to adopt radical social and economic policies. With his election in 1982, Brizola emerged as one of the most enduring political figures in decades. His reelection to the governorship in 1990 placed him in an excellent position to launch another campaign for the presidency in 1994, having placed third in the 1989 presidential elections.

The PDS consolidated its electoral control of the northeastern states in the November 1982 balloting. It retained a foothold in the West and North, and it defeated the opposition in two states in the South, Santa Catarina and Rio Grande do Sul.

While the voting for the governors was important, the results of the elections for Congress were viewed as critical; the composition of the electoral college that would elect the next president in January 1985 was drawn in great part from members of Congress. Only 211 deputies were reelected. The Congress that convened in March 1983 was the largest in the history of the country, having increased from 304 seats in 1946 to 479 seats in 1983.

The political party system underwent a period of severe stress after 1982. The Congress became the focus of attention in 1984, when an amendment to restore direct presidential elections in 1985 was introduced. The movement to restore civilian government mushroomed into a nationwide campaign—*Diretas Já* (Direct Elections Now)—that galvanized civil society. When the vote was taken in Congress on April 25, 1984, it was clear that the authoritarian state had leaned heavily on the party leadership. The vote was 298 to 65 in favor, including 55 "yes" votes from the government party. But the amendment failed because of 113 absences (112 from the PDS); the requirement was two-thirds of the total membership of Congress, not of those voting. The final count was 22 votes short.

Strains began to show within the government party in 1983–1984. A backbench revolt at the PDS national convention in July 1983 had nearly defeated the party leadership. The inability of President Figueiredo to provide leadership in identifying his successor for the 1985 indirect presidential election heightened the tension. Paulo Maluf, the former governor of São Paulo, waged a relentless campaign to capture the PDS nomination—and thus the presidency, he thought. Vice President Aureliano Chaves was the logical successor, but he was opposed by the most conservative of the president's advisors. Interior Minister Mario Andreazza was their candidate, and they planned to retain power after 1985 if he was elected.

Chaves and his pragmatic followers in the PDS abandoned the government party in mid-1984 to form the Liberal Front. It soon was apparent that a political deal was possible between the Front and the opposition PMDB. Another sign that shifts were taking place in the political party structure was the resignation of PDS president José Sarney to protest the Maluf campaign. Maluf received the PDS nomination at the party convention in August 1984, but it was a hollow victory. The Front and the progressive wing of the PMDB was determined to support Minas Gerais Governor Tancredo Neves and selected former PDS president José Sarney as his running mate. The Front and the PMDB formed the Democratic Alliance (AD) for the campaign.

The political parties were again under tremendous popular pressure. As the campaign proceeded, each member of the electoral college had to determine whether his interests were best served by supporting the unpopular Paulo Maluf and the PDS or taking a risk in endorsing Tancredo Neves and the AD. State governors, sensing the changing tides of the patrimonial order, moved to support Neves. By a vote of 480 to 180 on January 15, 1985, the electoral college selected Neves and Sarney. Of the votes received by the candidates of the AD, 271 were from the PMDB, 113 were from the Party of the Liberal Front (PFL), and 55 were from PDS dissidents. (A handful of smaller parties supplied the other 41 votes.)

Tancredo Neves was never inaugurated president. He took ill on the eve of the March 15 ceremony. José Sarney was sworn in as acting president; Neves died in April, and Sarney formally became the first civilian chief executive since 1964. Immediately, a new set of tensions arose in the party system. The progressive or "authentic" wing of the PMDB believed that it should have the dominant policy role in the new government. But Sarney, politically and philosophically, was opposed to many of its policy positions. He sought allies at the Center and Center-Right of the party spectrum. It soon became apparent that President Sarney's primary political support would come from the PFL and the military. Ulysses Guimarães, the leader of the PMDB in the Chamber of Deputies, emerged as the key leader of the opposition to Sarney.

Sarney's thoughts turned immediately to the November 1986 elections for state governors and Congress. To succeed—indeed, to survive—the president would have to build a new political coalition for those elections. The pre-1964 political parties were very much in evidence as the New Republic began to operate. The old PTB of Brizola and Goulart had been taken over by a small, conservative clique from São Paulo and never regained its former prominence. Those who still supported Brizola's form of populism joined his PDT (Democratic Labor Party), with which he had won the governorship of the Rio de Janeiro state in 1982. Many of the pre-1964 UDN members were in the PFL. The old PSD became the PDS with the reorganization of the party system in the late 1970s, and it remained a system-oriented, pro-government patronage entity.

Elections were held for mayor in November 1985 in the capital cities—the first such vote in over 20 years. In São Paulo, a coalition of the PTB and PFL elected Jânio Quadros with 37.5 percent of the vote. Brizola's PDT won in Rio de Janeiro and in Pôrto Alegre. The PMDB retained a majority of the mayoralty posts (19 of 25 races) but not in the major cities. The PT scored a dramatic victory in Fortaleza and Ceará. The PDS and the PFL fared poorly. The PMDB leadership became increasingly concerned that its historical position as the dominant party of the opposition was being eroded by new groups such as the PT or by old warhorses of national politics such as Brizola and his PDT.

In part, driven by a need to find an alternative program to win the November 1986 elections, the government adopted its heterodox economic shock program (the Cruzado Plan) in February 1986 (see Chapter 5). The PMDB and the PFL, the parties sustaining the Sarney administration, suddenly found their standing in the public opinion polls soaring. Warnings that the plan was out of control by mid-1986 were ignored by the jubilant government. The elections were of double significance, in that those elected would serve a four-year term as the national legislature and also would sit as a Constituent Assembly to write a new constitution.

Given the apparent success of the Cruzado Plan, the PMDB and the PFL were the big winners in November 1986. The PMDB won 261 federal deputies, giving it a definite majority in the 487-member Chamber of Deputies; the party took 45 seats in the federal senate. Twenty-two of the 23 governorships went to the PMDB. The PFL placed second, as expected, with 119 deputies and 16 senators. The big loser was the PDS, which elected only 33 deputies and 5 senators, less than half of its congressional delegation in the old legislature. The remaining seats were divided among the smaller—and disappointed—parties.

No sooner were the elections over than the system underwent another period of crisis. The immediate failure of the Cruzado Plan in late 1986 robbed the Sarney administration of much of its legitimacy. Seeking shelter, government party members began searching for new alliances and partners. The general tenor of the new Congress was moderate or Center-Right, its strength coming from the PFL, the PDS, a wing of the PMDB, and fragments of the smaller parties. The Left, which held about 25 seats, drew from the PMDB, the PDT, the PT, and smaller parties. It quickly became obvious that the decision to combine the work of the national legislature with that of the Constituent Assembly was almost unworkable.

Ulysses Guimarães of the PMDB was elected presiding officer of the assembly, which began its deliberations in February 1987. The next 15 months were spent drafting a new Magna Carta. Because of the divisions within the PMDB, the PFL assumed the leadership role in trying to represent President Sarney's interests and in drafting a moderate to conservative document. Throughout the period of drafting the constitution, President Sarney shifted cabinet membership in an effort to find a broader base of support. But as the economy moved from one crisis to another, and one shock plan after another, any coherence in the party system was quickly submerged by the desperate search for enough votes to pass a workable constitution.

The Left made early progress in the drafting process, but by late 1987, a temporary centrist coalition, with strong backing from the military, emerged. The Centrão (Big Center) defeated efforts to reduce Sarney's term of office to four years and to introduce a parliamentary system to curb its authority. The constitution was finally approved on September 22 and promulgated on October 5, 1988. Little important structural change was introduced. The presidential system was retained, as was the traditional position of the armed forces—after much debate. The states and municipalities received significant increases in the distribution of revenues.

Elections were held in 1988 for municipal offices. Mayors and city councilmen were elected across Brazil—more than 1.2 million candidates and a total electorate of just more than 75.8 million. The PMDB was the biggest loser, even though it elected almost 1,900 mayors and 17,000 councilmen and received about 25 percent of the vote nationwide. The PFL came in second, with almost 1,500 mayors and close to 17,000 council members, and it received more than 15 percent of the popular vote. The smaller parties turned in a lackluster performance, although the PT captured headlines with the election of Luiza Erundina as mayor of São Paulo city.

The 1988 municipal balloting opened the presidential succession campaign. The 1988 Constitution had established a runoff system for presidential elections to provide the new chief executive with an absolute majority of the national vote. The key issue, then, was to place first or second in the first round of voting. Early leaders in the polls were Brizola of the PDT and Lula of the PT. Then, out of nowhere, a newcomer appeared. Fernando Collor de Mello, candidate of his recently organized National Reconstruction Party (PRN), moved quickly to the top of the polls. The young, attractive governor of the Northeastern state of Alagoas captured the public's interest. He quickly formed an electoral alliance with three small parties at the margin of the party system, a move that provided him with additional time on television.

The PMDB chose the lackluster but honorable 73-year-old Ulysses Guimarães as its candidate. The Brazilian Social Democratic Party (PSDB) nominated Senator Mario Covas of São Paulo. Other parties looked to their traditional leaders to carry the party banner. Party realignment continued throughout the campaign. By the time of the election, the PMDB had slipped to under 200 federal deputies and the PFL to about 100. The PSDB grew slightly as members of Congress looked for a probable winner in the November voting. Collor de Mello's party slowly but inexorably expanded as federal deputies and senators sensed that he might have a chance to win.

An electorate of 82 million went to the polls on November 15, 1989. Collor de Mello of the PRN and Lula of the PT placed first and second, respectively. Lula barely displaced an outraged Leonel Brizola, who finished third. The next month was spent attempting to win over the parties that had lost the first round of voting. Two televised debates in December offered the voters stark contrasts between the candidates—in terms of appearance and of their programs. In December, 35.1 million Brazilians voted for Collor de Mello—over 53 percent of the valid vote; 31.1 million chose Lula.

Collor de Mello had pieced together a winning coalition, primarily among the poorer and small-town voters. Lula dominated in most of the state capitals. Collor also received the votes of the small but significant number of upper-class voters who feared Lula's socialist-statist rhetoric and his anticapitalist bias. But the president faced a difficult situation. While he was the first democratically elected president since 1960, he had few formal supporters in Congress, and elections were scheduled for October 1990 to choose new governors and a new legislature. The PMDB had about 28 percent of the votes, the PFL about 20 percent, the PSDB about 13 percent. The combined forces of the Left (the PDT, PT, PCB, PC do B, and PSB) had about 13 percent; the Right (PDS, PRN, PTB, PDC, PL) had about 23 percent.

But the problem was not one of being on the Left or the Right—or in the middle. The issue was once again party accountability. Lacking ideology or program, and responding to local and state interests, as well as to personalist leaders, the parties were unable to form either an alternative to the president or a strong coalition supporting him. The initial heterodox shock program (the Collor Plan) of March 1990 received grudging support from a majority because it was popular with the voters. But as the plan ran into trouble, so did Collor.

In the elections of October 3, 1990, Brazilians elected 1,600 governors, vice governors, senators, alternate senators, federal deputies, and state legislators. Local and regional issues dominated the campaign. In congressional balloting, the PMDB continued its slide in national representation. The PFL did well, although its vote remained concentrated in the Northeast. The PSDB turned in a mediocre performance; Collor's party, the PRN, made some strides, but it remained a small, minority force. On the gubernatorial side, the PFL did well: nine victories on its own and four additional seats through coalitions. The PSDB won only one governor. The PRN elected two governors. The PTB did well—reflecting a generally conservative trend in the national vote—with two governors. Brizola retook the governorship of Rio de Janeiro, and his party elected two governors. The PT did poorly and elected no governors.

By 1991, Collor faced in Congress continuing opposition to his attempts to legislate change. The dim prospects for the nation's economy robbed him of much of his original popularity. The president appeared to lack the negotiating skills needed to seek a workable coalition. And the parties, as always, reflected local and regional issues, not national topics. Ronald Schneider made the following comment in the early 1990s:

To say that a drastic restructuring of the party system is badly needed is not to imply that it is possible, much less likely. A major obstacle resides in the peculiar electoral system—one that not only minimizes both any degree of responsibility of representatives to constituencies or meaningful party discipline, but also encourages alliances of transitory electoral convenience at the state and local levels. These are often contrary to the parties' positions on the national level.[15]

President Collor de Mello reshaped his cabinet in early 1992 in an effort to broaden his base of support. The new cabinet members were either technocrats or experienced politicians. But before the president could reenergize his administration, corruption charges against him and his key associates resulted in impeachment proceedings in Congress. Collor resigned in September, and Congress voted for impeachment in December. There was little, if any, political party support for the president during the proceedings.

Vice President Itamar Franco, a traditional member of the PMDB in his home state of Minas Gerais, was inaugurated to complete Collor's term of office. Franco appointed a cabinet of friends and associates, among whom was São Paulo Senator Fernando Henrique Cardoso as foreign minister. Cardoso, who would soon become finance minister and the author of the Real Plan, was one of the founders of the PSDB.

Cardoso successfully used the Real Plan to support his presidential ambitions in 1993–1994. The apparent end of hyperinflation made him an increasingly popular figure. Before the Real Plan began to take effect, the presidential candidacy of Lula of the PT dominated the polls; but as the implications of low inflation became apparent throughout Brazilian society, Cardoso and his ticket of the PSDB-PFL (and supported by the small PTB) moved up quickly in the polls. His running mate from the PFL, Senator Marco Maciel, was a seasoned political leader from the key state of Pernambuco. There was no ideological coherence to the ticket, merely pragmatism. The PSDB drew votes in the more developed Southern region; the PFL was the leading vote getter in the more backward Northeastern area. The PTB hoped to benefit by appointments and political preference after Cardoso's election. The combination, for electoral purposes, made sense; from a programmatic viewpoint, it was in the classic Brazilian tradition.

The field of candidates was filled with traditional figures from the PDT (Leonel Brizola), PMDB (former São Paulo Governor Orestes Quercia), and the PPR (Progressive Renovating Party-Espiridao Amin). The PPR was the latest new political party. It was an amalgamation of the PDS (Party of Social Democracy), created by Governor Paulo Maluf of São Paulo, and the Christian Democratic Party (PDC).

The October 1994 elections were the first in decades to be held in an "inflation-free" environment. Nearly 78 million voters went to the polls to elect a president, vice president, state governors, the lower house of Congress, and two senators from each state, as well as all state legislators. Cardoso, riding a wave of popularity because of the Real Plan, and because of his own personality as a respected academic, a potential world leader, and a modernizer, was elected with 34.4 million votes compared to 17.1 million for the runner-up, Lula, thus avoiding a second round of voting. The candidate's coattails worked: governors sympathetic to Cardoso were elected in all of the major states of the federation. In elections for the Senate, a majority of those elected appeared favorable to the new chief executive; as always, the vote for the Chamber of Deputies was fragmented, with more than 15 parties gaining representation.

The Cardoso administration took office on January 1, 1995. Among some supporters of the new president, there was an expectation that Congress, although splintered along party lines, would rally behind the administration's reform agenda. This was not the case. The parties responded, as usual, to local and regional interests, driven by personal ambition and a search for "pork" in the form of projects and money that could be transferred back to the state and municipal leaders who had sent them to Brasília in the first place.

The first administration of Cardoso was characterized by continued volatility in party performance. As one observer notes, "Brazil now has easily the most fragmented party system in Latin America and one of the most fragmented in the world."[16] One of the most confusing aspects of the Brazilian political party system is the propensity of members to move from party to party without fear of reprisal or concern about coherence in their own political thinking. Again, "the extraordinary propensity of Brazilian representatives of the catchall parties to switch parties is unheard of among the other more developed nations of Latin America. . . . What makes the Brazilian case all the more remarkable is that many of the changes in parties are incongruous from the ideological point of view; politicians move from one party to its archenemy."[17]

While there are a few, small parties that maintain some programmatic consistency—the PT, the PCB, and the PC do B—these are small and relatively insignificant in defining the agenda. They often are found in opposition to the Cardoso government's plan of action, but they need to join forces with the more opportunistic of the parties to exert voting strength. Another problem the Cardoso administration has confronted is the weakness of the support of the president's own PSDB party. While the PFL, increasingly well organized and better disciplined than most, has been a stalwart in defending and voting for the president, members of the PSDB have defected on a number of occasions, making it more difficult to predict levels of party support for key legislative issues.

THE 1998 NATIONAL ELECTIONS AND POLITICAL PARTIES

The campaign for the October 1998 national elections opened early that year. The government candidate was clear—a constitutional amendment had been approved by Congress to allow an incumbent president to seek a second mandate. Fernando Henrique Cardoso and Marco Maciel would stand for the PSDB-PFL, plus a coalition of small parties. In the spring, there was a moment of uncertainty as the PMDB held a nominating convention to decide whether it would launch its own candidate or support Cardoso. Both former Presidents

Itamar Franco and José Sarney toyed with the idea of running, but the party, which had been courted by the presidential palace during the first term of office, opted to support the Cardoso ticket. The principal opposition, again, was the PT, which nominated Lula for a third run. In an astounding demonstration of the "feckless" party system, Leonel Brizola, the founder and titular leader of the PDT, and a sworn enemy and critic of Lula in the past, agreed to run as vice president. The ostensible goal was to unite the populist opposition forces. Former finance minister and Ceará governor Ciro Gomes launched his candidacy, but it was generally believed that he was positioning himself for the 2002 national election. Smaller parties indicated candidates, but few were viewed as viable.

Lula moved into first place in the polls during the summer of 1998, raising the usual concerns about a reversal of economic policy if he were to win in October in either the first or second round of voting. Most observers overlooked the fact that in each of his previous campaigns—1989 and 1994—he was also the front runner early in the campaign. By autumn, President Cardoso had taken the lead in public opinion polls. His use of free television time, allocated to each candidate on the basis of the number of parties supporting them, was a success. Moreover, Lula appeared honest but unconvincing, and he often seemed to be defending a now outmoded economic order. He was not helped by the brash and often confrontational statements of his running mate, who was seen by many as wanting to turn back the clock—politically and economically.

The October 4 election also determined the makeup of the Chamber of Deputies and the Senate. The Cardoso alliance of six political parties (the PFL, PSDB, PTB, PPB, PMDB, and PSD) lost one seat in the Senate and a dozen seats in the Chamber. But it retained comfortable, if formal, majorities in both houses of Congress (see Table 2.1).

A number of key state governorship races were held over for a second round on October 25. Voters gave the president a somewhat more complicated set of results. The government allies in key states lost to the opposition—Rio de Janeiro, Minas Gerais, and Rio Grande do Sul, which are among the most important in the federation. The election of PSDB Governor Mario Covas in São Paulo was an important win for the government. But Covas defeated former governor and mayor Paulo Maluf, leader of the PPB, which may complicate that party's support for the government program. But in total, the final tally on the gubernatorial races—14 were decided on October 4 and 13 in the runoff on October 25—gave the government 19 states, plus the Federal District of Brasília—while the opposition took seven governorships (see Table 2.2).

Following the election results, there again was talk in Brasília of the need for electoral reform. Highest on the list of initiatives was party loyalty—once elected, a member of Congress would have to vote with the party for the duration of the legislative term. Other topics under consideration were moving to a mixed proportional representation/district voting system to lend greater coherence to the voting process, and talk of stiffening the requirements to organize a national

Table 2.1
Composition of the National Congress in 1999

Party	Chamber of Deputies	Senate
PFL	106	20
PMDB	82	27
PSDB	99	16
PPB	60	4
PT	58	7
PDT	25	2
PTB	31	1
PSB	19	3
PL	12	0
PD do B	7	0
PPS	3	1
PSD	3	0
PMN	2	0
PV	1	0
PRONA	1	0
PRP	1	0
PST	1	0
PSL	1	0

Source: ''Dicas de Brasília 98,'' *PATRI*, April 30, 1998, p. 136; *Brazil Watch*, October 26–November 9, 1998.

Table 2.2
Party Control of Governorships, 1998–1999

Party	1998	1999
PMDB	8	6
PSDB	7	7
PFL	6	6
PSB	2	2
PTB	2	0
PT	1	3
PV	1	0
PPB	0	2
PDT	0	1

Source: Brazil Watch, November 9–23, 1998.

political party. But these suggestions have been discussed for a number of years, and any decision will await the recovery from the 1999 recession caused by the January 1999 currency devaluation.

NOTES

1. Scott Mainwaring, "Brazil: Weak Parties, Feckless Democracy," in Scott Mainwaring and Timothy R. Scully, eds., *Building Democratic Institutions: Political Party Systems in Latin America* (Stanford, Calif.: Stanford University Press, 1995).

2. For an excellent analysis of this period, see Robert M. Levine, *The Vargas Regime* (New York: Columbia University Press, 1970), and Robert Levine, *Father of the Poor? Vargas and His Era* (Cambridge: Cambridge University Press, 1998). See also Lourdes Sola, "O golpe de 37 e o Estado Novo," in Carlos Guilherme Mota, ed., *Brasil em perspectiva*, 9th ed. (Rio de Janeiro and São Paulo: Editora Difel/Difusão, 1977).

3. Samuel P. Huntington, *Political Order in Changing Societies* (New Haven, Conn.: Yale University Press, 1968).

4. Victor Nunes Leal, *Coronelismo, the Municipality and Representative Government in Brazil* (New York: Cambridge University Press, 1977).

5. Jean Blondel, *As condições de vida política no estado da Paraíba*, trans. Alcantara Nogueira (Rio de Janeiro: Fundação Getúlio Vargas, 1957).

6. Marcus Odilon Ribeiro Coutinho, *Poder alegria dos homens* (João Pessoa, Paraíbo: Gráfica "A Imprensa," 1965).

7. Marcos Vinícius Vilaca and Roberto Cavalcanti de Albuquerque, *Coronel coronéis* (Rio de Janeiro: Edições Tempo Brasileiro, 1965).

8. Anthony Leeds, "Brazilian Careers and Social Structure: A Case History and Model," *American Anthropologist* 66 (1964): 1321–1347.

9. Gláucio Ary Dillon Soares, "The Politics of Uneven Development: The Case of Brazil," in Seymour M. Lipset and Stein Rokkan, eds., *Party Systems and Voter Alignments: Cross-National Perspectives* (New York: The Free Press, 1967), p. 477.

10. Ibid., p. 490. For a theoretical interpretation of center and periphery in Brazilian politics, see Jorge Balan, ed., *Centro e periféria no desenvolvimento brasileiro* (São Paulo: Difusão Europeia do Livro, 1974).

11. For a comprehensive analysis of the party, see Ronald H. Chacote, *The Brazilian Communist Party* (New York: Oxford University Press, 1974).

12. For an analysis of the election, see Bolivar Lamounier and Fernando Henrique Cardoso, eds., *Os partidos e as eleições no Brasil* (Rio de Janeiro: Editora Paz e Terra, 1978).

13. Ibid.

14. The surge of popular support for the MDB and its implications for the political system are examined in Bolivar Lamounier, ed., *Voto de desconfiança: Eleições e mudança política no Brasil, 1970–1979* (São Paulo: Editora Brasileira de Ciencias, 1980).

15. Ronald Schneider, *Order and Progress: A Political History of Brazil* (Boulder, Colo.: Westview Press, 1991), p. 381.

16. Mainwaring, "Brazil: Weak Parties, Feckless Democracy," p. 375.

17. Ibid., pp. 375–376.

Chapter 3

The Patrimonial State
and Society in Brazil

If our analysis is correct, and the traditional definition of the patrimonial state is undergoing modification, we do not yet know how meaningfully or quickly it will impact Brazilian society. In previous editions of this book, we noted the weakness and ineffectiveness of the political party system. In addition to the party organizations, other groups historically have suffered a similar fate: the inability to oppose the interests of the central government and still survive. Groups and institutions seeking to maneuver within the restrictions of Brazil's patrimonial regime learned to cooperate or to allow themselves to be co-opted, otherwise they confronted unmitigated hostility. But if the patrimonial state is to be redefined, the relationship of society to the state needs to be reexamined. Relationships will undergo alteration—cosmetic or substantive—as the economic and financial reform processes proceed and as the general reform of the state moves forward in the twenty-first century. History cautions us to preclude dramatic ruptures, but it is likely that change will come.

In this chapter we will examine the traditional and the new and evolving roles of some of the key social actors in the patrimonial order in Brazil. Some have played a pivotal role in the past, while others have been marginal. All will find themselves creating or redefining their linkages, both to the central authorities as well as to the local and state elites. Of particular importance are the Roman Catholic Church, industrial groups, state employees, and the labor movement. Until very recently, most of these actors were either supportive of or poorly prepared to oppose the patrimonial order, save in exceptional circumstances. In spite of the continued weakness of the political party system, which should be the primary conduit for societal concerns and interests—but in Brazil is not— the issue is, can institutions in society replace the political parties, or must they redefine their relationship with the patrimonial order to provide greater "space" or autonomy in their attempt to either corner resources of the state or break loose from the traditional corporatist, bureaucratic ties imposed by the state? These are important questions for the twenty-first century if Brazil is to truly modernize. And they have added significance if we are correct in arguing that the traditional political elites will continue to ferociously resist any dilution of their power. As the authority of the central bureaucratic state is diluted, and the elites retreat into a position of stalling social reforms to continue to manipulate a significant portion of the population, will modernizing elements in Brazilian society demonstrate the capacity to confront the traditional political elites and either build alliances for change or, in the last instance, confront the elites and force them to address the long neglected social agenda?

To affirm that the patrimonial order has dominated group activity in Brazil is not to assert that it has totally destroyed such activity. Indeed, at times, political action by organized groups can signal a movement toward a transition in the patrimonial order to indicate a need for institutional adjustments to meet current modernization needs. The patrimonial order is not a totalitarian system; flexibility is its chief attribute. While it has been opposed to fundamental shifts in the distribution of power in Brazilian society, it accommodates, and at times encourages, public debate. The movement that began in 1943 to challenge the authoritarian state of Getúlio Vargas is one example. It came from those groups that favored a limited but constitutional public order. The events surrounding the overthrow of João Goulart in 1964 demonstrated the capacity of group activity to indicate the need for action to preserve the patrimonial order. The campaign for direct elections—*Diretas Já*—in 1983 and 1984 gave impetus to the transition process that resulted in the restoration of a civilian regime in 1985. After 1990, the business sector became an important advocate for economic liberalization and reform.

The return to civilian government in 1985 followed a period of rapid political mobilization by a broad coalition of societal groups. The *diretas* movement had widespread support. But when the constitutional amendment came to the floor of Congress for a vote, the military regime was able to muster enough votes to defeat it. The direct election forces, rather than continue to fight, made the decision to accept their defeat and to retreat, at least temporarily. The most recent, and dramatic, example of the capacity of the patrimonial order to survive was the defeat of Luis Inácio da Silva ("Lula") in his three attempts to build a counter-elite coalition in presidential elections (1989, 1994, and 1998). Confronted with a coalition of the old populist Left, the political elites coalesced behind "safer" candidates—Fernando Collor de Mello and Fernando Henrique Cardoso.

Traditionally, the shift from an open to a closed political system, or the reverse, has not represented a dismantling of the patrimonial system. The basic attributes have remained in place. The political actors may change, and indeed, the personalities will undoubtedly be different, but the underlying commitment of a particular government or regime, and the way in which that regime or government acts to guide political action, has been able to determine the survival of the patrimonial order. Policy shifts, personnel changes, direct rather than indirect elections, and so forth historically have not meant a repudiation of the patrimonial concept. They have been part of the evolving context within which the state sought to maximize its position of dominance.

Philippe Schmitter has stated that, over time, "A history of paternalism and patrimonialism has made association leaders and followers ready to leave initiation to higher authorities and to regard the government as the supreme *patrão* of the society."[1] The willingness of the populace to "leave it to the state," the lack of interest group activity, and the corporatist nature of Brazilian society—the "belief in and acceptance of a natural hierarchy of social groups, each with its ordained place and its own set of perquisite responsibilities"—confirm the reality of the patrimonial order in Brazilian society.[2] But, once again, we must remain open to the possibility that the complicated process of reform during the first Cardoso administration—and the earlier economic liberalization efforts of Collor de Mello—have set the stage for an alternative scenario. There is no guarantee that the commitment to modernization will succeed. Indeed, the "track record" of the first Cardoso government offers evidence both in favor of and against societal change. However, for the first time in Brazilian history, the economic reform process is going to reduce the size of the central bureaucracy. State companies have been sold; public employees have been dismissed; and all new capital flows and technology will help modernize Brazilian industry and commerce. These are significant changes, all of which are taking place within an unprecedented process of globalization, in which Brazil wants to play an increasingly important role. But it cannot do so if the traditional "veto" of the political elites over needed institutional modifications continues. Many of the traditional actors, instead of embracing change, fear it, and they have reacted accordingly. To understand why, we need to examine the evolution of the key actors.

THE ROMAN CATHOLIC CHURCH

Frank Bonilla has stated that, historically, "the military and the Church lay claim, in part justifiably, to being the only genuinely national institutions" in Brazil. The Church, he continues, believes "itself the receptacle and instrument of a moral and spiritual unity that binds Brazilians together in ways that political loyalties have never matched."[3] After the victory of the March 31, 1964, movement, the Church found itself the only institution with the autonomy and resources to criticize the military regime publicly. But its central role in the opposition coalition diminished as nonclerical actors took the lead in restoring democracy in 1985. And as the authority of Pope John Paul II, an orthodox leader of the Church in Rome, asserted his primacy in Brazil and appointed a generation of careful conservatives as leaders of the Church, the hierarchy retreated from political confrontation. On the one hand, the Church undertook a valiant defense of the indigenous peoples and the poor—responding to the pastoral mission of the Church—but avoided "politicization" in response to the Pope's admonition. But in the 1990s, a peculiar metamorphosis occurred within the Church in Brazil. The leadership came to identify economic and financial reforms with an effort by the elites to further marginalize the poor. The Church grew to become a vociferous opponent, for example, of privatization, of foreign capital, and of efforts to modernize the state. How this evolution occurred is a fascinating "case study" of the changing role of patrimonial institutions in Brazil.

Background

The Church in Brazil, during the Empire, provided one of the principal supports for elitist monarchical rule. With the advent of the Old Republic in 1889, church and state were separated. During the Old Republic, the Church operated without governmental interference. In a nation in which more than 90 percent of the population were at least nominal members, the Church continued to play an important social and educational role.

With Vargas's victory in 1930, the archbishop of Rio, Cardinal Sebastião Leme, informally renegotiated many of the prerogatives the Church had previously enjoyed. The 1934, 1937, and 1946 constitutions refer to God in the preambles, and the provisions relating to marriage and education explicitly recognize the preeminent place of Roman Catholicism. Members of the clergy enjoy full political rights, and many have served in Congress. Informal ties between church and state continue, particularly in the areas of health, education, and social welfare. It is a necessary and an expected aspect of all state ceremonies that a ranking member of the clergy attends and participates. Thus Brazil remains a deeply Catholic country, not as measured by church attendance but by the respect and projection into society that the Church enjoys.

The Church Modernizes

Only after 1945 did segments of the Church begin to assume a more militant role in social and political questions. The issue of the Church as an institution versus the Church as a movement was deeply debated. Its institutional need "entails an intrinsic involvement with politics that often leads to cautious, generally conservative positions on most political questions. This involvement has frequently led to the Church's 'sacrilizing' [*sic*] tradition and becoming a key element in social control and norm maintenance by its conferral of religious legitimacy on established social structures and authority patterns."[4]

After 1945, the writings of the French Left deeply influenced activist Catholics, particularly those of Jacques Maritain, Emmanuel Mounier, and the French Dominican priest L. B. Lebret. The need to bring the Church into the twentieth century was recognized in Rome. The Latin American Episcopal Conference

(CELAM), created in 1955 to analyze Latin American problems, was followed in 1958 by the Papal Commission for Latin America. The National Conference of Brazilian Bishops (CNBB) had been founded in 1952 with Bishop Hélder Câmara as its secretary-general.

The international Church became more activist with the election of Pope John XXIII in 1958. The influence of the international Church, one of the "supra-national actors," cannot be overlooked in assessing the development of the Church in Brazil. John XXIII's encyclicals, *Mater et magistra* (1961) and *Pacem in terris* (1963), and the meeting of Vatican Council II (1962) provided important support for indigenous Catholic forces convinced that the Brazilian Church, to survive, must become relevant to the needs of the poor.

The CNBB, under Hélder Câmara's influence, became increasingly vocal in analyzing outstanding social issues. The Church was instrumental in supporting the creation of the Superintendency for the Development of the Northeast (SU-DENE) in 1959. Church action groups in the Northeast had been expanding the Church's role for a number of years before Juscelino Kubitschek announced, at a regional meeting organized by the CNBB, that the federal government would actively seek to resolve the extraordinary misery of the nine-state area.

The pastoral letters of the Brazilian bishops issued in 1962 and 1963 reflected the newfound social calling. One such document, issued in 1962, was an "Emergency Plan" of the CNBB for the Church in Brazil.

Hélder Câmara also served as national secretary of the Catholic Action movement during these years. His spirit of innovation permeated the youth movements, particularly the Catholic University Student Organization (JUC), which became a leading proponent of radical Catholic action. The concern of the students in the JUC focused on making existing institutions more responsive to the needs of national development. In 1962, the JUC actively participated in the formation of Population Action (AP), a new, radical, Roman Catholic action group. *Brasil urgente*, a radical Catholic paper published in 1963 and 1964, publicized the platform of change that AP advocated. AP was not a church-affiliated entity, as was Catholic Action. It was a "political ideological" and "nonconfessional" organization that hoped to attract all Catholics in Brazil who were committed to change.[5] The radical Catholic movement had penetrated the National Union of Students (UNE) and, with Communist student backing, succeeded in electing four consecutive presidents of the organization prior to 1964.

The increasing militancy of AP enraged "traditional" Catholics. Its identification with the "basic reform" movement of the Goulart administration disturbed the military. As the 1963–1964 crisis mounted, the Church organized peasant unions in the Northeast; it also sponsored, through the Basic Education Movement (MEB), a program of rural education reaching 180,000 peasants over 25 radio stations. The MEB approach combined literacy education with *conscientização*, instilling in the peasants a consciousness of their conditions and rights.

The MEB had been organized in March 1961 as a collaborative effort of the

CNBB and the Brazilian government to utilize radio to reduce illiteracy among the people of the underdeveloped regions of the country. President Quadros had been impressed by the radio education programs initiated in the late 1950s in Natal, Rio Grande do Norte, and Aracajú, Sergipe, as part of the Church's social awakening. The Church agreed to organize the program, and the government financed it.

The radio schools spread throughout the North and Northeast from 1961 to 1964. Organized by the CNBB, the MEB became an independent agency directed nationally by a council of bishops appointed by the CNBB. A good deal of autonomy was allowed, and encouraged, at the state and local levels. The MEB began to move toward a more radical position in late 1962. Adopting the theme of *conscientização* and social action, the MEB prepared a controversial textbook, *Viver é lutar* (To Live Is to Struggle), in 1963, which, when printed in January 1964, was seized by Governor Lacerda of Guanabara because it was, in his opinion, Communist inspired.

One of the principal proponents of *conscientização* as an instrument for attacking illiteracy and social deprivation was Professor Paulo Freire of the University of Recife. The *método Paulo Freire* (Paulo Freire method) stressed relevance and equality in its teaching methods. The vocabulary to which the peasants or workers were exposed was drawn from their own experiences and related to their social and political needs. There were no "teachers," in the traditional sense, in the courses organized by Freire and his followers. "Coordinators" guided the literacy classes, but every effort was made to equalize relations among all of the participants, instructors and students alike.[6]

Freire used the Cultural Extension Service of the University of Recife to administer the program. Attracting a vigorous and dedicated group, primarily university students and instructors, as well as intellectuals, he had hopes of reaching millions of illiterate Brazilians with his dynamic method of learning. Unfortunately, the 1964 coup intervened, and Freire went into exile.

Another instrument of *conscientização*, in this period before 1964, was the Movimento de Cultura Popular (Movement of Popular Culture, or MCP), which attracted strong radical Catholic support as well as the aid of the Communist Party. An important MCP center opened in Recife under Mayor Miguel Arraes in 1960. In its early days, Paulo Freire had cooperated with the Recife program, but he moved to the Cultural Extension Service as the MCP came under increasing criticism as a subversive organization. Cultura Popular programs were espoused by a number of student and Church-related groups.[7] Plays, outdoor assemblies, pamphlets, and films were used to arouse the masses. At a congress held in Recife in September 1963, one delegate stated the movement's purpose as follows: "Cultura Popular assumes the character of a struggle. Apart from forming an authentic national culture, this struggle promotes the integration of the Brazilian man in the process to socioeconomic and politico-cultural liberation of our people."[8]

With the coup d'état of 1964, the military moved to emasculate AP, JUC,

UNE, MEB, and other radical Catholic and popular organizations; many leaders were imprisoned or exiled, and their programs were condemned as being subversive and "anti-Brazilian." With the purge of the student and lay groups, the Church leadership itself divided over the proper institutional role it should occupy.

The national Church had to steer a delicate course between social advocacy and institutional survival between 1964 and 1985. The national hierarchy spoke out against the government when priests and nuns were arrested and tortured for political activities. A period of tension occurred from 1964 to 1967, when the clergy supported the growing militancy of the UNE and guerrilla kidnappings of diplomats. In November 1967, the Central Commission of the CNBB issued a document entitled, "Why the Bishops Cannot Remain Quiet," which criticized government policies.

Pope Paul VI's 1967 encyclical, *Populorum progresso* (On the Development of Peoples), and his visit to Bogotá, Colombia, in 1968 to address the Second General Conference of CELAM, gave renewed impetus to the responsibility of the Brazilian Church in the area of social reform. That message served to justify the continued attempts of the progressive clergy to make the patrimonial order more responsive to the needs of the poor. At the same time, such efforts aroused hostility and, at times, violent opposition of groups such as the Command to Hunt Down the Communist and the Society to Defend Tradition, Family, and Property, located in São Paulo. The latter, an organization of conservative Catholic youth, had as its objective the purification of the Church by ridding it of radical influence.

It is important to note that the response of the Church was in large part motivated by a political catalyst. Social and political change became acceptable to a majority of the hierarchy when it was perceived that the Church was under attack from strong, ideologically motivated forces, such as the Communist Party. Moreover, it was in those areas most politicized, the Northeast especially, that the leadership felt compelled to respond with action programs to preserve the institutional influence of the Church.

The leadership of the Church was by no means unified in supporting an action program. Many conservative bishops saw such a program as contrary to the mission of the Church and against the best interests of its members. Slowly, through attrition and new appointments, the profile of the Brazilian bishops moved from modest-conservative to moderate-progressive in the 1960s. But it must be remembered that the shift came in response to a growing awareness of a political challenge that required Church action.[9]

The post-1964 political climate inexorably drew more moderate Church leaders to a higher level of awareness of the need for a more progressive Church mission. Not only was that mission a legitimate one, but accusations that the bishops and priests were acting subversively were firmly rejected. Indeed, those who condemned Church social action were the subversives: "The Church is not subversive. Subversives are those who criminally deprive the majority of Bra-

zilians of bread, basic education, and participation in the benefits of technological progress."[10] A growing number of bishops and priests believed that, "If
the Church was close to the people, as Christ was, it could speak for them and
denounce the injustice that plagued them."[11]

The question that soon brought the church and the state into open conflict
was that of violations of human rights. The regime's efforts to wipe out terrorist
activity in the late 1960s and early 1970s had led to the creation of a widespread
security apparatus that employed severe interrogation and torture techniques to
elicit information from prisoners. In June 1972, the CNBB issued a statement
condemning the use of physical, psychological, and moral torture by police
authorities. The conference urged the restoration of habeas corpus, which had
been suspended for political crimes by Institutional Act No. 5.

In November 1976, in a "Pastoral Communication to the People of God,"
the CNBB condemned torture, censorship, and the absence of civil liberties and
social justice. The impunity of police who acted illegally, the absence of land
reform, the plight of the Indians, and the suffering of the poor were frankly
analyzed. The regime's doctrine of national security was attacked; the right of
individual security was defended.

With the beginning of authoritarian liberalization in the late 1970s, the Church
intensified its efforts to identify with the plight of the average Brazilian. Increasingly, it turned to the defense of the Brazilian Indians in the frontier region,
who were being forced from their land, and of the urban poor in the slums
surrounding the cities. Foreign priests became the object of tense confrontations
between the Church and the state; often assigned to the frontier areas or to the
slums, the European and North American priests were frequently militant advocates of the rights of their parishioners. Since at least half of the priests in
Brazil were (and are) foreign, the potential for conflict was high, and it remains
so.

One important organizational response to the lack of priests and the increasingly pastoral mission of the Church in Brazil is the Basic Christian Communities (CEB). Thomas Bruneau wrote that, "the most important single
innovation in both theological and social terms of the Church in Brazil has been
the formation of the Basic Christian Communities or CEBs."[12] The CEBs, some
80,000 in all, bring together local residents to discuss immediate needs and
concerns. While normally begun under Church initiative, they are more than
Church-dominated units. The communities serve grassroots constituents and
have come to play an important political role in evaluating political parties and
their platforms and urging members to take political action to defend their rights.
It remains to be seen, though, whether the CEBs can stem the flow of Catholics
to other faiths—whether a "People's Church" can keep Brazil's masses beneath
the Catholic umbrella.[13]

Challenges to the Church

The capacity of the Catholic Church to influence the patrimonial order, as it did in the 1970s, has diminished to the degree that the Church itself has become weaker as a national institution. Since the late 1970s, the Church has been challenged by the rapid growth of Pentecostal congregations in Brazil. The Pentecostals are replacing the more traditional Protestant churches in Brazil as an alternative to Roman Catholicism, and they are drawing substantial numbers of converts from Catholic ranks. In addition, folk Catholicism, heavily influenced by the African cults and local religious habits of the hinterlands, continues to dominate religious life outside of the large coastal cities. It is estimated that some 30 million identify with some form of African religion. The leadership of the Catholic Church has repeatedly criticized the "Africanization" of religion in Brazil.

The progressive wing of the Church leadership—those advocating a "People's Church"—has always argued that the CEBs are an important way to maintain Church loyalty among Brazil's poor, as well as useful in reducing the attraction of the Pentecostal groups and the Afro-Brazilian religions. The more conservative wing of the Church, while deploring the rise of alternative religions, has argued against the CEBs as a politicization of the work of the Church—in effect, abandoning any pretensions to influence the patrimonial order by mobilizing the Church faithful against the state.

The Church's involvement in criticizing the military regime's policy on human rights in the 1970s and early 1980s served to attract new political supporters during the *abertura* period, but it does not appear to have strengthened doctrinal and institutional requirements of the Church. The Church's power is that of moral leadership, and its emphasis on social action is a role to which both the patrimonial state and the Church itself continue to adapt. Alone, the Church can do little to further the cause of social justice in Brazil. In collaboration with similarly minded groups, it can seek to focus the attention of the regime in power on the human and social needs of the Brazilian people. Still, with the Church facing mass defections to other faiths—only 75 percent of Brazilians were considered nominally Catholic when the Pope visited Brazil again in 1991—it remains to be seen whether the Church can remain the preeminent moral leader in Brazil indefinitely.

With the end of the Military Republic, the political space within which the Church had been able to maneuver narrowed considerably; as many of the demands of civil society were met in the early 1980s, the willingness of the patrimonial order to listen to social agitators decreased. Scott Mainwaring observes:

By the March 1985 inauguration of a democratic government, Catholic groups had lost part of their political impact, both as a result of their own political ingenuousness and of the consolidation of a traditional Brazilian pattern of elitist style politics. Yet while Catholic movements became marginalized during the political struggle of the first half of the 1980s, this certainly does not mean that they have lost their relevance. The political issues they raise remain as important as ever in Brazil. Questions of popular participation, grass-roots democracy, and socioeconomic justice have been relegated to a secondary role in the last years of Brazilian politics, yet it is evident that these issues have hardly been resolved.[14]

An important component of the Brazilian Church's strategy after 1985 was driven by the papacy of the new Pope. Soon after his election in 1978, Pope John Paul II made it clear that he rejected any political role for the clergy. His particular concern was with the more radical versions of the doctrine, known as the theology of liberation. The doctrine involves the use of Marxist analysis and has been used to justify the activism of Roman Catholic priests and nuns in Latin America since the early 1970s.

The basic tenets of liberation theology were endorsed at the second conference of Latin American bishops, held in Medellín, Colombia, in 1968. At that conclave, the bishops of the region issued a series of documents that supported a "preferential option for the poor" and denounced institutionalized violence and other social ills that were—and are—rampant in Latin America. Military governments in the region saw this "preferential option" as a thinly veiled criticism of the lack of social policy within the then-dominant bureaucratic-authoritarian regimes. The newly elected Pope, concerned with the destruction of Marxism, saw little to support in a movement that endorsed elements of the doctrine that he was dedicated to erasing in eastern Europe and the Soviet Union.

At the third conference of Latin American bishops, held in Puebla, Mexico, in 1979, Pope John Paul II made it clear that he wanted the region's religious to divest themselves of all political ideologies. The Puebla conference was an important turning point in the relations between the Catholic Church in Brazil and the central administration of the Church in the Vatican. The most "liberated" clergy were clearly in Brazil. A number of the theorists of the theology of liberation wrote and lectured in Brazilian religious institutions.

A series of books by a Franciscan friar, Leonardo Boff, aroused the anger of the Vatican in the early 1980s. When Boff published *Church: Charisma and Power—Liberation Theology and the Institutional Church* (1981), the Vatican's Sacred Congregation for the Doctrine of the Faith decided to act to curb both Boff and the too-radical Brazilian Church. A 36-page essay, titled "Instructions on Certain Aspects of the 'Theology of Liberation,' " was prepared by the congregation and ordered to be published by the Pope in September 1984.

It was made clear at the Vatican that the document was viewed as the most thoroughgoing critique of what the Pope and the Church's conservative majority considered the political radicalization of doctrine and clergy, both in Latin America and among left-wing Roman Catholics elsewhere. To emphasize the strong disapproval of liberation theology, Friar Boff was summoned to Rome by the congregation's head, the powerful Joseph Cardinal Ratzinger, a close conservative ally of the Pope. After further deliberation, the congregation condemned Boff for his criticism of the Church hierarchy in his writings. In a statement issued in March 1985, the congregation rejected Boff's arguments. Boff immediately issued a conciliatory statement and said that he accepted the reservations of the congregation: "I prefer to walk with the church rather than walk alone in my theology."[15]

In May 1985, the Vatican ordered Friar Boff to maintain a period of "penitential silence," and he was forbidden to write, publish, or attend conferences for an unspecified period of time. The decision of the Vatican increased the tension between the still-liberal leadership of the Brazilian Church and the Vatican. In a tense three days of meetings in March 1986, 21 senior bishops met with the Pope and Vatican officials in Rome to attempt a reconciliation. As a result of that meeting, the Vatican, a few weeks later, canceled the "penitential silence" of Friar Boff.

While a 1986 Vatican statement condemning "unbridled capitalism" as well as "Marxism" softened the confrontation between the Brazilian Church and Rome, the Pope continued to use his most powerful tool: the appointment process. It became obvious in the mid-1980s that all vacancies in the Brazilian Church hierarchy were being filled with conservative bishops. The more progressive leaders were transferred to lesser positions whenever possible. The message was clear: To prosper in the Church of John Paul II, one had to espouse conservative theological positions.

But the progressive leadership of the CNBB continued its struggle. In February 1988, it lashed out at the government of President José Sarney. A letter entitled "The Urgency of Great Decisions" warned that "national frustration" and dissatisfaction with the government and the political establishment had reached levels that could bring "catastrophic consequences" for the country. Most damagingly, the letter backed widespread claims that corruption was worse than under the military regime.[16]

The release of a letter from Cardinal Paulo Evaristo Arns, Archbishop of São Paulo, to Fidel Castro on the thirteenth anniversary of the Cuban Revolution outraged conservative Roman Catholic opinion in Brazil and abroad. The Vatican took the occasion to divide into two the São Paulo diocese in March 1989. Arns was left with the city's core, which was heavily middle class—and conservative. Four new dioceses were created in the impoverished periphery of São Paulo, where Arns had established his reputation in the 1970s when he worked with the labor movement in opposing the military regime. Conservative bishops were appointed to all four dioceses. And in September 1989, two seminaries in the Northeast city of Recife were closed—they were seen by the Vatican as schools dominated by the theology of liberation.

At the twenty-ninth General Assembly of the CNBB in April 1991, which was called to prepare for the forthcoming visit of Pope John Paul II to Brazil, the Brazilian Church restated its priorities. In documents released following the meeting, emphasis was given to workers' issues, violence in the countryside, indigenous peoples, and Brazil's youth. And during his October 1991 visit, the Pope addressed these issues with vigor and passion.

In the 1990s, the leadership of the Church has developed and deepened the commitments undertaken in 1991. And this, possibly, may be the new role that "relegitimates" the Catholic Church as an important societal player in the "new" Brazil. The Church has been at the forefront of defending indigenous and workers' rights. Of increasing concern to the Cardoso government has been the "political" action of the clergy on the frontier, working to support rural workers' rights. The Church pastoral commission does not view this as political but humanitarian, fulfilling Pope John Paul's admonition. But it has brought the Church into growing conflict with the government, which is constrained from introducing meaningful land reform because of the opposition of the traditional patrimonial forces in the countryside. A poignant example of the rural crisis in which the Church is very involved was a massacre of poor rural folk several years ago. As reported in the *New York Times*:

Twelve settlers died, including a 7-year-old girl, and many more disappeared, feared murdered. Hundreds were injured. The graves of the victims were marked by number, not name. "Some people say this is where Brazil ends," Father Geraldo [the local Catholic priest] told a newcomer chilled by the brutality. "I say it's where Brazil begins."[17]

To the degree that the Cardoso government is prevented from addressing the legitimate needs of the rural poor, the Catholic Church can find a new role and continue its strident defense of their rights. That will entail conflict with the political authorities, but it also places the Church on the side of the poor and marginal, the majority of Brazil. And, if we are correct about the patrimonial order shifting, it may provide an important future role for the Church.

But the Catholic Church is constrained from even greater militancy because it is seriously understaffed. New priests are few. European and American priests have come to Brazil to fill the void, but they present a different sort of political issue—they are foreigners who are easily targeted by local elites as intervening in the internal affairs of Brazil. In a country in which race and class will become more significant, there are few priests of color. As noted earlier, the growth of Afro-Brazilian religious movements in recent years has attracted many of the black population, further diminishing the pool of parishioners for the Church. Pentecostal groups are active through religious television ministries and at the street level in neighborhoods across Brazil. They can operate from storefront churches, and they have taken advantage of the absence of the Catholic Church by organizing religious activities and offering informal pastoral guidance on a daily basis by community spiritual leaders.

The Catholic Church, then, confronts a number of issues. Can it compete with the new—and the old—religions? Will it avoid a political confrontation with the state over its increasingly confrontational position in defense of the poor and landless? Are the resources available to the Church to continue to administer to its traditional urban, middle- and upper-class constituencies and to integrate people of color, poor, and uneducated? The Church in Brazil is a player, but it currently lacks the financial and manpower resources needed to become a central player. It remains torn between its traditional role and the perceived need to address social inequalities, both rural and urban. But to the degree it achieves the former, it may alienate the latter.

THE LABOR MOVEMENT

The pre-1964 Brazilian labor movement has been described accurately in the following terms:

Labor relations with both the government and with employers evolved from a pattern of paternalism inherited from the colonial social structure which was dependent upon slavery. This accounted for much worker apathy toward the labor union movement, making *personalismo* the basis of control of labor. In effect, the characteristics of the whole labor movement have often been a reflection of individual leaders, and until the late 1950s, attempts by labor union leaders or political parties to inspire a general class consciousness among workers received little popular support.[18]

The labor movement in general has provided an excellent example of the co-optation policy of the patrimonial state. Rather than allow the growth of an independent and perhaps a destabilizing labor movement, each regime since 1930 used its power to tie labor to the government. This effectively precluded the creation of an autonomous, politically active interest group to represent workers' concerns, until the late 1970s, as we shall see.

The Labor Party (PT), organized in 1928, did not survive the Vargas coup in 1930. Vargas, identifying labor as a potential source of strength for his regime, quickly moved to co-opt the workers by providing them with benefits that they had not requested. He interfered in labor's organizational efforts and tied labor to the government, legally and personally.

In November 1930, the Transitional Republic created by decree the first Ministry of Labor. Labor unions were legally recognized, and new unions were stimulated. As a result of this new freedom, a number of strikes marred the early Vargas years. The 1934 Constitution outlawed strikes and placed unions under police supervision. By 1937, any hint of an independent labor movement had disappeared.

The 1930–1937 period was one of mutual experimentation. To survive and flourish, the union leadership accepted government interference and direction; to ensure social class conciliation and a dependent working class, the regime guaranteed union survival in exchange for its freedom. The concept of popular participation in labor policy never evolved in Brazil.

With the Estado Novo (New State) in 1937, a new labor policy was enunciated, a policy that would dominate the life of Brazilian workers for four decades. Employers and workers were set up in parallel organizations. The basic units were the *sindicato* (union), the state federation, and three or more state federations joined in a confederation. An inclusive national labor organization was forbidden. This structure was never fully applied to employers. And despite the rise of an independent labor movement in the late 1970s, much of the Vargas era structure survives today.

Government recognition for all unions was required, and labor courts replaced the concept of collective bargaining. Each worker needed a *carteira profissional* (identification card), issued by the government, to be employed. An *imposto sindical* (union tax) was required for all nonagricultural workers, employers, and the self-employed. For the worker, the amount was one day's pay. Payments were made to the Bank of Brazil in the name of the worker's union. The tax funds were at the disposal of union leaders for education, welfare, and professional purposes, as well as for a wide variety of political purposes. In later years, the union tax was called a "contribution."

In 1943, Vargas consolidated the paternalistic labor legislation, which remained virtually unchallenged and unchanged until 1977. It brought together the impressive welfare legislation of the Transitional Republic: a minimum wage, regulated working hours, improved health facilities, educational programs, and a carefully structured procedure for resolving conflicts with employers.

Two forces were influential in the post-1945 labor movement. The Brazilian Communist Party (PCB), legalized in 1945, took an active role in the union movement, openly until 1947, when they were again banned, and clandestinely until 1964. The PCB actively supported the creation of the National Confederation of Workers, which was banned in 1948. The other active organization was the Brazilian Labor Party (PTB), organized by Vargas to capture the working-class vote after 1945. A PTB member was minister of labor for most of the post-1945 period. During the presidency of Eurico Dutra, labor did not play an important role in national life, nor was it encouraged to do so by the conservative administration.

During the 1951–1954 period, union elections were permitted, minimum wage levels were raised, and unions were allowed to affiliate with international labor organizations. The policy of nonharassment continued under Kubitschek (1956–1961), and more collective bargaining was allowed. With the succession of Goulart as president in 1961, labor moved into its period of greatest independence—ironically. As labor minister and PTB leader, Goulart had successfully posed as labor's advocate, regardless of government policy. As head of the government, he found himself pressured for inflationary wage increases, greater welfare legislation, strike protection, and so on, all issues that would further weaken his administration if granted. Labor became more militant. The General Workers Command (CGT), an illegal entity formed to coordinate the confederations in the absence of a national organization, served as a goad for increased radicalism. By 1964, the confederations and the CGT were heavily influenced by the Communist Party.

Philippe Schmitter captures well the modus operandi of labor leaders during the early 1946 Republic.

The syndical leadership of long standing, closely associated with the bureaucrats of the Labor Ministry and the Retirement and Social Welfare Institutions and loyal to the idea of a paternalist reformist state as the protector and benefactor of the labor movement, retained its hold on the top posts.[19]

This symbolic relationship between union leadership and government would not be challenged until the late 1970s.

With the March 31 movement, the CGT was abolished, unions were taken over by the government, and close government supervision was reestablished. Communist leaders were purged. By 1966, most of the tainted unions had been ''purified'' and returned to dependable hands. The military regime's program of *novo trabalhismo* (new labor movement) in 1966 and 1967 sought to recapture labor's loyalty through assistance to the unemployed and scholarships for the children of workers' families.

Deliberate steps were taken by the regime to exclude organized labor from patronage channels and the political influence that it had enjoyed in the early 1960s.

In order to prevent labor leaders from using their participation in tripartite policy making bodies as a source of union power, the government restructured the social security system into one single National Social Welfare Institute (INPS), in 1966, and had it placed under strict bureaucratic control. One step further in the same direction was taken in 1974, when the government withdrew the INPS from the Ministry of Labor and placed it under the new Ministry of Social Security and Welfare (MPAS). The corporatist arrangements inherited from the Estado Novo (1937–1945) were not dismantled but a further note was added to it—rigid bureaucratic control of union life.[20]

Even though the authoritarian regime appeared unconcerned about labor militance by the early 1970s, conditions had begun to change dramatically in the union ranks. The economic miracle had expanded the industrial base of Brazil dramatically. Tens of thousands of new workers, skilled and unskilled, flocked to São Paulo and its new industrial suburbs. Foreign companies expanded their domestic plants. Brazil's export-led model of growth increasingly sought to emphasize industrial goods as well as agro-industrial and traditional crops and minerals. The first efforts to assert workers' grievances through strikes in 1968 were suppressed, but they did highlight a new reality within the working class:

In the Populist period the mass strikes in 1953 and 1957 had been organized and channeled by the official trade union movement, and the unions had looked to the State for resolution of their grievances. After 1964, the unions faced a hostile State, and this forced them increasingly to try and negotiate with their employers and openly oppose the State.[21]

It was the industrial working class, now employed and living in the new industrial suburbs, that was no longer willing to accept government-led unions. It began to look for different means of expressing its demands. That process slowed in the repressive years of the Médici government in the early and mid-1970s. But by the time President Ernesto Geisel took office in 1974, circumstances were appropriate for a new effort to organize Brazil's industrial workers. Press freedom had been restored. The early discussion of *abertura* had begun. The time was ripe to sow the seeds of what would later be called the "new unionism."[22]

National attention became focused on the workers' demand for restitution of lost wages in 1973 and 1974. The unions argued that, in those years, the government's inflation numbers were deliberately falsified; since wage raises were tied to inflation, the workers had been denied a fair salary increase. The government finally admitted in 1977 that, indeed, that was the case. The metalworkers' federation was particularly vociferous in demanding restitution of lost income. Led by Luis Inácio ("Lula") da Silva, a young, charismatic head of the union in São Bernardo, an industrial suburb of São Paulo, the wage restitution issue was used to raise the level of consciousness of the industrial working class in Brazil.

In May 1978, the São Bernardo metalworkers' union called a strike that gained the support of over 30 percent of the labor force in the region. They were joined by workers in other auto plants and then by the other metalworkers in the region (known as the ABC, which were the initials of three of the industrial suburbs). The impact of the autoworkers' strike spread to other industries and workers that year. A main element in the wave of strikes was that the unions insisted on negotiating with the employers and not with the state—to which the factory owners agreed. Agreements were reached after protracted negotiations. Immediately, plans were made for the next year's negotiations. Once again, the metalworkers led the workers in striking in May 1979. But this time the state intervened to bring the strike to a halt. It was a violent confrontation between unions and the state that demoralized the union leaders. But other strikes in the industrial areas of southeast Brazil continued.

In November 1979, the government decreed a new wage law that remained in effect until February 1983. It agreed to adjust wages every six months rather than every year (as had been done), according to a single national consumer price index (INPC). Those workers earning one to three minimum salaries (one to three times the legal minimum wage in Brazil) received an increase equal to 110 percent of the change in the INPC.

The wage decision coincided with the end of the metalworkers' 1979 strike effort. While the government had reorganized wage policy, the unions received only a few of their demands. It was also clear that the militant attitudes of the metalworkers of São Bernardo and the heavy-industry region around the city of São Paulo were not shared by all workers, either in the state of São Paulo or in other industrial areas.

In 1980, the metalworkers' strike became a national event. It received widespread support from the Church, students, intellectuals, and many other groups in Brazilian society. Even though the union was taken over by the government, and its leaders—including Lula—were imprisoned, the strike continued. Confronted by massive state and private-sector opposition, the workers accepted defeat after 41 days.

The strenuous efforts to define an independent political position for urban industrial workers led to the formation of the Workers Party (PT) during the period of party reorganization in 1979–1980. Led by Lula and his colleagues, the new grouping attracted widespread support in the industrial cities and suburbs of the Southeast. The PT wanted to avoid the pre-1964 relationship between the unions and the PTB and create an autonomous political power base. Plans were made to nominate PT candidates for local and state office in the November 1982 national elections.

In February 1981, Lula and his colleagues were brought to trial under the National Security Law because of their conduct during the 1980 strike. They were convicted, but the Supreme Military Tribunal, which exercised jurisdiction in the case, annulled the proceedings and ordered a retrial. At the new hearing, in November 1981, the group was again sentenced. Being found guilty under the National Security Law the tribunal prohibited Lula from standing as a candidate for office in the November 1982 elections. Finally, in May 1982, as part of the liberalization process, the Supreme Military Tribunal rescinded jurisdiction over the case, and the charges were dropped. Lula immediately became the PT candidate in the São Paulo governor's race.

The PT was not the only organized political voice of the workers in the early 1980s. The PCB, the Communist Party of Brazil (PC do B), and other radical Marxist and Trotskyite factions competed for worker support, both within the unions and at the polls in November 1982. The election results were disappointing for the PT. Lula lost his race for governor of São Paulo, placing fourth among five candidates. His party's candidate in Rio de Janeiro placed fifth among five in the race for that state's governorship. The party elected only eight federal deputies, the smallest number of the minor parties, and no senators. The party's poor showing was attributed to its inexperience, the widespread impression that it was a party for workers only, and the poor organization and financing that had characterized the campaign.

In addition, by 1982, the economic recession in Brazil had entered its second year. Unemployment was rising, and labor militancy had become less attractive. Soon after the elections of November 1982, the government was forced to alter the wage law extensively, something that would happen with frequency throughout 1983 as the government attempted to reassure the International Monetary Fund (IMF) and the private commercial banks about the country's financial plans before it received new loans to finance the foreign debt and needed imports. The PT strenuously opposed the various packages proposed by the government, and it was the small PTB that finally provided the votes the government needed in November 1983 to approve the latest wage legislation. The divisions in the ranks of organized labor became more evident in 1983.

The various labor groups did come together in São Paulo in July 1983, when workers in a state petroleum refinery called a strike to protest the government's efforts to restrict wage increases. The minister of labor immediately intervened in the union and dismissed its president; a number of workers lost their jobs. The government was highly sensitive to the fact that the refinery was responsible for producing about one-third of the gasoline in Brazil; a prolonged work stoppage would have had a negative impact on industry and on middle-class consumers. It was noted that other unions in different industrial areas of the country did not declare a general strike, although many staged sympathy demonstrations. The general strike in São Paulo was peaceful and served to remind the government that even with the economic crisis and high levels of unemployment, organized labor had the capacity to act politically, with potentially damaging implications for the nation's economy.

Following the July 1983 strike, over 5,000 delegates organized to create a new Central Workers' Organization (CUT). The CUT was the first central trade union body organized since 1964, when the CGT was disbanded. The minister of labor immediately declared the CUT illegal under the existing labor code. The CUT also faced opposition within the labor movement from those sectors that gave priority to negotiating with the government and sought to avoid confrontation.

The groups opposed to the CUT coalesced around a less centralized structure, forming the National Coalition of the Working Class (CONCLAT) in November 1983. Composed largely of former union leaders (of the state-sponsored unions), the CONCLAT pursued a more accommodationist line and was superseded in importance by the CUT, whose confrontational strategy and effective internal coordination won concessions from employers. The CONCLAT subsequently shifted toward a somewhat more centralized structure and renamed itself the General Confederation of Labor (CGT). It has remained less powerful than the CUT, largely because of its links to the government in Brasília.

By the early 1990s, the CUT had consolidated its position as the leading union confederation in Brazil. It also had taken an unambiguous position of opposition to the liberal policies of the Collor de Mello government. Throughout the 1980s, the unions, as we have seen, played an important role in the Diretas Já campaign and in the transition to civilian government in 1985. Union autonomy was recognized in the 1988 Constitution, which upheld

- the right to strike;

- the right of unions to be free from direct government intervention;

- respect for the financial autonomy of the unions; and
- recognition of the existence of union confederations.

While the confederations had operated openly and with increasing aggressiveness in the late 1970s and 1980s, they did not have legal status until 1988. In addition to the CUT and the CGT, the Brazilian labor movement is composed of

- Força Sindical, a relatively new offshoot of the CGT, created by the former Communist union leader Antônio Medeiros. The powerful metallurgical workers in São Paulo are the backbone of the CGT. Medeiros is a centrist politically and has attempted to work with the Collor de Mello government; and
- União Inter-Sindical, an extremely small corporatist-type confederation with a very conservative orientation and little national influence.

Of the four entities, the CUT is the largest and controls nearly 90 percent of public-sector unions, about 50 percent of those in Brazilian-owned manufacturing establishments and 50 percent of those in multinational companies. Its power base has always been in heavy industry in the São Paulo area, and, in particular, in the automobile industry. In addition, it has a large constituency in Minas Gerais and Rio de Janeiro, the other two main hubs of industrialization in Brazil.

The CUT has a strong working link with the PT and strongly supported Lula's candidacy for the presidency in his three presidential races. During the Collor de Mello government, the CUT led labor criticism of his policies on wages and wage-related issues. It used strikes, threats of a general shutdown of industry, and other tactics to attempt to intimidate the government.

The government's strategy in the early 1990s was to encourage the growth of Força Sindical as a union alternative to the CUT. The Labor Ministry has channeled funds to the Força Sindical in an effort to strengthen Antônio Medeiros and to undercut CUT leaders. The CUT and the Força Sindical were involved in strong competition to influence nonaligned groups of workers in the struggle to build a broader national following. But the CUT has remained a militant and dominant voice for Brazil's working class, especially state employees. It has strong links to the PT; it has a powerful base of support in both the public sector and heavy industry; and it appeals to the deep concerns of the working class regarding the perceived challenge of the economic reforms of the Cardoso administration.

Almost invariably, the unions have been at the forefront of opposition to the privatization process. Why? Because some union members will definitely lose their jobs and entitlements. Ideologically, unions remain wedded to a ''big'' paternalistic state; and union leadership perceives that it will be reduced in importance as a societal actor to the degree that free markets are introduced into Brazil. Competitiveness means more technology and fewer workers, the unions fear. New policies are needed in Brazil to educate, retrain, and relocate workers, but this is a daunting task in the short run (as it is in many of the industrial countries). It is safe to predict that the reality will continue to be adamant opposition to the Cardoso government's plans. As reported in July 1998, when Telebras, the national telephone company, was privatized, "riot police clashed with thousands of protestors—mostly students, labor unionists, and members of Brazil's radical landless movement—who accused the government of selling the national patrimony to foreign interests."[23] There is no question that the CUT, and to a lesser degree the other union organizations, will continue to work against the government's reform program. But, ultimately, that program will succeed. Both the union movement and the government will need to carefully evaluate the political as well as the economic consequences of that "success" in the twenty-first century if a modicum of social peace is to be achieved.

THE RURAL LABOR MOVEMENT

The rural labor movement in Brazil may pose the greatest social threat in decades for the patrimonial regime, and it may be one of the major crises of the second Cardoso administration. The rise of the Movement of Landless Rural Workers (MST) in the 1990s has provided the first effective and aggressive resistance to the traditional patrimonial order in the vast Brazilian countryside. According to an article in the *New York Times Magazine*,

from the arid northeast to the fertile south, tens of thousands of Brazilians are claiming their rights to settle unused lands in their country. Hundreds of millions of acres of rich soil lie untouched—the legacy of land grants awarded to the ruling class 400 years ago. . . . Leading families and business groups keep their estates as a hedge against inflation or as an investment, while rural workers toil in near-feudal conditions or, cast off when jobs run out, wander the countryside.

Today, the government pays lip service to this ideal [the land should belong to the one who works it], pledging to buy unused farmland and give it to workers. But, in practice, the process can be derailed by local judges and the military police, who often side with the large landholders.[24]

The history of rural poverty, landless peasants, routine violence, and repression is long-standing in Brazil, no matter what the public bureaucrats of the patrimonial order state publicly. They, of course, are aligned with the local power brokers—the landowners and their cronies. It is a fact in Brazil that early labor legislation specifically excluded rural workers or, when rural legal rights were mentioned, they were never implemented. Not until March 2, 1963, did Congress pass the Rural Labor Statute, which provided a means of enforcing existing legislation for the benefit of rural laborers. Even before Congress acted, as part of the basic reform strategy of the Goulart government, the unionization effort in the Northeast had gained considerable momentum.

The first organized program of collective peasant action was the Peasant

Leagues (Ligas Camponesas) in Pernambuco. Organized in 1955 by Francisco Julião, a state assemblyman and lawyer and the son of a landowning family, they grew out of a mutual-assistance burial association. When peasants asked Julião for legal help, he introduced a bill to have the state government expropriate three unused plantations for distribution to the workers. Julião immediately became a hero. *Ligas* spread quickly into neighboring states, with an estimated membership of 100,000 concentrated in the humid farming strip along the northeastern coast, called the Zona da Mata. Tenant farmers and sharecroppers were the major participants.

In the early 1960s, competition for the support of the peasants emerged from within the Church. Bishops such as Dom Eugenio Sales moved to counter Julião and the growing Communist influence over the peasants. Fathers Paulo Crespo and Antonio Melo in Pernambuco organized the first statewide federation of rural workers in 1962. By April 1964,

more than 100 peasants' associations (leagues and Catholic unions) existed in Pernambuco. Their combined membership was estimated to be about 280,000. Direct control of peasant organization was no longer solely in the hands of Julião or the Catholic Church. Between 1962 and 1964, representatives of the Brazilian Communist Party (PCB, the Moscow-oriented group), the Communist Party of Brazil (PC do B, influenced by the Chinese doctrinal position), the Leninist Vanguard (Trotskyite), the administration of the state's governor, Miguel Arraes, and the administration of President João Goulart also competed for the privilege of organizing Pernambucan peasants.[25]

Anthony Leeds has characterized Julião's leadership of the *ligas* as being in the typical paternalist mold of Brazil.[26] The same can be said of the Goulart administration's motives in moving to organize rural unions. The rural labor movement was a movement from ''on top'' with the benefits handed down to the waiting peasants. Little peasant initiative appeared in any of the unionization efforts; the struggle was among competing national elite groups: the Church, university students from JUC and AP, the politicians, and the ideologues.

The First National Congress of Rural Workers and Laborers, held in Belo Horizonte in November 1961, was indicative: it was divided by the competing groups that sought to use it for their own ends. By November 1963, and the organization of the National Confederation of Agricultural Workers (CONTAG), Julião had been elected to Congress and was a marginal leader in the movement. A coalition of Communists and radical Catholics defeated the more moderate Church group for control of the confederation; the *ligas* had not participated in the meeting.

By late 1963, then, there was a good deal of activity in the countryside. The protection of national labor legislation had been extended into the rural area for the first time. A number of groups fought with each other to organize the peasants under the new legal provisions for their own political or institutional advantage. The issues of agrarian reform, the eradication of illiteracy, and the standardization of a living wage and just working conditions for rural workers produced an extraordinarily confusing convergence of diverse interests. The resulting mobilization of the peasants terrified the rural oligarchy and raised the specter of massive internal disorder for the military. The presence of the Communists and the obvious influence of Fidel Castro and his revolutionary message in the work of many of the groups convinced a large number of military figures that the movement was subversive.

With the 1964 coup, all units were closed. CONTAG and its federations and unions were taken over by the government. After a year of cleaning out the rural movement, the military regime followed a policy of cautious corporatism and paternalism in the countryside. With the passage of an agrarian reform law in 1965 and the creation of land-reform institutes and agencies, the issue became one of control and censorship by the government. Rather than the radical agrarian reform called for at the National Congress of Rural Workers in 1961 and repeated by CONTAG in 1963–1964, the government sponsored colonization projects in the Amazon and education and welfare programs. The small but real advances made in the countryside before 1964 were neutralized during the Military Republic.

The rural workforce in the Northeast was most susceptible to a restoration of the patrimonial order following the 1964 Revolution. Landowners and rural security forces quickly dismantled incipient organizations, and traditional forms of control were reinstituted. Chronic underemployment in the rural areas helped depoliticize the peasantry. The economic miracle of the late 1960s and early 1970s drew large numbers to the industrial Southeast of the country, while many returned to the North and Northeast during the crisis years of the early 1980s, most remained in the South. The population of the Northeast dropped throughout the 1970s. Government planning in the 1970s deliberately ignored the social needs of the Northeast, and investment was encouraged in capital-intensive activities.

Given the absence of heavy industry in the Northeast, agriculture has remained the mainstay of the workforce. While agro-industry and technological innovation have been introduced into Brazil's Central and Western states, they have made few inroads in the Northeast, except in areas growing sugarcane, which is essential for the production of alcohol as a substitute for expensive petroleum imports. However, the majority of the distilleries are found elsewhere in Brazil.

Contrary to superficial observation, a significant development took place in the 1970s among rural workers:

All unionists were obliged to confront the suffocating institutional reality in the 1964–1985 period. Many succumbed to the government's project of making rural worker unions into welfare-dispensing local agencies of the military state. Yet a distinct and powerful minority attempted to keep alive the call for agrarian reform that had worried prominent sectors of the Brazilian elite in the period preceding the 1964 military coup.

This minority faction of the rural union movement even managed to take command of the National Confederation of Agricultural Workers (CONTAG), the union movement's peak organization between 1965 and 1985. At CONTAG, the progressives were in a position to set the agenda for the trade union apparatus as a whole (without raising the ire of the military state) during a critical period of its political development and physical expansion.[27]

Biorn Maybury Lewis's study of the rural union movement in this period explains the survival and the success of the leadership in terms of the "politics of the possible": the capacity to avoid the repression, to employ scarce political "space" for sustaining grassroots militancy, and to undermine the institutional constraints on labor. This allowed the rural unionists to rebuild and expand a union network—under the eyes of the Military Republic. Intelligently, the rural leaders used the rules and regulations of the regime to accomplish their goals.

As a result of this strategy, in the early 1980s, the proletarianized workers of the coastal areas took a cue from the ABC area in São Paulo and the example set by militant Church groups, political parties, and labor organizers. Workers began to demand higher wages and better working conditions. The battle was slow, particularly given the Northeast's political position as the bedrock of the government party in elections. The federal funds that were generously distributed in the region prior to the elections went to traditional political and social groups, with the understanding that they would maintain the status quo ante. A *New York Times* reporter noted that Northeasterners "have grown so dependent on local authorities for the basic necessities of survival that the Establishment has become fixed and unassailable."[28] But the success of the CONTAG-led militants—and the not-so-militant ordinary citizens seeking their rights after 1964—resulted in the creation and growth of the MST, which emerged as a key actor in the late 1980s.

The MST formally organized in 1984 in the south of Brazil as a pressure group for agrarian reform. The organization currently operates in 22 Brazilian states and is coordinated by a congress of 65 people, representing the states in which it operates and a national board of directors of 15 members. The MST receives strong support in the urban areas from the PT and the CUT. Perhaps its most important ally in the countryside is the Pastoral Land Commission (CPT) of the Catholic Church.

The MST wants to introduce land reform that reduces the emphasis on huge plantations of grain, cotton, and soya beans and to "organize production to supply the population of Brazil with the food they need, giving incentives for small-scale production of poultry and pigs," comments one of its national leaders, João Pedro Stedile.[29] This programmatic approach is supported by, ironically, the UN Food and Agricultural Organization, which produced a report in 1998 urging the Cardoso government to encourage more family-run smallholdings that, it argued, would be more efficient than vast ranches. And the World Bank, in the same year, issued a report that demonstrated that when land in the Northeastern state of Piaui was redistributed to small farmers, yields increased by up to 40 percent on naturally irrigated farms and up to 70 percent on those that were artificially irrigated.[30]

All of this makes good sense, and the Cardoso government has paid greater attention to agrarian matters than any of its predecessors. The Ministry of Agrarian Reform was resurrected, and a known advocate of reform was appointed as its first minister. Token gestures have been made by the government. But the reality is otherwise. The powerful landowning lobby has immense political clout. In the 1980s, it formed a political party, the Rural Democratic Union (UDR), to protect its interests, and its leader was a presidential candidate in 1990. The UDR disbanded in the early 1990s and was resurrected as the rural delegation in the national Congress ("bancada rural"), which has played an influential role in stalling substantive progress in agrarian matters. The Cardoso administration often has had to turn to the bancada rural to trade its votes for government legislation in exchange for "slow motion" on rural matters. Sensing an opportunity for greater political space, the UDR was revived in 1996.

The militancy of the UDR has been met increasingly by the countermilitancy of the MST and its allies in the Church and the urban labor movement, as well as increasing sympathy from average Brazilians. In 1997, 25,000 rural workers in Brasília demonstrated against the government's land reform program; the Roman Catholic bishops simultaneously launched a fierce attack on the government's economic policies, blaming those policies, in part, for the impoverishment of the poor. The Brasília demonstration was the culmination of a two-month protest march by MST members from São Paulo to Brasília and coincided with the first anniversary of the murder of 19 rural workers by local police in the Northern state of Pará. In response, President Cardoso met with the leaders in his office and promised to accelerate its land reform policy, including a proposal to set up a new credit system for loans to recently settled families.

Dissatisfied with the government's response, the MST in 1998 moved into the urban areas of Brazil, threatening violence and further demonstrations. The MST is now closely aligned with university students and urban intellectuals, the CUT, and the Catholic Church. It actively participated, as we noted, in the demonstrations in 1998 against the privatization of the state telephone company when it was auctioned to foreign investors.

The rural union movement has come of age in Brazil. Long marginalized, it renewed itself after 1964. Slowly but surely, it built its institutional structure, state by state, in the 1980s and early 1990s. Finding succeeding governments unresponsive, it became more militant in the late 1990s. No serious observer believes that it will either disappear or be overwhelmed by its adversaries until it achieves its goals. Given its network of support, the MST represents the most recent, militant attack against the local political elites of the patrimonial order. The Cardoso government confronts a difficult political decision—to support the landless or run the risk of losing the support of the rural landowners and power brokers. How it responds will determine to some degree the profile of Brazil in the twenty-first century.

THE INDUSTRIALISTS

Industrial groups traditionally have experienced great difficulty in exerting pressure on government policy making. Unlike the earlier industrial societies, both freewheeling entrepreneurship and the give and take of competitive pluralistic politics bypassed Brazil until very recently. The dominant role of the patrimonial state determined economic policy in Brazil throughout the nineteenth and twentieth centuries until 1990, when trade liberalization opened vast new opportunities for business. While business as business has flourished in the 1990s, the community has found it difficult to exercise concerted political influence. Let us see why.

Historically, a tradition of government protection of, and intervention in, economic affairs began with the agricultural producers of the nineteenth century, particularly the coffee planters in São Paulo. The government manipulated exchange rates and devised price-support programs to maintain prices in the face of overproduction. Similar policies were instituted for the uneconomical sugar producers of the Northeastern coast.

The intervention of the government in the industrial sector began with the cotton textile industry in the last half of the nineteenth century. "Creeping protection" characterized the government's policies.[31] Tariffs and surtaxes were among the instruments employed to protect the fledgling industries of Brazil. When the participation of the government was sought by manufacturers, the willingness of the patriomonial state to intervene in an area of new activity was evident.

With the increasing importance of industry in the Brazilian economy after World War I, the state moved into a position of influence and domination through protection and preemption of economic policy initiatives of private groups. Equally important, the impetus for industrialization often came from the old traditional families or with their cooperation and forbearance. The result, Fernando Henrique Cardoso says, is that the industrial bourgeoisie in Brazil never developed a class consciousness that would facilitate group action; it remains a very heterogeneous group. There was no need for a coordinated industrialists' party with regard to organized labor, because the state carefully controlled the working class. Because of the high level of profits in industry, supported by government favors and protection, industrialists "accept traditional practices and act more like groups linked to the old dominant classes than as a group that aspires to power."[32]

The only political action acceptable to the industrialists in Brazil has been that which complements the policies of the state:

It consists of the personal participation in the game of compromises that patrimonial style politics, still dominant, offers to those that have resources to deal with the burden of clientelist politics. This participation is highly rewarding for the industrialists, for by having access to the Congress and the President, they are able to gain economic advantages for their business groups without having to be concerned about any redefinition of the traditional political style.[33]

Thus, the business culture necessary to nurture a truly indigenous *and* internationally competitive industrial sector was suffocated from the outset. Warren Dean, in his study of industrialization in São Paulo, notes that after 1945 "the industrialists still shared most of the attitudes and interests of the planters, and when they did not, they were still willing to defer."[34] The result, by the later 1950s and 1960s, was that "perhaps half of the industrial capital in São Paulo's private sector . . . was foreign-owned or controlled."[35] Dean concludes his analysis by stating that "the manufacturers were plainly disqualified from embarking their society upon a conscious policy of industrialization."[36] Domestic industry gained the reputation of being of inferior quality; manufacturers bought local raw materials with reluctance, thus postponing the installation of basic industry. And the manufacturer, so dependent on the government for monopolies and special price fixing, and with a penchant for political "deals," never gained a positive image among his countrymen. "His success was not admired, nor did he embody the aspirations of the masses."[37]

In practical terms, this has meant that the patrimonial state held the preeminent leadership role in defining the path of Brazil industrialization. An Economic Commission for Latin America analysis of postwar economic policies in Brazil highlighted the preponderant role of the government in the economic realm:

Brazil's public sector owns . . . the country's maritime . . . and rail transport facilities and its installation for the production of petroleum . . . controls most of the steel making sector, and is rapidly becoming the principal producer of electric energy. It . . . markets a considerable proportion of the exportable production; it is also the principal iron ore producer and exporter. It exercises direct . . . control over the exchange market. . . . It constitutes . . . the major commercial banking enterprise since it accounts for about 35 percent of the general credit extended to the private sector through the Banco do Brasil, and most of the agricultural credit. . . . Through other specialized financial agencies it grants the wages, the interest rates, rents, and staple commodity prices. It sets minimum agricultural prices and is beginning to . . . operate a large-scale storage and marketing system for agricultural commodities. . . . It determines the composition of private investment and intervenes in the capital market.[38]

Nathaniel Leff comments that, given the political context of Brazilian economic development after World War II, "Private sector industrialists were not able to stand in the way of the large expansion in the scope of the government's controls and regulation, or to curb its direct investment and production activities."[39]

The economic miracle of the late 1960s and 1970s produced a new generation of entrepreneurs in Brazil, more oriented to production for export and more willing to take risks with their capital. As the economic role of the state in

Brazil continued to grow in the 1970s, and as the multinational corporation retained its position of strength in the internal market, the Brazilian private sector grew restless. Confronted by a complex array of institutions that decided the state's industrial policies, after little consultation with the entrepreneurs themselves, the quiescent position of the Brazilian industrialists began to give way to a more assertive role. This development did not change the basic distribution of power within Brazilian society or in the economy. It did not represent a willingness of the regime to reverse the trend of public participation in the economy or to turn against the multinationals. At best, it represented a "coming of age" of younger industrial leaders, concerned with preserving some area of independence for themselves in the rapidly growing economy.

The younger generation of industrialists moved quickly in the 1980s to re-direct the public image and the private influence of the São Paulo business class and their supporters in other industrial centers in Brazil. With the abrupt response of Brazilian society to the April 1977 package that resulted in widespread demonstrations during the months of June, July, and August 1977, the new business elite joined in calling for a restoration of a state of law in Brazil. In some instances, study groups were formed to prepare documents exploring social and political issues—unheard of in previous years.

In 1978, a prominent group of business leaders issued a document stating that economic and social development would be possible only "under a political arrangement that permits the ample participation of all." In 1983, a successor document called for a number of changes in national economic priorities and stated that "full democracy is a great national desire." The contribution of the businessmen to the transition in 1985 was important, but they remained frustrated with the inept economic policies and the closed economy of the Sarney government (1985–1990). While many business sectors profited from the high inflation and economic uncertainty, it was clear that the Brazilian economy needed basic reorganization.

The Collor de Mello government dramatically reduced tariffs and opened up the country to competition for the first time. New business opportunities flourished. But the failed economic policy of the administration, and the fact that it survived for such a short time, offered little hope for a new set of economic priorities and opportunities. Only with the onset of the Real Plan in 1994 has business been able to realistically think about competing globally, attracting new capital and technology, developing new products, and upgrading Brazilian competitiveness. While business has been highly successful since 1994 in profiting from the wave of privatizations (in which Brazilian businessmen have been actively involved) and benefitting from the attractiveness of Brazil to foreign investors (with whom it has formed joint ventures), the truth is that,

on the public stage, business has had little collective influence. . . . The transition to democracy in Brazil forced the nation's big industrialists to rethink their political activities and reorganize themselves for articulating focused political influence. In their efforts to organize business politics over the last decade, two elements stand out. First, business leaders have been very creative and inventive; they have experimented with many new organizations and channels of influence. Second, the experimentation has resulted in few concrete victories for aggregate business lobbies. The experimentation . . . reflects the continuing frustration of big business with its lack of collective influence in Brasília, especially in Congress.[40]

In part, as Ben Ross Schneider further explains,

Brazil's industrialists are individually powerful yet collectively weak. Individual industrialists . . . have regular access to economic ministers . . . yet the captains of industry lack
formal organizations that adequately aggregate their interests. Industrialists have neither
a strong peak association, research institutes, lobbies, nor closely associated political
parties.[41]

This reflects, of course, the historical reality of the patrimonial state in which individual actors were politically handicapped. And the more senior members of the industrial and business elite are comfortable with the old way of doing business. But the more modern leaders of business are seeking a new role and voice in the rapidly evolving economic development of Brazil. While there is a plethora of business organizations, these groups are not key players and often serve more of a social/convocational purpose than real planning or lobbying units. Brazil is one of the few major countries in the region that lacks a multi-sector peak association that brings together industry, finance, and commerce. The hope for the business sector is that new leaders and new strategies will emerge in the National Confederation of Industries (CNI) and FIESP (the São Paulo State Federation of Industries), both of which are seen as the most apt to carve out a new role for the business community in its relations with Brasília.

Brazil's business community has been reluctant to become involved in the major social issues of the day. It remains wary of the union movement, urban and rural. It is unwilling to take a stand on land reform. It does not appear to be particularly concerned, as a community, with the continuing social inequal-ities in its society, save as it is reflected in low global competitiveness, which is a reflection of poor educational opportunities. It may well be a generational question. While the post-1990 opportunities have been many, the development of a political and social mission and the appropriate institutions through which to channel those concerns has yet to emerge. Until this happens, the business community will be a critical component of the country's economic and financial success, but it will carry little weight, either in the political party structure or in the ongoing debate about whether the patrimonial order is—or should be—in retreat.

THE STATE BUREAUCRACY

In April 1983, *Veja*, a weekly newsmagazine, ironically spoke of "the country of the suffix 'brás,' which is an island of social well-being surrounded by Brazil on all sides,"[42] referring to the 560 state companies that became a powerful economic force under the Military Republic. The reference to the country of "brás" refers to the fact that many of the state entities have names such as Petrobrás, the state oil company, Nuclebrás, the state nuclear firm, and so on. The workers in these companies number more than 1.3 million; if one adds the government employees in the judicial and legislative branches, those in the armed forces, and those at the state level, the total is more than 4 million public employees. The issue of the state bureaucracy became, in the early 1980s, a major controversy in Brazil. The state company employees emerged as being among the strongest supporters of the patrimonial order—and not unexpectedly, since they are among the major beneficiaries of the growth of the public sector since 1964.

The growth and influence of the federal bureaucracy and, perhaps as important, the reasons for its expansion are rooted in Brazilian political history. The expansion of the Portuguese Empire necessitated a large administrative structure. With the Napoleonic wars and the move of the royal court to Rio de Janeiro in 1808, public positions (*cargos públicos*) as sinecures became an accepted part of Brazilian administration.

Under Vargas after 1930, with authority and control concentrated in the presidency, the bureaucracy expanded rapidly. In 1938, the Administrative Department of Public Service was created to serve the administrative system; it seldom, if ever, succeeded in sheltering the bureaucracy from the realm of patronage. Time and again, efforts were made to create an elite career service, but the political needs of the executive always intervened.

The efforts of the national government since 1964 have aimed at controlling the proliferation of the bureaucracy in order to make it a more efficient instrument for economic modernization. The group within the bureaucracy that has received the most attention is the *técnicos* (technocratic planners), as opposed to the *burocratas* (traditional administrators). The *técnicos* are development oriented, concerned with reform and necessary structural modification; they are "scientific," in that their plans are elaborated after careful study and, supposedly, with little concern for politics—that is, the old-style, pre-1964 politics. The *burocratas* are concerned with preserving the traditional political system and their positions in it. They execute the decisions made by others and do not see their role as being a dynamic, innovative one. Octávio Ianni states that the *burocratas* function to maintain the status quo, while the *técnicos* are concerned with reform and change. In many societies, the role of the *técnicos* is one of both initiating and responding to new social and economic needs; in Brazil, their role since 1964 has been limited to the more narrow economic area.

Before 1964, the *técnicos*, while present in the federal bureaucracy, were outnumbered and their efforts vetoed by the political needs of the post-1964 governments. After 1964, new men were introduced into the bureaucracy; a large portion of the spoils bureaucracy was dismissed; the ministries and agencies of the government were purged; and a major governmental reorganization allowed the *técnicos* free rein to plan the future economic transformation of the nation. Those *técnicos* who were considered politically "sage," such as Roberto Campos, were utilized by the military; others, such as Celso Furtado, lost their political rights and went into exile.[43]

The emphasis on central planning began after Varga's fall from power in 1945. But only since 1964 have the technical and political aspects of planning coincided. During the 1946 Republic, lip service was paid to the concept of planning—plans were elaborated, but they were vitiated by the practical political problems of the era. After 1964, the military was able to control the political system and, simultaneously, endorse the technical aspects of central planning as a means of legitimizing its rule through economic success. Civilian administrations since 1985 continue to lean on the planning model instituted by the military, perhaps more to maintain control over the spoils the bureaucracy has to offer than to shape a coherent national development scheme.

Two missions from the United States, one in 1942 and the other in 1943, assisted the Brazilian government in drawing up lists of investment priorities, but they had limited effect on government policy. In 1946–1947, the Dutra government prepared the SALTE Plan[44] to coordinate existing plans, but it was not approved by Congress until 1950.

Some progress was made during Vargas's presidential term of 1951–1954 in utilizing the SALTE Plan, but a more important development was the contribution of the Joint Brazil–United States Technical Commission. Organized in 1948, it carried out its work from 1951 to 1953. Its principal task was to provide needed technical assistance in preparing loan applications for development projects to be submitted to international lending agencies and the United States. An important result of the work of the commission was the organization in 1952 of the National Bank for Economic and Social Development (BNDES), which employed and trained many of the nation's *técnicos* during the succeeding decade and preserved the concept of rational, scientific planning. The work of the commission resulted in little else of substance; with the inauguration of the Eisenhower administration, there were few public funds available in Washington for development support.

When President Kubitschek took office in 1956, he announced a program of 30 goals to be achieved by the end of his five-year term. He organized the Council of Development, a planning and advisory unit for the chief executive. The program had a mixed record by 1961, but it had succeeded in focusing attention on planning throughout Kubitschek's term of office.

João Goulart's Three-Year Plan for Economic and Social Development (Plano Trienal, 1963–1965) was written under the direction of Celso Furtado, who was then serving as planning minister as well as superintendent of SUDENE. Based on an impressive array of economic and social data, the plan contained a series of policy directives, which represented little of the current political and economic realities in Brazil. The plan failed because of the political use to which it was put by the Goulart government. In addition, Brazilians tended to accept or reject the document in accordance with their political beliefs: those who supported Goulart generally favored it; those opposing the president denounced the plan. Eventually, even political supporters of the president criticized the document, and it was dropped after accomplishing some short-term political goals of the administration.

Although a number of regional development plans were drawn up between 1946 and 1964, the most prominent was that of SUDENE, prepared by Celso Furtado and his staff. A five-year plan, to be updated annually, it was endorsed by Congress after a bitter debate and opposition from the traditional interests in 1959; it was funded only in 1961. The master plan for the Northeast emphasized infrastructural investment, but it also served to gather regional support for social and political change in the underdeveloped area. SUDENE lost its autonomy in 1964 and became part of the federal government's overall planning effort.[45]

After the 1964 coup, Minister of Planning Roberto Campos (a former president of the BNDES and former Brazilian ambassador to the United States) masterminded the Program of Economic Action of the Government (PAEG) for 1964–1966. For Campos and fellow *técnicos*, PAEG represented

an essentially "technocratic" approach to the complex problems of economic policy. Their diagnosis did not differ radically from previous planning documents, even that of the Goulart government. The sharp contrast lay in the team's determination to follow through on their full implementation, confident that the President should extend his full backing rather than sacrifice financial stabilization measures in the face of the inevitable political protests from labor (over wage freezes) and producers (over credit restrictions).[46]

PAEG was followed by the Strategic Program of the Costa e Silva government and the Goals and Foundations for the Action of the Government of President Médici. The Médici government issued the First National Development Plan (1972–1974). In September 1974, President Ernesto Geisel unveiled the Second National Development Plan (1975–1979), which was followed during the Figueiredo administration by the Third Plan (1980–1985).

Strategic decisions were made by civilian technocrats or administrators within broad development and security parameters established by the armed forces. The authority of the technocrats was enormous. Working in the growing government bureaucracy, with the large variety of state companies at their disposal and the full backing of the patrimonial regime, the independence of this group was impressive. The bureaucratic-authoritarian state that dominated Brazil between 1964 and 1985 was managed on a day-to-day basis by a large group of highly sophisticated and well-educated planners, economists, and administrators.

It was only with the downturn in the economy that began in the late 1970s that the state bureaucracy became a political question. While the businessmen in their various statements in the 1970s had criticized the powerful role of the state corporations in the economy, they had not singled out the employees themselves. By the early 1980s, it was not only the influential, and often unsupervised, role of the state companies that was a matter of alarm, the special perquisites granted to state company employees also began to create grave concern.

By the early 1980s, the state corporations represented 30 percent of the gross domestic product (GDP) of Brazil and more than 60 percent of the foreign debt in dollars, much of which had been borrowed with only vague central government approval or knowledge. The 10 largest state companies represented 35 percent of the global disbursement of the public sector in Brazil. Moreover, the leadership of the state corporations often came from the senior bureaucratic and military leadership of the 1964 Republic. President Ernesto Geisel had been president of Petrobrás; the president of Electrobrás during its development of the Itaipú hydroelectric power project, retired army general José Costa Cavalcanti, was an individual of power and influence. The corporations not only became powerful economically but also clearly represented a segment of the power elite that expected—and received—deference.

So did their employees, it seems. As pressure grew in 1982 and 1983 to cut public spending, the government turned to the state sector, long viewed as an area of overspending and poor planning. It was discovered that the massive borrowing of the state companies had added immeasurably to the foreign debt burden. It also became obvious that the benefits enjoyed by state employees were highly inflationary. For example, it was possible to work for only nine months in a state company and receive the equivalent of 16 months' salary. Many retired as early as age 50 with full benefits. Promotions were frequent. Special health facilities and discount shops were available. Low-interest loans were provided, and there was almost no unemployment in the public sector, compared to the country in general in the early 1980s.

The issue was dramatically illustrated in the summer of 1983. The central government decided to cut the benefits and salaries of the state company employees as part of their negotiations with the IMF and the private commercial banks. The state employees threatened to close down Brazil by calling a strike, which was forbidden by law. As a show of their influence, a major demonstration was staged in which the employees refused to accept a cut in benefits. The draft decree-law, which was ready to be issued, was quickly revised during a hastily arranged meeting between Planning Minister Delfim Netto and the presidents of the state companies in Brasília. The resulting decree was less harsh and dealt primarily with the investments of the companies and less with employee benefits, although some adjustments were introduced.

Ironically, the *tecnoburocratas* (bureaucratic technocrats) of the state corporations became opponents of the government as the regime attempted to reduce state spending and eliminate obvious causes of inflation. Long thought of as a problem-solving elite, they had become part of the problem by the 1980s and 1990s.

The Sarney government (1985–1990) compounded the problem. The administration, desperate to build support for a five-year term of office for the president, and highly susceptible to appeals for public funds from state and local officials in the North and Northeast (President Sarney's home state, Maranhão, greatly benefited from his presidency), would hear nothing of fiscal restraint. Contracts were awarded for unneeded construction projects; new public-sector positions were authorized when there was a surplus of workers in the government; and little interest was manifested in privatization—selling off the inefficient and overstaffed state corporations.

The Collor de Mello government, as it took office in March 1990, announced that privatization would be given a high priority. The drain on the budget of having to finance the companies, the cost of public-sector salaries, and the inefficiencies of the corporations were the reasons given for the commitment to privatize. But the bureaucratic process became interminable; 1990 came and went, and it was not until late 1991 that the first state company—USIMINAS, a steel producer—was sold.

Unfortunately, the USIMINAS sale, while ultimately successful, aroused a great deal of passionate opposition from the labor unions representing the public-sector workers and from nationalist politicians such as Governor Leonel Brizola of Rio de Janeiro state. A scheduled sale was suddenly canceled amid chaos in late September 1991. The auction had to be postponed because of lawsuits in three courts challenging its legality and union members throwing eggs at potential investors attempting to enter the Rio stock exchange to bid. Finally, in October, with riot police and left-wing protestors hurling rocks and tear gas canisters outside of the stock exchange, investors bid $1.1 billion for controlling shares of the state steel company.

Because of the violence and apparent nationalist backlash against privatization, foreign bidding was very low. It had been the hope of the Collor administration that the sale of the state companies would prove attractive to foreign investors. But, ironically, the two largest buyers were in Brazil's state sector: the state minerals company, Companhia Vale do Rio Doce, and Previ, the pension fund of Brazil's state bank, Banco do Brasil. As the Collor de Mello government collapsed in 1992, no further progress was made. The interim administration of Itamar Franco (1992–1995) was not very interested in privatization until the appointment of Fernando Henrique Cardoso as finance minister. But his principal preoccupation was inflation and the creation of the Real Plan in 1994. When elected that year as Itamar Franco's successor, his government gave high priority to privatizing the myriad of inefficient and outdated state corporations.

But precisely because they were "corporatist," these entities had built-in constituencies viscerally opposed to privatization. The workers were supported by the union movement, which represented them, and by the old populist forces, wary of foreign investors and free market forces. The first confrontation took place in 1996 over the sell-off of the giant natural resources concern, Cia. Vale do Rio Doce (CVRD) (Company of the Rio Doce Valley)—an iron ore, gold, copper, and pulp concern that had a net worth exceeding $10 billion. It was reported at that time that

an unlikely alliance of populists and military men is mounting a last-ditch bid to block the privatization . . . led by two former presidents, José Sarney and Itamar Franco, the bid to keep Vale in state hands has brought together strange bedfellows: populists opposed to privatization on principle and national-defense hawks who consider the sale of the natural resources a threat to Brazil's security. Opponents are also courting any interest group holding a grudge against President Fernando Henrique Cardoso, such as a rural legislature angry at recent alternations in the farm tax.[47]

Finally, in May 1997, after more than 120 legal challenges were filed around the country, a consortium led by the National Steel Company (CSN), Brazil's largest steel maker, and itself recently privatized, paid $3.08 billion for the company. But once again, prior to overcoming the legal obstacles, "Police used tear gas and a water cannon against protestors, mainly from trade unions and left-wing political parties, who returned fire with stones and bottles."[48]

The successful sale of the CVRD resulted in a quickened pace of privatizations at the state and local levels. The next battle was the sale of the huge state telephone company, which finally took place in July 1998, but two years of politics were needed to set the stage for the sale. In June 1997, Congress reluctantly passed a bill creating a regulator for the industry and establishing the rules for its privatization. There were doubts about whether the government would be able to overcome political opposition in 1998 which, again, saw a replay of the CVRD scenario—legal entanglements and street demonstrations by the unions, students, and the MST, backed by the Catholic Church. Overcoming all odds, the auction took place successfully and opened the country to a new period of expanded investment in technology, critical to its continued development and modernization.

The only major state corporation that remains is Petrobrás, the state oil company. While the Cardoso government has been able to "liberalize" the petroleum sector, it has been reluctant to call for its privatization. The steps taken thus far are important and will open the sector to new foreign investment. Perhaps the second Cardoso government will be able to find a way to further reduce the public-sector burden by the privatization of the oil company.

Two other areas in which the government has met with partial success are changes in the social security system and administrative reform. Both have added enormously to the federal deficit over many years' time. Both also attack the heart of the bureaucratic structures of the patrimonial order. A reduction of the number of public employees and their benefits will immeasurably add to government efficiency and the competitiveness of the national economy. But both reforms undermine the corporatist nature of Brazilian society. Equally, both public servants and retirees have been the backbone of the traditional elites who have curried favor with those social actors by supporting an expansion of supports and services without the courage to raise the revenues needed to fund them.

The Cardoso government attempted in 1998 to move both issues front and center on the reform agenda with only partial success. The first, and most successful of the reforms, was achieved in early 1998 when the federal Senate finally approved legislation to slash the personnel costs of the federal government. Among the major components of the bill were:

- civil servants may be laid off for unsatisfactory work or simply if they become excess to requirements, but only if payroll costs amount to more than 60 percent of revenue and if all non-tenured posts have already been abolished;
- any pay increase must be in accordance with the new legislation; and
- money-losing public-sector corporations must be privatized or closed down within a two-year deadline.

The legislation took more than two years to work its way through both houses of Congress. The debates engendered strong and often violent demonstrations by public workers and their union representation. But the decision of Congress was one that was driven by a public perception that public-sector workers were overpaid and underworked, and that the exigencies of the new economy required a leaner and less expensive state bureaucracy.

Social security reform, the critical component of the federal budget deficit, was more difficult to achieve during most of the first Cardoso administration. After deeply emotional debates over a three-year time period, Congress, in mid-1998, defeated the government initiative by one vote on a critical bill—to remove a clause that would, for the first time, establish a minimum retirement age. Under current pension rules, some Brazilians can collect public pensions as early as their mid-forties. The government had hoped to establish a minimum retirement age of 60 for men and 55 for women.

Returning to the fray a few weeks later, the government rebounded and won votes to defeat four opposition amendments. As a result, the bill maintained a planned 30 percent reduction in pensions for civil servants and the establishment of a minimum retirement age of 53 for men and 48 for women who were currently working. But the opposition, in June, was able to defeat the government proposal to restrict civil servants' rights to retire with full pay. The Cardoso bill would have reduced by up to 30 percent the pensions of public employees earning more than $1,040 a month.

Brazilians currently retire according to their length of service, but loopholes in regulations allow many public servants to retire with more than full pay while still in their 40s. While Congress approved a general bill in May 1998, procedures permitted the opposition to remove items from the approved legislation for a separate vote. The opposition did this with three items. But with the onset of the national electoral campaign, the administration was unable to move the legislation beyond that point, and it was assumed that new initiatives awaited

1999. But the fiscal crisis that erupted in the middle of the national electoral campaign allowed the government to take up social security in November and to finally win approval of measures intended to reduce imbalances between the public and private pension systems. In arguing for the reforms, Finance Minister Pedro Malan stated that civil service pensions, which were expected to run a $35 billion deficit in 1999, were draining the country.

Malan said that the imbalance between the systems was crippling Brazil: while $46 billion went to provide benefits for 18 million workers in the private system, the government spent $33 billion on pensions for less than 3 million retired public employees. The new measure bases retirement in the private sector on the number of years a worker has contributed to the plan rather than on the number of years worked. It also sets new minimum retirement ages in the civil service of 53 for men and 48 for women, provided that the men have paid into the pension system for 35 years and the women for 30 years. The government failed to do away with the generous system of giving civil servants full salaries until their death. But Cardoso was expected to issue an executive order that will require civil service pensioners collecting over $1,000 a month to pay up to 20 percent of their benefits back into the system.

In a classic example of the bargaining that takes place in exchange for votes, the administration had to promise a bloc of 37 legislators representing agricultural businesses that it would delay repayment of more than $1 billion in farmers' debt in return for their support. The government also granted farm businesses $280 million in concessions in exchange for their support. But, as we shall see in Chapter 5, the urgency of reform escaped the Congress in December 1998, after the government and the IMF had agreed to a deep fiscal reform package in exchange for substantial financial support for Brazil. The failure of the legislature to approve additional fiscal cuts scared away skittish international investors. Currency speculators tried—successfully—to undermine the stability of the Brazilian currency, and the Cardoso government was forced to devalue the *real* in January 1999. The Congress was then convinced to approve the government's fiscal program, but only after prolonged bargaining and exchange of favors. The lack of support in Congress resulted in a deep recession in 1999, higher unemployment, and a sharp drop in living standards for a majority of the population.

CONCLUSION

In this chapter we have analyzed important new dynamics in Brazil. A new, aggressive labor movement challenged the military regime and won. But the union movement, and the political party that represents its interests, the PT, have been unable to fundamentally influence policy in favor of the working class. The Roman Catholic Church, understaffed and still identified more with those who have than with those who do not, is seeking to redefine its role. It may have found the best, most appropriate mission in standing with the poor and dispossessed—rural and urban. But alternative religious institutions pose an institutional threat, and considering the degree to which the Church is seen to support the local political elites, it may find it difficult to fulfill its new mandate.

Rural labor emerged in the late 1990s as an aggressive force seeking to undo centuries of neglect and repression in the countryside. Its militancy shocked many, in both government and society. But the social and economic disparities in Brazil are so cavernous that it was only a matter of time before a movement emerged to challenge one of the fundamental pillars of the patrimonial society— a quiescent, controlled, rural population. And the principal beneficiaries of the new market-oriented economic reforms, the industrialists and the businessmen, are not key political actors. They have yet to find an appropriate way of either working with or supporting the needed social and economic reforms that will make Brazil a more just society. The state bureaucrats, threatened by the privatization program of the Cardoso government, have thought only of their own interests in fervently opposing economic change. They have too long profited from the patrimonial system and are understandably reluctant to see their perquisites—undreamed of by the rural poor and urban marginals—diminished for the greater good.

This presents a complicated, rapidly evolving overview of Brazilian society at the end of the twentieth century. The basic power base of the patrimonial state is being undermined by both social and economic forces. But the political elites of the system either do not understand the wave of change or refuse to acknowledge and accept it. They will not surrender without a struggle, as they have demonstrated in their ability in Congress to delay and stretch out the reform process during the first Cardoso government. And, if *The Economist* is correct, "The new Congress [will] be more rebellious than the present one, not least because the national mood is sourer than it was in 1994, when goodwill was running high for Mr. Cardoso." And, it continues:

Mr. Cardoso's five-party alliance will again enjoy a majority larger than the 60 percent required to approve constitutional changes. But that is on paper. Not only are the two large parties allied with the government internally divided, but some congressmen swap party allegiance rather frequently.[49]

This confirms our analysis in Chapter 2, where we discussed the political party system. And it again underlines the difficulty that Cardoso and his well-meaning team will confront in the second term—on the one hand, growing militancy for social justice and economic opportunity; and on the other hand, a determination of the traditional political elites to stall or preclude change at all. Congress, a logical mediator in most political systems, is not prepared to play that role in Brazil. Civil society remains weak and hesitant—and groups such as businessmen are unsure of how far reform should actually go, critical institutions such as the Church seek a new role but have not yet found it; and important institutions such as the labor unions, which are so vital to the restoration of democracy, have now become a major impediment to progressive economic reform. This situation plays to the advantage of the vestiges of the patrimonial regime in Brazil. The question is whether this is a transition or a long, potentially conflictive stalemate.

NOTES

1. Philippe C. Schmitter, *Interest Conflict and Political Change in Brazil* (Stanford, Calif.: Stanford University Press, 1971), pp. 380–381.

2. Ibid., p. 98.

3. Frank Bonilla, "Brazil," in James S. Coleman, ed., *Education and Political Development* (Princeton, N.J.: Princeton University Press, 1965), p. 216.

4. Luigi Einaudi and Alfred C. Stepan, III, *Latin American Institutional Development: The Changing Catholic Church* (Santa Monica, Calif.: RAND Corporation, 1969), p. 47.

5. Thomas G. Sanders, "Catholicism and Development: The Catholic Left in Brazil," in Kalman H. H. Silvert, ed., *Churches and States: The Religious Institution and Modernization* (New York: American Universities Field Staff, 1967), p. 95.

6. See Paulo Freire, *Educação como prática da liberdade* (Rio de Janeiro: Editora Paz e Terra, 1967).

7. Emanuel de Kadt, *Catholic Radicals in Brazil* (London: Oxford University Press, 1970), p. 105.

8. Einaudi and Stepan, III, *Latin American Institutional Development*, Sec. 2.

9. For a discussion of these themes, see Thomas C. Bruneau, *The Political Transformation of the Brazilian Catholic Church* (New York: Cambridge University Press, 1974) and *The Church in Brazil: The Politics of Religion* (Austin: University of Texas Press, 1982).

10. Quoted in Bruneau, *The Political Transformation*, p. 208.

11. Ibid., p. 207.

12. Thomas C. Bruneau, *The Catholic Church and the Basic Christian Communities: A Case Study from the Brazilian Amazon* (Montreal: Center for Developing-Area Studies, McGill University, 1983), p. 2.

13. For a more detailed discussion, see Rowan Ireland, "Catholic Base Communities, Spiritist Groups and the Deepening of Democracy in Brazil," in Scott Mainwaring and Alexander Wilde, eds., *The Progressive Church in Latin America* (Notre Dame, Ind.: University of Notre Dame Press, 1989).

14. Scott Mainwaring, "Grass-roots Catholic Groups and Politics in Brazil," in Scott Mainwaring and Alexander Wilde, eds., *The Progressive Church in Latin America* (Notre Dame, Ind.: University of Notre Dame Press, 1989), p. 185.

15. "Text of Statement by Friar," *New York Times*, March 21, 1985, p. 1.

16. "Church Condemns Sarney Government for Corruption," *Financial Times* (London), February 4, 1988, p. 4.

17. Diana Jean Schemo, "The Dispossessed," *New York Times Magazine*, April 20, 1998, p. 42.

18. U.S. Army, *Area Handbook for Brazil* (Washington, D.C.: U.S. Government Printing Office, 1964), pp. 513–514.

19. Schmitter, *Interest Conflict and Political Change in Brazil*, p. 129.

20. Amaury de Souza and Bolivar Lamounier, "Escaping the Black Hole: Government-Labor Relations in Brazil in the 1980s," p. 7 (Mimeo).

21. John Humphrey, *Capitalist Control and Workers' Struggle in the Brazilian Auto Industry* (Princeton, N.J.: Princeton University Press, 1982), p. 25.

22. For a lucid account of "new unionism" and the transition to democracy, see Margaret E. Keck, "The New Unionism in the Brazilian Transition," in Alfred Stepan, ed., *Democratizing Brazil: Problems of Transition and Consolidation* (New York: Oxford University Press, 1989).

23. Anthony Faiola, "Brazil Sells Phone Giant," *Washington Post*, July 30, 1998, p. A26.

24. Schemo, "The Dispossessed," p. 42.

25. Cynthia N. Hewitt, "Brazil: The Peasant Movement of Pernambuco, 1961–1964," in Henry A. Landsberger, ed., *Latin American Peasant Movements* (Ithaca, N.Y.: Cornell University Press, 1969), pp. 374–375.

26. Anthony Leeds, "Brazil and the Myth of Francisco Julião," in Joseph Maier and Richard W. Weatherhead, eds., *Politics of Change in Latin America* (New York: Praeger, 1964), pp. 190–204.

27. Biorn Maybury-Lewis, *The Politics of the Possible: The Brazilian Rural Workers Trade Union Movement, 1964–1985* (Philadelphia: Temple University Press, 1994), p. 2.

28. Warren Hoge, "Rural 'Colonels' of Brazil: Their Power Never Dies," *New York Times*, January 25, 1983, p. 2.

29. Brian Homewood, "Ploughshares into Swords," *New Scientist*, December 7, 1996, p. 18.

30. Ibid.

31. Stanley J. Stein, *The Brazilian Cotton Manufacture* (Cambridge, Mass.: Harvard University Press, 1957), p. 81.

32. Fernando Henrique Cardoso, *Empresário industrial e desenvolvimento econômico* (São Paulo: Difusão Europeia do Livro, 1964), p. 161.

33. Ibid., p. 165.

34. Warren Dean, *The Industrialization of São Paulo, 1880–1945* (Austin: University of Texas Press, 1969), p. 236.

35. Ibid., p. 237.

36. Ibid., p. 238.

37. Ibid.

38. "Fifteen Years of Economic Policy in Brazil," *Economic Bulletin for Latin America*, November 1964, pp. 196–197, quoted in Nathaniel Leff, *Economic Policy-Making and Development in Brazil, 1947–1964* (New York: John Wiley, 1968), p. 35.

39. Leff, *Economic Policy-Making*, p. 52.

40. Ben Ross Schneider, "Organized Business Politics in Democratic Brazil," *Journal of Interamerican Studies and World Affairs* 39, no. 4 (Winter 1997–1998): 96.

41. Ibid., p. 97.

42. Marcos Sá Correa, "Alta privilegiatura," *Veja*, April 13, 1983, p. 74.

43. See Leff, *Economic Policy-Making*, pp. 143–153, for a discussion of *técnicos*.

44. The acronym SALTE refers to the four areas of the plan: *saúde* (health), *alimentação* (food supplies), *transportes* (transportation), and *energia* (electric power).

45. See Riordan Roett, *The Politics of Foreign Aid in the Brazilian Northeast* (Nash-

ville, Tenn.: Vanderbilt University Press, 1972), for a discussion of Furtado, SUDENE, and the Northeast.

46. Ronald M. Schneider, *The Political System of Brazil: Emergence of a "Modernizing" Authoritarian Regime, 1964–1970* (New York: Columbia University Press, 1971), pp. 150–151.

47. Matt Moffett, "Brazil Seeks Buyers for a Mining Giant Amid Effort to Block Key Privatization," *New York Times*, November 26, 1996, p. A17.

48. Geoff Dyer, "Late Legal Bid to Force Brazil Mining Auction," *Financial Times*, April 30, 1997, p. 14.

49. "Brazil Prepares for Cardoso Without Coat-Tails," *The Economist*, August 1, 1998, p. 29.

Chapter 4

The Military in Politics

In commenting on the military pressure in 1954 to force Getúlio Vargas from power, Thomas Skidmore points out that "the decisive voice now came from the army, always the ultimate arbiter in Brazilian politics."[1] Analyzing the period of democratic transition in the 1980s, Alfred Stepan demonstrates that in Brazil "the military relinquished their control of the presidency in 1985 only after intense informal negotiations that left many military prerogatives unchallenged."[2] But just a decade later, with the inauguration of Fernando Henrique Cardoso, a Brazilian observer of civil-military relations comments that "Cardoso is creating a new pattern in the relationship between the political authority and the armed forces."[3] This new relationship is based on the 1996 National Defense Policy of the Cardoso administration.

We have posited that the armed forces have been an integral component of the patrimonial state for more than 150 years. They served, when necessary, to preserve that state and were frequent participants in its construction and implementation. The advent of the Cardoso administration raises a number of intriguing questions about the long-term survival of the patrimonial order in Brazil. If economic changes, such as privatization and the restructuring of the civil service, reduce the size and influence of the bureaucracy, will the new National Defense Policy establish, for the first time, complete control of the military by civilian authorities? And if it does, does this weaken the patrimonial state significantly as we enter the twenty-first century? These are important questions that we will need to consider. This chapter considers, first, the important historical background of the military in Brazil through 1985 and the termination of the Military Republic. Second, it examines the transition regimes of José Sarney (1985–1990), Fernando Collor de Mello (1990–1992), and Itamar Franco (1992–1995). Finally, it looks at the current situation of the Brazilian armed forces in the post-

Cold War period, a new emphasis on regional cooperation—especially with Argentina, a traditional geopolitical adversary—and Brazil's changing role in world affairs. We will then be in a position to evaluate whether the new policies of President Cardoso represent a meaningful reduction in the influence of the military and whether the patrimonial order will change as a result.

A relatively unimportant institution prior to the War of the Triple Alliance (1865–1870), the military precipitated the overthrow of the emperor in 1889 and remained front and center in Brazilian political life for the next century. From the establishment of the Old Republic in the 1890s through the 1960s, the traditional role of the armed forces was one in which they " 'moderated' the political system during times of crisis but never actually assumed governmental power itself."[4] New perceptions, ideologies, and perceived threats to the status quo dramatically revised the traditional role in 1964.

Over the course of the 1946 Republic, the military became increasingly uncertain that civilian politicians were prepared to deal with Brazil's developmental agenda. The boundary between the armed forces and political party actors began to erode. The military was strengthened in this conviction by its involvement in the Superior War College (ESG), which gave it the confidence—and the doctrine—needed to push aside civilian government in 1964. Perceptions of mass mobilization worried many military officers, who feared that the Cuban Revolution was undermining fragile civilian governments throughout Latin America. Brazil seemed particularly vulnerable to the officer class, given the fragmented political party system, the legacy of Getúlio Vargas's populism, and the few resources available to the regime to address pressing social needs. Finally, by 1964, a growing majority of the military leadership concluded that the threat to military hierarchy had gone far enough. Insubordinate enlisted men, rebellions by noncommissioned officers, and the use of political criteria in officer promotion decisions had reached alarming proportions.

Thus the qualitative difference in 1964 was that the military was determined to exercise public power, for the first time since the 1890s, by occupying the governmental/bureaucratic offices of the patrimonial regime. Previously, military intervention had occurred to rid the system of a destabilizing influence and had been followed by the return of political control to the civilian elites. In 1964, totally disillusioned with the national experience of civilian government, the military opted for direct rule in an attempt to restore equilibrium to Brazilian society.

It is at the level of critical policy choices and the interplay of key members of the patrimonial elite that we will find the root causes for traditional military intervention in Brazil and for the decision, in 1964, to retain power. It is that dynamic, also, which will explain the decision of the armed forces to create a controlled transition in the late 1970s and 1980s. We will need to examine the evolution of civil-military relations after the transfer of authority to a civilian government in 1985 to understand the current dynamics of the armed forces as an institutional force in Brazil today.

THE MILITARY ENTERS POLITICS

After successfully concluding the war against Paraguay in 1870, the Brazilian military did not "unbuckle their swords or relinquish their sense of military honor before entering political chambers."[5] Unable to gain satisfaction for its demands from the imperial government, the military toppled the monarchy in 1889 when it became clear that the other major props of the Empire—the Church and landowning aristocracy—had withdrawn their support.

The military ruled Brazil from 1889 to 1894. During that period, the armed forces assumed the position of guardians of the republic, a position that was confirmed in the Constitution of 1891 and in succeeding documents. A navy revolt in 1893–1894 demonstrated the existence of conflicting factions in the armed forces. Basically an intramilitary struggle for leadership between army and navy, the rebellion was put down by the central government and the army, with the help of São Paulo state militia. In exchange, São Paulo received army support for the election of a Paulista civilian to the presidency in 1894.

The armed forces played an important role behind the scenes in the Old Republic. They were not united, however, so the civilian oligarchy played one branch against the other. To offset the influence of the army, the Republican government tended to favor the navy's requests for larger appropriations and the latest equipment. In addition, the central government encouraged the creation of state militias, with the understanding that they would be at the service of the federal government if it was challenged by the army. The tension between army and government resulted in frequent denunciations of civilian policy in the Clube Militar in Rio de Janeiro. With the victory of the only army officer to occupy the presidency after 1894, Marshal Hermes da Fonseca, the civilian oligarchy's fears of an increase of the army's influence in politics were confirmed.

The involvement of the military in the affairs of the Old Republic increased during and after World War I. While the senior officials by and large defended the existing order, some junior officers reacted unfavorably to the continued elitist domination of the society. Their disorganized protests provided the opening shots of the campaign that defeated the Old Republic.

The *tenentes*, the young army officers who worked for reform in Brazilian society after World War I, at first confined their campaign to the army. Within a short time, they sought allies against the Republican Party regime at the local and regional levels. The *tenentes* revolted in 1922 in Rio de Janeiro and in 1924 in São Paulo. By 1930, when they endorsed Vargas, they had turned to the national level for implementation of their vague, but sincere, objectives.

Vargas's rebel army, commanded by Lieutenant Colonel Pedro Góes Montero, moved on Rio de Janeiro from Rio Grande do Sul in late 1930. Many officers and enlisted men had joined its ranks. The Northeastern states fell before the challenge posed by Captain Juarez Távora's rebel column. The military commanders in Rio de Janeiro deposed President Washington Luís and formed a junta. That group turned the government over to Vargas on October 24, 1930.

At first, Vargas tolerated a diffusion of power in his provisional government. Slowly, he consolidated his position, however, and the senior military officers transferred their allegiance to him. The *tenentes* fragmented; some remained loyal to the president throughout the Transitional Republic, while others became disillusioned with Vargas's authoritarian manner and eventually abandoned his cause. They emerged after 1945 in the opposition to the PSD-PTB coalition.

The military remained an essential underpinning of Vargas's authority from 1930 to 1945. It endorsed his direction of the patrimonial regime when it became clear that he favored maintaining the status quo and that the new urban groups he mobilized and aided would not become a destabilizing factor. Vargas carefully placed faithful supporters in positions of influence in the army. General Eurico Dutra became war minister in 1936, and General Góes Monteiro became army chief of staff in 1937. Both advocated a strong, united army in a well-governed state. They successfully weakened the state militias and actually sought to give the national army a clear monopoly on force. During Vargas's preparation of his coup in 1937 and the announcement of the New State, the army stood by him:

The Army command had been planning an authoritarian solution of Brazil's political crisis since the Communist revolt of November 1935. The higher military were skeptical of Brazil's ability to withstand the confusion and indecision of open political competition, and they were frightened by the prospect of further gains by radicals of the left—who, if ever in power, might succeed in removing the Armed Forces as the ultimate arbiter of political conflict.[6]

With the end of World War II in sight, Vargas promised an opening of the political system. The military, loyal to the regime after 1937, in part because of the large role it was given in the nation's industrial development, understood that it was time for a change. The authoritarian political system of the Transitional Republic would not serve Brazil after the war ended. When Vargas appeared to renege on his promise to hold open elections in December 1945, the military had little compunction in issuing an ultimatum that forced Vargas into retirement. Generals Dutra and Góes Monteiro, the willing supporters of the 1937 coup, masterminded the 1945 ouster. Once again, as in October 1930 and November 1937, the military determined the fate of the nation with limited, if any, significant civilian political input. The growing criticism of the dictator and of his authoritarian government brought into question the legitimacy of the Transitional Republic. Once the military high command decided that Vargas's continuation in power would endanger governmental authority, it acted in its role as a constitutional guardian.

1945–1954: The Military as Guardian

The military presided over the creation of the 1946 Republic. Góes Monteiro resigned as war minister but accepted the new and powerful position of commander in chief of the army. The two major candidates were military: Dutra for the PSD and Eduardo Gomes for the UDN. The civilian politicians looked to the army to guarantee the new political order. The December 1945 election that selected Dutra and the Constitutional Assembly that wrote the 1946 document both had army protection.

The Dutra administration maintained the patrimonial system with the superficial trappings of democracy. Decisions were made at the center with a military imprimatur. The elites of the Vargas era, with the PSD as their stronghold, welcomed the relative calm of the placid Dutra administration.

The tensions of 1945 reemerged in 1950 as Getúlio Vargas prepared his campaign for the presidency on the PTB ticket. Although elected to the federal Senate in 1945 on the PSD ticket, he used his continuing popularity with the working class to build the organizational strength of the PTB. Vargas tried to have Góes Monteiro accept the vice-presidential nomination on his ticket, but he refused, saying he was committed to the Dutra-PSD candidacy.

Vargas accepted the nomination of both the PTB and PSP (Social Progressive Party) in 1950. The opposition was divided; both the PSD and the UDN nominated candidates (Gomes again for the UDN). The army high command remained neutral, although it was unhappy about Vargas's candidacy. His victory in October 1950 opened a four-year period of chaos in Brazilian politics.

One segment of the military was drawn to Vargas's talk of development nationalism. It believed that Brazil had to industrialize to be great, and it was willing to accept Vargas if he provided the necessary leadership for a program of industrialization. Another wing adopted a "wait and see" attitude. If the president did not attempt to upset the balance of social and political forces created in 1946, he could remain in office. If he acted to polarize Brazilian society, he would have to bear the consequences. A third group maintained its implacable opposition to Vargas and sought to undermine his authority.

Although the majority of the armed forces were probably "legalists" in 1950—they would let Vargas assume office if he was popularly elected—it is clear that their "protection" was not unlimited. Góes Monteiro said that Vargas was acceptable as long as he "respected not only the Constitution but, in addition, the inalienable rights of the Armed Forces."[7] Although Vargas's war minister, General Newton Estillac Leal, was sympathetic to the leftist nationalists in the armed forces backing the president, he did not speak for all of the officer corps. In March 1952, Estillac Leal had to resign under pressure from the anti-Communist, anti-Vargas wing of the military.

By 1954, the economy was in serious trouble. Inflation and high prices had badly eroded the economic position of the urban groups, the working and middle classes upon whom Vargas had depended for political support. One middle-income group that was quite conscious of its decreasing purchasing power was the officer corps. In February 1954, a group of concerned junior officers protested to the war minister about their low salaries. Many in this group blamed the economic slowdown on Labor Minister João Goulart, Vargas's deputy in

PTB-labor politics, who had been appointed in June 1953. Military officers feared a continuing decrease in their economic position to satisfy labor's never-ending cry for higher wages and increased benefits. To assuage military discontent, Vargas dismissed Goulart in early 1954. The president could not risk open rebellion among the officer corps; the labor minister was a convenient and an acceptable scapegoat.

Suddenly, a crisis erupted. A Presidential Palace-inspired assassination attempt against journalist Carlos Lacerda—a UDN member and muckraker who had waged war against the Vargas administration—failed, but it did kill an air force major. The anti-Vargas military demanded his resignation. On August 22, the president rejected an air force demand for his resignation; the next day, the army made the same demand. On August 24, defiantly refusing to resign, Vargas committed suicide, leaving an impassioned letter to the Brazilian people. His conduct ensured his immortality in the nationalist pantheon.

1954–1964: The Military as Participant

Within the context of the multiparty, competitive system there were military coups in 1954 and 1964, an attempted coup in 1961, and the beginnings of a coup in 1955 that brought about a countercoup in defense of the constitutional regime. The 1954 coup removed Vargas from office once again after his 1950 election as constitutional president. The 1964 coup sent President Goulart into exile after a stormy three years in office. The 1955 attempt tried to prevent President-elect Juscelino Kubitschek and Vice President-elect Goulart from assuming office. In 1961, the three military ministers unilaterally announced their unwillingness to accept Vice President Goulart as a successor to President Jânio Quadros, who had resigned suddenly after eight months in office. Neither coup had the support of a majority of the military high command or widespread popular support among the civilian political elite. A small segment of the armed forces favored the coups but, without further political justification, the unilateral military decisions were not considered legitimate. The authority of the civilian constitutional order was upheld in spite of the open dissidence of powerful segments of the military establishment.

The 1954 and 1964 coups were political acts with widespread support among the political elite, both civilian and military. They also received endorsement from a majority of the participant sectors of the civilian population. The conduct of President Vargas in 1954 and President Goulart in 1964 provided sufficient justification for the coalescing of civilian-military opinion in favor of their removal from office through military action.

In 1955, the coup was supported by only one of the political parties, the UDN, but the defeated standard-bearers of the party in the election denounced the attempts of their political supporters to subvert the legal order. Such restricted partisan appeals for military force—those supported by only a narrow cross section of the political elite—are generally unable to succeed in a praetorian society, for fear that a civil war will erupt among the major political contenders for power.

The 1961 attempted coup was an immediate reaction by the military ministers that provoked immediate and widespread indignation. They had misjudged the depth of support for the maintenance of the constitutional order by both civilians and military officers. An important factor was the margin of political support provided by the governor of Rio Grande do Sul, Leonel Brizola, the brother-in-law of President Goulart, and the anticoup sentiments expressed by the commander of the Third Army, located in Pôrto Alegre, the capital of Rio Grande do Sul. The civilian-military elite was unwilling to risk bloodshed to impede Goulart's taking office. Without wider popular and institutional support, the coup was doomed. The military did, however, succeed in limiting Goulart's authority with the imposition of a parliamentary system of government.

These attempted coups of 1955 and 1961 indicate the limits of freedom allowed the military establishment before 1964. The armed forces, although the most powerful social institution in Brazil, were not the only actors possessing a power potential. The military, or coup-prone segment of it, could be thwarted by widespread opposition from within the military and/or the civilian sector of society.

The 1954 coup removing Vargas from office for the second time (which ended in his suicide) was an example of the military's playing its role as moderator in the political system. Vargas had mobilized and manipulated the urban working class throughout his term of office. His populist politics frightened the traditional conservative elites, who feared that the president would next turn his attention to the social and economic prerogatives they possessed. The elites' extensive questioning of presidential authority convinced the military that internal peace required the president's removal. In addition, the widespread stories of corruption and misadministration strengthened the argument against Vargas. The postwar concern of the military with economic growth and technological and industrial development, along with its basic disapproval of populist politics that seemed to represent a threat to law and order, combined to unite the military forces behind Vargas's dismissal.

The 1955 coup attempt grew out of the presidential election of that year. The PSD-PTB ticket was made up of Governor Juscelino Kubitschek of Minas Gerais and former labor minister and PTB leader Goulart. It was clearly a successor government to Vargas. The UDN nominated General Juarez Távora, an old *tenente* who had broken with Vargas in the 1930s. The PSD-PTB victory had been won with only about one-third of the votes cast. Adhemar de Barros and the PSP drew off about 25 percent with his populist campaign reminiscent of Vargas.

The conservative military was furious, but War Minister General Henrique Teixeira Lott was determined to support the constitution and guarantee the inauguration of the PSD-PTB team. With rebellion among the right-wing officers in the air, Lott heroically defended a constitutional transition. But to do so, he was forced to depose an acting president of the Republic in November, who had sided with the conservatives. When President João Café Filho, who had taken a medical leave of absence, attempted to return to office, the armed forces decided to retain the new acting president. To do so, Congress approved a military request for a state of siege (a form of martial law), which only lapsed with the inauguration of President Kubitschek in January 1956.

The Kubitschek years (1956–1961) were politically the most tranquil of the 1946 Republic. By maintaining political stability and a relatively high rate of economic growth, the administration achieved a large degree of legitimacy. By combining nationalism and economic development, Kubitschek received sufficient popular support to ward off any challenge from either civilian or military dissidents.

õ   The military was well treated by Kubitschek, who did not repeat Vargas's error of ignoring the officers' standard of living. Pay raises and new equipment were delivered as requested. General Teixeira Lott returned to the government as war minister and effectively maintained a nonpolitical stance. The president reassured skeptics who believed he was sympathetic to the Communists by repeatedly and publicly criticizing them and by supporting the United States in its Cold War diplomacy.

As a reward, in part, for his defense of Kubitschek and Goulart in 1955, the PSD-PTB coalition turned to General Teixeira Lott as its presidential candidate in 1960. Goulart again was nominated for vice president. The opposition UDN selected Governor Jânio Quadros of São Paulo and Senator Milton Campos of Minas Gerais as its nominees. In the November 1960 election, Quadros and Goulart won (the vote for president and vice president in the 1946 Republic was separate). Both were sworn in without incident in January 1961.

The National War College

An important influence in determining the armed forces' role from 1961 to 1964 was the doctrine of national security (*segurança nacional*) elaborated at the Superior War College (Escola Superior de Guerra, or ESG) in the 1950s and early 1960s. Founded in 1949 under the direction of General Osvaldo Cordeiro de Farias, with advice from a U.S. military mission, the ESG's mission was to prepare "civilians and military to perform executive and advisory functions especially in those organs responsible for the formulation, development, planning and execution of the politics of national security."[8]

The emphasis in the curriculum of the ESG was the study of basic problems involved in the development of foreign policy and its coordination with the need for national security. Both civilians and military officers attended the school's seminars and discussion groups. The civilians were expected to have a university education and to have demonstrated achievements in their profession. Selected by the armed forces general staff, the military officers, normally colonels or brigadiers, were approved by the president. It is estimated that by 1964, two-thirds of the active-duty generals were ESG graduates.

The ESG provided a framework for the armed forces to work with members of the civilian elite to develop a fairly sophisticated conception of Brazil's future development. By combining the issues of military security and national development, very broadly interpreted, the post-1964 civilian and military elites worked together in the years preceding the coup d'état that brought down the Goulart government. A common understanding of the political, social, and economic needs of the nation and a determination to defend the permanent national objectives of Brazil became deeply ingrained in the military through the functioning of the ESG. After the 1964 coup, the ESG continued to serve as an important center for the training of leaders in the Military Republic.

1961–1964: The Movement Toward Intervention

When Jânio Quadros suddenly resigned from the presidency in August 1961, his action took civilian and military leaders by total surprise. Though during the preceding months Quadros had demanded additional powers to govern, no one expected him to abdicate when he failed to get them. Against this backdrop, the anti-Vargas military was confronted with the possibility of Vargas's heir as president. Would the armed forces sanction the succession of Goulart? Given Goulart's absence in the People's Republic of China on a trade mission, the president of the Chamber of Deputies became acting president. It was immediately clear that the military and civilian elites were seriously divided.

The military ministers, led by War Minister General Odílio Denys, opposed Goulart; the legalists favored his inauguration. Acting President Ranieri Mazzilli informed Congress on August 18 that "for reasons of national security" Goulart should not return to Brazil. Congress equivocated and recommended that Goulart become chief executive, but with reduced powers under a parliamentary form of government.

The military ministers, in a manifesto dated August 29, 1961, reiterated their opposition. Marshal Teixeira Lott called for Goulart's acceptance and was placed under house arrest by General Denys. The commander of the Third Army in Rio Grande do Sul suddenly proclaimed his support for the vice president. Was civil war a possibility? Unlike the political crises of 1945, 1954, and 1955, the war minister of 1961 had failed to gather support for his position from the army field commanders. The Third Army's endorsement of a legalist solution—Goulart's succession—deeply divided the armed forces. The war minister, unwilling to risk the unity of the military and bring about a civil war, compromised and accepted the parliamentary solution. The vice president arrived in Brasília on September 5, 1961, and took the oath of office two days later.

The Coup of March 31, 1964

The period from September 1961 to March 1964 was one of crisis in Brazil. The military was deeply divided over the Goulart government. For the first time, the militant nationalist segment of the officer corps received open support from the Presidential Palace.

Soon after its creation, the parliamentary system proved unworkable. In a short time, Goulart had appointed and lost three prime ministers. The nation was convulsed by riots and strikes, and inflation was beginning to escalate alarmingly. The military was alert to the possible repercussions of a continuation of the political instability. The constitutional amendment of September 1961, instituting the parliamentary system, called for a plebiscite in 1965, but the government lobbied for one sooner. The military ministers issued a manifesto in August 1962, supporting an early vote. Congress set the election for April 1963, but Goulart wanted an earlier vote, possibly to coincide with the gubernatorial and congressional elections of October 1962. Goulart's fourth and final prime minister, Hermes Lima, was a well-known supporter of the vote. Congress finally agreed to set January 3, 1963, as the date of the national plebiscite. With assurances that public order would be maintained, the plebiscite resulted in an overwhelming victory for Goulart, who recovered the full powers of the presidency.

Goulart proceeded to do precisely what the moderate military feared. He began to campaign for "basic reforms" in education, housing, the tax system, and land tenure. Inflation continued to haunt the government, and in May 1963, a group of officers petitioned Goulart for pay increases, which Congress finally voted in July.

The attempts at economic stabilization had clearly failed by mid-1963. The growing debate over the political direction of the regime had politicized students, labor union members, and peasants. On September 12, 1963, hundreds of noncommissioned officers and enlisted men in the navy, air force, and marines revolted in Brasília. They held the president of the Chamber of Deputies and a Supreme Court justice prisoner. Though quickly subdued, the incident caused widespread alarm among civilian and military leaders.

Information about a government-inspired military plot to arrest Governor Carlos Lacerda of Guanabara, the vociferous UDN critic whose assassination the Vargas administration had plotted, and Governor Miguel Arraes of Pernambuco, a rival of Goulart on the political Left, became public shortly thereafter. While both plans failed, Goulart insisted on disciplining an officer who had refused to participate in the plot against Lacerda.

Gradually a large number of officers became convinced that Goulart posed a real threat to public order. The leader of the planners was Army Chief of Staff General Humberto Castello Branco, who had recently left his command of the Fourth Army in the Northeast (Recife). The challenge to the neutrality of the armed forces posed by Goulart and his cronies deeply concerned the high command. Discipline and hierarchy were under attack; the officer corps was fragmented badly between those supporting and those condemning the chief executive; the mandate that the armed forces held to protect the constitution was being called into question by the leftist, antidemocratic suggestions of reform emanating from the government.

The drift to the Left accelerated with a rally in Rio de Janeiro on March 13, during which Goulart publicly signed two decrees as part of his new reforms. One nationalized all private oil refineries; the second stated that the "under-utilized" properties of over 1,200 acres located within six miles of federal high-ways or railways, and land of more than 70 acres situated within six miles of federal dams or irrigation or drainage projects, would be liable to expropriation. The radicals had won control of presidential policy making. The themes of the March 13 rally were repeated in Goulart's annual presidential message to Congress on March 15. While the Left had won the president's ear, it was still a divided Left, ranging from the fiery Leonel Brizola, the president's brother-in-law (the "negative" Left) to San Tiago Dantas (the "positive" Left).

A memorandum by General Castello Branco to his staff, distributed on March 20, convinced many legalist officers that the armed forces had no alternative but to take the offensive against Goulart. The memorandum confirmed the "historic role" of the military as the defender of the constitutional order and the laws of the nation.

Finally, on the weekend of March 27–29, an issue of military discipline persuaded doubting officers that the time had come for action. The navy minister moved to punish a sailor who had been actively organizing a labor union of enlisted men. The sailor had been part of the leftist national student organization before his induction. In response to the minister's action, more than 1,000 sailors and marines rebelled on March 26 and barricaded themselves in a labor union building in Rio de Janeiro.

Goulart dismissed the navy minister, replacing him with an aged retired admiral who had been endorsed by the General Confederation of Labor, an ally of the radical Left. The new navy minister offered full amnesty to the rebels. On March 30, Goulart addressed a gathering of sergeants in Rio de Janeiro. The nationally televised speech was bellicose; the president refused to separate himself from attacks on military discipline.

The armed forces acted within 24 hours. The first troops moved on Rio de Janeiro from Juíz de Fora in Minas Gerais. The civilian UDN governors in Guanabara and Minas Gerais cooperated fully. The troops sent from Rio by Goulart to crush the rebellion joined the rebels. Appeals by Goulart for popular demonstrations of support failed, and he fled from Rio to Brasília and then to Pôrto Alegre in Rio Grande do Sul. The president of the Senate declared the presidency vacant the same night; the president of the Chamber of Deputies, following the constitutional directive, became acting president.

The military intervened to remove President Goulart because he had attempted to utilize popularity to offset the potential "coercion" of the armed forces. Once again, when the military decided that the chief executive had attempted to change the operating rules of the game—thereby violating the constitution, disrupting the "civil tranquility" of the nation, and undermining the neutrality and effectiveness of the military establishment—the military acted collectively to remove him from office and to restore the status quo ante.

By 1964, the armed forces came to believe that they possessed a constitutional mandate to remove Goulart from office. The constitutions of 1891, 1934, and 1946 stated that the military existed as a national institution with the responsibility of maintaining public order and guaranteeing the normal functioning of the three branches of government. But the constitution also stipulated that while the military was subordinate to the chief executive, its obedience was required only when the president acted within the limits of the law. In the final analysis, the military held the discretionary power to determine whether the chief executive was acting within constitutional limits.

In addition, the stimulus provided by the development doctrines of the ESG motivated the armed forces to reconsider their previous unwillingness to assume power. Given the inability of the Goulart government to progress in its reform program—which many officers doubted was either sincere or appropriate—the ESG alumni came to believe that their program was superior to that of the administration in power. With the support of key civilian groups, possessing a doctrine of development and convinced that they could effectively govern Brazil themselves, the armed forces assumed power.

The Military Republic, 1964–1985

The period from 1964 to 1985 (the Military Republic) was unique in Brazilian history. The armed forces had been actively involved in the political process for decades. But there had never been a collective decision to overthrow a civilian regime and retain power; prior interventions had resulted in a rapid restoration of a nonmilitary government.

What characterized the Military Republic was its determination to rapidly modernize the Brazilian economy while ignoring social issues and emasculating the political process. The military transferred key decision-making areas to a new power elite: the technocrats. Often foreign trained, and normally economists or planners, they operated with the full support of the military and without regard for either the social or political consequences of their decisions.

There were three phases of the post-1964 period: the first, from 1964 to 1968, was the period of controlled government, in which civilian influence declined steadily, but it was not yet clear that the armed forces and their supporters would so abruptly centralize power in the authoritarian state; the second, from 1969 to approximately 1979, was the period of authoritarian government—and the high point of the economic miracle; the third phase, called authoritarian liberalization, had its origins in the final years of the military and opened in 1979, with the inauguration of President João Figueiredo, and terminated with the transfer of power on March 15, 1985, to a civilian government.

THE REVOLUTION DEFINES ITSELF: THE INSTITUTIONAL ACTS

The Institutional Acts were a significant event in Brazilian political life. These documents constituted the justification for military intervention and also provided a political framework within which major institutional and structural reforms were made. While not canceling the constitution, the acts superseded and restricted the purview of that document. They represented the efforts of the armed forces to restore the influence of the patrimonial regime after 1964. As such, they represented a running commentary on the inadequacies of the 1946 Republic, as well as formal notification to the nation that the changes introduced in 1964 were to be considered permanent.

After 1964, 17 Institutional Acts and more than 100 Complementary Acts were issued. The Complementary Acts spelled out the specific intent of the more general principles involved in the Institutional Acts. The 1967 Constitution emerged, in part, from a feeling that the changes brought about by the early Institutional Acts and the Complementary Acts required incorporation into a new legal framework. With the First Constitutional Amendment of October 1969, it became clear that the 1967 Constitution was an impermanent document to be ignored when required by the interests of the armed forces in their efforts to restore the status quo to Brazil. Not until the mid-1970s would a slow process of juridical normalization begin with the cancellation of the Institutional Acts. The final step in that process was the promulgation of the 1988 Constitution during the Sarney government (1985–1990).

Institutional Act No. 1, April 9, 1964

The presidency of Brazil was declared vacant on the night of April 1, 1964, and the president of the Chamber of Deputies was sworn in as acting president early on April 2. The nation—and the civilian political elite—waited. After a week of negotiation over the course of the March 31 coup, the armed forces decided to act unilaterally. The political initiative passed to the military; it remained there throughout the second half of the 1960s. On April 9, the three military ministers issued an ''Institutional'' Act. The act did not rest on any constitutional justification; its authority derived from the moral force of the Revolution itself. No further justification was deemed necessary by the armed forces.

The preamble of the act states the reason for its issuance:

The successful Revolution invests itself with the exercise of the Constituent Power, which manifests itself by popular election or by Revolution. This is the most expressive and radical form of the Constituent Power. Thus, the successful Revolution, like the Constituent Power, is legitimized by itself. The Revolution dismisses the former government and is qualified to set up a new one. The Revolution holds in itself the normative strength inherent to the Constituent Power, and establishes judicial norms without being limited by previous norms.

The act vastly strengthened the powers of the chief executive. While the 1946 Constitution remained in force, it was subject to modification by the act. The president received the power to propose amendments to the constitution, which Congress had to consider within 30 days; only a majority vote, as opposed to the two-thirds vote stipulated in the 1946 Constitution, was needed for approval. Only the president could submit expenditure measures to Congress, and Congress could not increase the amount stipulated in the bills. The power to declare a state of siege without congressional approval was given to the president, and the executive was granted the power to suppress the political rights of ''political undesirables'' for 10 years. On April 11, 1964, General Humberto Castello Branco, a leader of the March 31 coup, was elected president by a cowed Congress.

Article X of the act, which gave the president the right to revoke the legislative authority of the elected officials and to suspend political rights, was to expire on June 15, 1964. The military government moved quickly to revoke the mandates of those members of Congress identified with the defeated Left. By the deadline, former president Goulart, as well as six governors and more than 40 members of Congress, plus some 300 individuals active in political life, had their rights suspended. Under Article VII, which gave the president the power to expel people from the civil service without regard for existing legislation guaranteeing employment, it is estimated that approximately 9,000 people were fired by November 9, the cutoff date stated in the act.

As the military became accustomed to its new political role, it was clear that its task would not be completed by January 1966, when the presidential term of Castello Branco was scheduled to terminate. In July 1964, a constitutional amendment extended the president's term of office until March 15, 1967; new presidential elections were set for November 1966.

With the decision to extend the president's term, implying a military commitment to retain power for an indefinite period, a number of events in 1965 helped determine the political strategy of the regime. The first was the election, in the São Paulo mayoral race in March 1965, of a candidate backed by former president Quadros. This was viewed as an affront to the armed forces.

On July 15, 1965, two laws dealing with elections and political parties were announced. These represented the first substantive revision of the pre-1964 political rules of the game. The electoral code reduced the number of parties by increasing the minimum requirement that parties had to meet to achieve or maintain legal status. Electoral alliances were forbidden; candidates were required to reside in the area which they sought to represent; voters were required to cast ballots for slates of candidates for local, state, and federal offices, rather than individual candidates; and the running mates of successful gubernatorial and presidential candidates were automatically elected. These reforms were an attempt to deal with one of the problems perceived by the military as most debilitating in the pre-1964 era: the weak and diffuse multiparty system. It was hoped that these reforms would introduce some coherence into the political system.

The Political Party Statute stipulated stringent procedures for the organization of new political parties. Individuals were forbidden to run for more than one office in any election. Residence and party membership requirements were spec ified for candidates. It was thought that this law would help control the problem of representation, so abused before 1964, when there were few requirements linking a candidate to his constituency.

Also promulgated on July 15 was the Ineligibilities Law, which barred former ministers in the Goulart government (those appointed after the January 1963 plebiscite) from candidacy. Its primary purpose was to prevent the candidacy of several prominent antiregime politicians in the upcoming state elections.

The gubernatorial elections of October 1965 were a critical event in the un-folding of the military regime. Despite the warnings and fears of many members of the armed forces, the Castello Branco government was determined to hold open, competitive elections. Two candidates for governor, identified as oppo-nents of the regime and both supported by former president Kubitschek, were victorious. Immediately, the military hard-liners pressed the government to annul the elections. To fulfill his promise to allow the inauguration of all candidates elected, President Castello Branco promulgated Institutional Act No. 2. With its publication, the military regime made a basic decision to restructure national politics to try to ensure that the legacy of the 1946 Republic would be effectively neutralized.

Institutional Acts Nos. 2, 3, and 4

Institutional Act No. 2 determined that only the president could create new positions in the civil service; further restricted the time allowed to Congress to consider legislation before it became law automatically; increased the number of members of the Supreme Court (which had been viewed as a last holdout against the more blatantly unconstitutional actions of the Revolutionary govern-ment); reserved the right of nomination of all federal judges to the president; reorganized the Supreme Military Tribunal; stipulated that civilians accused of crimes against national security were to be subject to military justice; decreed the indirect election of the president and vice president by an absolute majority of the federal Congress; permitted the president to declare a state of siege for 180 days to prevent "the subversion of internal order"; extended the right of the Revolution to suspend individual political rights for 10 years; established restrictions on the activities of those whose political rights were removed; gave the president the right to intervene in the states for reasons other than those stipulated in the constitution, in order to ensure the execution of a federal law or in order to prevent or punish the subversion of order; abolished existing political parties and canceled their registration; excluded from judicial competence all acts of the Supreme Revolutionary Command and the federal government in Institutional Acts Nos. 1 and 2 and in the Complementary Acts to follow, plus resolutions, passed since March 31, 1964, of state assemblies that canceled the mandates of legislators; and gave the president the power to recess Congress, legislative assemblies, and chambers of municipal councillors. The second act was to remain in force until March 15, 1967, the date of the inauguration of Castello Branco's successor.

The political party situation was further modified by Complementary Act No. 4 of November 20, 1965, which provided for the provisional registration of political organizations sponsored by at least 120 federal deputies and 20 senators. Two parties emerged, replacing the 13-party system of the 1946 Republic: a government-sponsored entity, the National Renovating Alliance (ARENA), and the opposition group, the Brazilian Democratic Movement (MDB). ARENA became a UDN stronghold with some PSD support; MDB attracted the remains of the PTB and some PSD elements.

Institutional Act No. 3, issued on February 5, 1966, replaced the direct election of governors with selection by state legislatures on September 3, 1966, scheduled legislative elections for federal senators and deputies and state deputies for November 15, 1966, and eliminated the election of mayors of all capital cities (henceforth they would be selected by the governors of the states).

The Complementary Acts announced through 1965 and 1966 served to implement or elaborate on the Institutional Acts. Perhaps the most notorious Complementary Act promulgated during this time was No. 23 of October 20, 1966, which confirmed the growing centralization of power in the hands of the military and strengthened the determination of the government to allow little, if any, organized opposition to its plans. Complementary Act No. 23 decreed the recess of the federal Congress until November 22, 1966—after the scheduled elections. The act stated that in the Congress there was "a group of counterrevolutionary elements whose objective was to disturb the public peace and upset the coming election of November 15, thus compromising the prestige and the authority of the legislative power." A precedent had been established, allowing the executive power to quiet the legislative branch whenever it suited the government's needs.

With the indirect election by the national Congress of Marshal Artur Costa e Silva to follow Castello Branco, the succession issue was settled. Costa e Silva ran unopposed; attempts by the MDB to launch a rival candidacy had failed. Federal senators and deputies, state deputies, mayors and municipal councilmen were selected in direct elections on November 15. ARENA won overwhelmingly, electing senators from 15 states and approximately two-thirds of the new deputies.

Institutional Act No. 4 of December 7, 1966, convoked an extraordinary meeting of Congress to vote and promulgate a new constitution. The preamble stated that it had become necessary to give the country a new constitution that would "represent the institutionalization of the ideas and principles of the Revolution."

The constitution was promulgated on January 24, 1967. It further strengthened the executive power and weakened any hope of opposition groups to use the constitution to justify opposition to the regime.

The Failure of the Opposition to Unite

With the inauguration of President Costa e Silva on March 15, 1967, the Revolution entered a new phase. The early efforts at controlling inflation appeared to be working; the needed structural reforms of the political system had been undertaken; and the crisis of confidence within the military seemed to have been overcome with the acceptance by Castello Branco of the Costa e Silva candidacy.

The main political event of the first year of the second military government was the futile formation of a united front of opposition forces. It was an ill-fated attempt by leaders of the pre-1964 regime to offer an alternative to the Military Republic. The front aroused little popular interest; it did not provide a focus for civilian protest; and the new leaders of the untried political parties were unwilling to lend their support. Faced with regime hostility, it quickly dissolved.

The Crisis of December 1968

Throughout the last half of 1968, it became apparent that divisions within the regime had deepened between those who supported a moderate, semiconstitutional policy favoring limited civilian participation and the hard-line nationalists who argued for military preeminence in all matters. The president seemed to favor a more moderate line, but many officers disagreed. They believed that Brazil could no longer ignore its underdeveloped regions; such a policy of neglect threatened national security and modernization. To achieve these goals, the regime had to avoid fractious partisan politics and further concentrate decision making in the executive.

The two positions were brought into confrontation over a speech made on the floor of Congress by a young Congressman who urged Brazilians to boycott military parades on Independence Day and asked that parents not allow their daughters to date military personnel. The nationalists found this address disgraceful and expected that the government would take appropriate action against the deputy. President Costa e Silva attempted to utilize legal channels to convince Congress to remove the deputy's congressional immunity, but Congress balked.

On December 12, 1968, Congress met to consider the insistent request of the government, that it lift Moreira Alves's immunity. The vote was 216 against the government, 141 in favor, and 15 blank votes. The government's demand had been rejected. In the face of this blatant disrespect for military authority, the government moved quickly to regain control of a rapidly deteriorating situation. The decision was made to issue yet another Institutional Act.

Institutional Act No. 5, December 13, 1968

The fifth Institutional Act stated that the "revolutionary process unfolding could not be detained." The very institutions given to the nation by the Revolution for its defense were being used to destroy it, stated the preamble of the act. The fifth act empowered the president to recess the national Congress, state legislative assemblies, and municipal councils by Complementary Acts. These bodies would convene again only when called by the president. In addition, the president could decree intervention in the states in the national interest, without regard for the constitutional restrictions on intervention; he could suspend political rights of any citizen for 10 years and cancel election mandates without regard for constitutional limitations. The national state of siege was prolonged; the confiscation of personal goods illicitly gained was allowed; the right of habeas corpus was suspended in cases of political crimes and crimes against national security and the social and economic order; and the restrictions to be placed on those who lost their political rights were increased and more explicitly designated.

Complementary Act No. 38 of December 13, 1968, decreed the recess of Congress. With the closing of the legislature, the regime had determined the immediate future of the Revolution of March 31, 1964. It would be a period of outright military rule, without the inconvenience of elected, civilian interference. The economic planning process, which represented the only significant accomplishment of the regime, would continue unfettered. The possibilities for "humanizing" the Revolution gave way to the need for internal security—that is, precluding overt opposition from civilian political groups—and development, to be determined by the military regime and its civilian supporters.

The first eight months of 1969 saw a flurry of revolutionary legislation. Institutional Act No. 6 (February 1, 1969) amended the 1967 Constitution (Article 113) and stipulated that the Supreme Court would consist of 11 members nominated by the president. It also said that the Supreme Military Tribunal would be responsible for trying all of those accused of national security crimes.

Institutional Act No. 7 (February 26, 1969) regulated the functioning of state legislative assemblies and municipal councils. It suspended interim elections for executive and legislative positions and decreed government intervention in case of vacancies. The president was empowered to set a new date for elections when he felt it useful.

Administrative reform of the states and municipalities, to conform to the model of the federal government, was decreed by Institutional Act No. 8 (April 2, 1969). A constitutional amendment facilitating government expropriation of, and compensation for, rural lands constituted Institutional Act No. 9 (April 26, 1969). The tenth act (May 18, 1969) further elaborated on the penalties that

accompanied the suspension of political rights and the removal of elected officials. Institutional Act No. 11 (August 14, 1969) established dates for the election of municipal officials; local voting had been held in abeyance since the
seventh act.

The President Incapacitated

Two dramatic events in August and September 1969 demonstrated both the
potential vulnerability of and the military's predominance in the 1964 regime:
the incapacitation of President Costa e Silva and the kidnapping of U.S. Ambassador C. Burke Elbrick.

A massive stroke incapacitated President Costa e Silva in late August. Under
the 1967 Constitution, Vice President Pedro Aleixo, a civilian from Minas Gerais, was next in succession. Within 48 hours of the president's illness, Institutional Act No. 12 (August 31, 1969) was issued. The military had decided
against the constitution. The ministers of the navy, army, and air force promulgated the act "in the name of the president of the Republic . . . temporarily
impeded from exercising his functions for reasons of health." The document
stated:

The situation that the country is experiencing . . . precludes the transfer of the responsibilities of supreme authority and supreme command of the Armed Forces, exercised by
his excellency, to other officials, in accordance with the constitutional provision.

As an imperative of National Security, it falls to the ministers of the Navy, of the
Army and of the Air Force to assume, for as long as the head of the Nation is incapacitated, the duties given to his excellency by the constitutional documents in force.

The Nation can have confidence in the patriotism of its military chiefs who, in this
hour, as always, will know how to honor the historic legacy of their predecessors, loyal
to the spirit of nationalism, the Christian formation of its people, contrary to extremist
ideologies and violent solution, in moments of political or institutional crises.

The document stipulated that the military ministers would act on behalf of
the president, that the previously published Institutional and Complementary
Acts would remain in full force, and that all of these acts would be beyond
judicial purview.

The U.S. Ambassador Disappears

On Thursday, September 4, 1969, U.S. Ambassador Elbrick was taken at
gunpoint from his limousine in Rio de Janeiro. His kidnappers left a note in
which they identified themselves as members of revolutionary movements; they
demanded the release of 15 political prisoners held by the regime in exchange
for the life of the ambassador. A note found in the ambassador's car, addressed
"to the Brazilian people," stated:

With the kidnaping of the Ambassador we want to demonstrate that it is possible to defeat the dictatorship and the exploitation if we arm and organize ourselves. We show up where the enemy least expects us and we disappear immediately, tearing out the dictatorship, bringing terror and fear to the exploiters, the hope and certainty of victory to the midst of the exploited.

The demands of the kidnappers were that their manifesto be published and that the 15 prisoners be taken to Algeria, Chile, or Mexico, where they would be granted political asylum. A time limit of 48 hours was stated. The manifesto ended with a warning to the regime from the terrorists: "Now it is an eye for an eye, and a tooth for a tooth."

The government responded immediately. The 15 political prisoners were rounded up from their places of detention and placed aboard a plane for Mexico; the manifesto appeared in the Brazilian newspapers. The list of prisoners included some of the leading critics and opponents of the regime. Amid rumors that members of the officer corps were "unhappy" over the government's decision, Institutional Act No. 13 (September 5, 1969) appeared, which empowered the executive to banish from the national territory any Brazilian considered dangerous to national security.

Institutional Act No. 14, issued on the same day, stated: "[It is considered] that acts of adverse psychological warfare and revolutionary or subversive war, that disturb the life of the country and maintain it in a climate of intranquility and agitation, deserve more severe repression." The act amended the constitution (Article 150) and established a penalty of death, perpetual imprisonment, banishment, or confiscation of goods for those guilty of participating in psychological, revolutionary, or subversive war against the state.

THE URBAN GUERRILLA MOVEMENT IN BRAZIL

The kidnapping of the U.S. ambassador dramatically publicized the existence, previously deemphasized by the regime, of a network of guerrilla bands operating in the cities of Brazil. The movement posed a serious threat to the stability of the regime during the period 1967–1969. By challenging the authority of the government, the terrorists hoped to weaken the support for the military among the middle- and upper-urban sectors. If the government could not secure public order, what else justified its continuation?

The terrorist group stemmed from dissident elements of the Moscow-oriented Brazilian Communist party (PCB), led for decades by Luis Carlos Prestes. The first offshoot had been the revolutionary Communist Party of Brazil (PC do B) with a decidedly Maoist or Fidelist orientation. Other fragments represented Trotskyite and Marxist variants. Prominent among the groups was the National Liberating Alliance (ALN), founded early in 1967 and led by former Communist Party Deputy Carlos Marighella.

A group that worked closely with the ALN but maintained its own identity was led by ex-Captain Carlos Lamarca. Called the Popular Revolutionary Vanguard, it merged with the National Liberation Command from June to July 1969 to form the Armed Revolutionary Vanguard (VAR), referred to as VAR-Palmares. (Palmares, in the Brazilian Northeast, was the site of an unsuccessful slave revolt in the late nineteenth century.) Under Lamarca's daring leadership, the VAR-Palmares became a romantic symbol of protest against the regime and attracted many students to its ranks. Disillusioned by military rule, they accepted Lamarca's leadership in, and Marighella's ideological justification for, armed insurrection. A pamphlet entitled *The Mini-Manual of the Urban Guerrilla*, by Marighella, which appeared in the middle of 1969, offered a sophisticated and an incisive summary of the bankruptcy of the regime and the necessity of undermining it by urban revolutionary warfare. The murder of Marighella in São Paulo on November 26 weakened the revolutionary Left considerably. The loss of Marighella and the continuing fragmentation of the radical Left were accompanied by increasingly effective repression by the regime.

By 1972, the guerrilla challenge had been neutralized. The terrorist groups had not weakened the regime in the eyes of its strongest supporters, the middle and upper sectors. On the contrary, these groups believed that the guerrilla movement justified strong and effective government. The death of Carlos Lamarca in a gun battle with security police in September 1971 deprived the guerrillas of their principal leader.

While the period following the 1964 Revolution had witnessed strong and often arbitrary conduct by the Military Republic, the opening of the guerrilla offensive legitimated the expansion and consolidation of a complex security and intelligence network. At both the state and federal levels, coordinating institutions either emerged or were reorganized to confront and destroy the subversive offensive and its adherents. Given the diversity of Brazil, the differences in state police and federal military jurisdictions, the level of perception of threat by individual security and military commanders, and the operation of death squads in São Paulo, the challenge of coordinating intelligence efforts was overwhelming. Inevitably, excesses occurred that were unknown or overlooked at the national level. As the armed forces became deeply involved in cooperating with police and security units working within each of the four army regions, allegations of direct military involvement in torture and interrogation sessions grew.

Although they were widely discussed, press censorship in Brazil prevented an open examination of these violations of human rights. International press coverage, critical of the regime, provided increasingly disturbing accounts of detention, interrogation, and physical torture. U.S. congressional committees considering foreign aid for Brazil drew attention to the reports. Public action and church groups in the United States and Europe condemned the inability or unwillingness of the Brazilian government to curb or terminate violations of human rights. The U.S. presidential campaign in the autumn of 1976 introduced the issue into American politics, with Democratic Party candidate Jimmy Carter openly referring to Brazil as a violator of human rights. The visit of First Lady Rosalynn Carter to Brazil in 1977, and her widely publicized meeting in Recife with North American missionary priests who had been mistreated by Brazilian authorities, further exacerbated the tension between the two governments.

In response to a U.S. State Department report on human rights in Brazil, required by 1976 congressional legislation, Brazil canceled its 25-year-old military assistance treaty with the United States in March 1977. The Brazilian Foreign Ministry said the report constituted an intolerable interference in its internal affairs.

With the lifting of press censorship in late 1977 and 1978, these events and the judicial proceedings under way against accused torturers received widespread attention. The Brazilian Bar Association and the Roman Catholic Church took the lead in demanding an end to violations of human rights. It is now clear that President Geisel personally deplored the excesses of the military and security forces.[9] A priority of his government was the elimination of the violations of human rights, but he was constrained by the authoritarian nationalists within the regime who condoned or promoted such violations in the name of vigilance against subversion. Geisel took two steps of importance in signaling his displeasure with the human rights violators and his intention of halting their actions. In January 1976, he removed the commander of the Second Army in São Paulo, General Eduardo D'Avila Mello, because of growing public clamor over continued torture and detention of citizens. General D'Avila was not personally accused of torture, but Geisel held him accountable for what his subordinates were doing. His replacement moved to control human rights violations, and by 1978 the situation had improved dramatically.

The second crucial decision taken by Geisel was the dismissal of his minister of the army, General Silvio Coelho da Frota, in October 1977. Frota had become a strong advocate of the status quo and looked with alarm at Geisel's liberalizing tendencies. In a daring power play, Geisel fired him and implicitly challenged the other members of the high command to veto his decision. None did. Geisel's appointee to succeed Frota restored the nonpolitical nature of the office of army minister.

The dismissal of D'Avila and Frota, combined with the growing pressure for a change in the nature of the regime, resulted in the virtual elimination of human rights violations as a major political issue by 1978. While the question of generalized police brutality and violence continues in Brazilian society, the armed forces quickly abandoned such practices and no longer used the argument that potential or actual leftist subversion justified such conduct. There was never a threat from the Left—indeed, many observers commented that the real threat in Brazil came from the Right.

CONSTITUTIONAL AMENDMENT NO. 1, OCTOBER 20, 1969

As the regime surmounted the challenge to its authority represented by the kidnapping of the U.S. ambassador, it became clear that President Costa e

Silva's incapacitation was permanent. The country confronted the task of selecting its fifth chief executive in 10 years.

On October 14, 1969, with the announcement of Institutional Act No. 16, the military high command decided that

considering that the superior interests of the country require the immediate and permanent filling of the office of the President of the Republic . . . considering that Institutional Act No. 12 [of August 13, 1969] . . . attributes to the military ministers the right to substitute for the President of the Republic in his temporary incapacitation . . . Article 1. The position of the President of the Republic is declared vacant . . . Article 2. The position of Vice President of the Republic is also declared vacant.

By using an Institutional Act, with Congress in recess, the prerogatives of that body were exercised by the executive power. By precluding the constitutional succession of the civilian vice president, the military prepared the way for the creation of a more rigidly authoritarian government to succeed Costa e Silva. The officer corps of the three services were polled. General Emílio Garrastazú Médici, a supporter of the stricken president and commander of the Third Army, located in the state of Rio Grande do Sul, ranked highest. He became the next chief executive on October 25, 1969, with a rapid vote by a demoralized Congress.

Institutional Act No. 17 of October 14, 1969, gave the president the power to transfer to the reserves any military officer guilty of violating the cohesion of the armed forces. The preamble of the act stated that ''the Armed Forces as institutions that serve to sustain the constituted powers of law and order, are organized on a basis of the principles of hierarchy and discipline.'' The act can be interpreted as a warning to those officers in disagreement with the decision of the military high command in favor of Médici. Also, the act gave the new president a ''legal'' means of imposing the military's will on the armed forces without having to resort to other forms of coercion or intimidation.

In a flurry of activity, the military ministers issued Constitutional Amendment No. 1 on October 17, in effect as of October 30. The amendment, among other changes, reduced the powers of Congress still further; the size of Congress was reduced when the criterion for the number of seats was shifted from population (benefiting the more backward states with a large illiterate population) to registered voters (benefiting the more urban states in the Southeast)—the new Chamber of Deputies was reduced from 409 to 293; the state assemblies were reduced from 1,076 seats to 672 seats; and the centralized control of the chief executive over the introduction of new legislation, especially money bills, was confirmed.

The amendment represented the determination of the military to ensure a presidential succession unmarred by dissent or protest. It provided the new chief executive with all of the power required for governing and controlling the nation. By moving to promulgate these decisions before the election of General Médici, the military high command assumed collective responsibility for the political decision to decimate the 1967 Constitution.

The indirect gubernatorial elections of October 3, 1970, saw ARENA candidates elected in all states except Guanabara. The MDB victory there had been ratified previously by the government. The new governors were cognizant of the group they needed to please most: the military. In the direct elections of November 1970 for a new chamber and two-thirds of the Senate, ARENA won an overwhelming victory.

With the consolidation of internal security and a period of dramatic economic growth following the stabilization period of 1964–1974, a new development emphasis emerged in the Médici government's domestic program. While the unity of the armed forces was by no means guaranteed, a combination of skillful administration, popular and pragmatic policies, and luck indicated that a majority of the officer corps was willing to support the Médici government's social and economic initiatives.

As part of the *Metas e Bases para a Ação do Governo* (Goals and Bases for Government Action), published in September 1970, the government announced its Program of National Integration (PIN). The goals of PIN for the first phase, which was to extend from 1971 to 1974, were to expand the agricultural frontier to include the Amazon Valley; to continue the integration programs of the Northeast and the Amazon; to incorporate the population of these regions into the national economy; to create an effective program for transforming agriculture in the semiarid regions of the Northeast; to reorient the internal migration of Northeasterners toward the North and away from the overcrowded cities of the Center-South states; and to ensure federal support for the industrial development of the Northeast region.

Complementary programs in the overall national integration effort, in addition to PIN, included the Program of Land Redistribution and Stimulation of Agriculture and Cattle Activities in the Northeast and North and the Program for the Development of the Center-West. The Program of Social Integration (PIS), announced in August 1970, provided an opportunity for the working class to share in the national income through the Participation Fund. Both the federal government and the private sector contributed to the fund, from which workers drew loans for the purchase of apartments or plots of land. The extent of a worker's participation was determined by level of employment and length of service.

In September 1971, President Médici sent to Congress the first National Development Plan, for the period 1972–1974. Its principal goals were to maintain annual growth rates of between 8 percent and 10 percent; to further national integration in the Northeast and Amazon regions (as outlined in the programs discussed previously); to create a modern, efficient, and technological economy; and to continue planning for a higher level of social integration.

Though the euphoria of the pre-OPEC crisis of 1973 allowed for a dramatic surge in economic growth (low international oil prices were key to growth, since Brazil remained highly dependent on petroleum imports) and infrastructural development during the Médici government, the regime did not loosen its political controls. The drive against subversives continued unabated. The president announced that elections for state governors, scheduled for 1974, would be indirect. In September 1972, press censorship tightened, and new regulations were announced that precluded criticism of economic policy, comments on political liberalization and amnesty for prisoners, and speculation on the presidential succession.

In June 1973, President Médici announced that General Ernesto Geisel, the head of the state petroleum company, was his choice in the January 1974 presidential elections. Geisel was a former aide to President Castello Branco. In addition to his reputation as an administrator, he had the good fortune that his brother had served as war minister in the Médici cabinet. Because of his identification with the Castello Branco wing of the armed forces, it was hoped that his election would signal the possibility of liberalization of the Military Republic.

In December 1973, President Médici reported to the nation that the economic growth rate that year had surpassed 10 percent. Exports rose, foreign investment continued to flow into the country, and the economy promised to continue to expand and diversify. But shortly thereafter, the head of the National Petroleum Council announced that from September 1973 to February 1974, the price Brazil paid for crude oil had risen 350 percent. Against the backdrop of this dramatic economic shock, the inauguration of General Ernesto Geisel as the fourth president of the Revolution took place on March 15, 1974.

THE FOURTH GOVERNMENT OF THE MILITARY REPUBLIC: GENERAL ERNESTO GEISEL (1974–1979)

Geisel emerged as the key figure in the post-1964 Military Republic. His commitment to authoritarian liberalization—innovation directed and determined at the apex of the political system—profoundly changed Brazil. The five years of the Geisel government witnessed a determined movement away from the grandiose overtones of the Médici team with its emphasis on *grandeza* (greatness), the building of monumental public works projects, and its disdain for civil liberties and human rights. Slowly but inexorably, Geisel charted a course of liberalization that won increasing support from all sectors of Brazilian society, including the armed forces. When he transferred power to his chosen successor, General João Figueiredo, in March 1979, Geisel had earned the respect of the Brazilian nation for his honesty and probity.

Geisel demonstrated his desire to separate himself from the Médici government in the organization of his cabinet and palace advisory team. His chief political advisor was General Golbery do Couto e Silva, a disciple of General Castello Branco and a key architect of the coming liberalization. Golbery had been one of the founders of the National Intelligence Service (SNI) after the Revolution and had served as president of Dow Chemical of Brazil. General

João Figueiredo, chosen to direct the SNI, was a military officer who had worked with both the Castello Branco-Geisel and the Costa e Silva-Médici groups since 1964. His selection was seen as a guarantee that the SNI would be conducted as a professional operation. The key economics position went to Mário Henrique Simonsen, a well-known economist and banker, who became the finance minister, and João Paulo de Reis Velloso, a holdover from the Médici group, who retained the post of planning minister. Other appointments appeared to indicate a preference for either competent technocrats or civilian political leaders with prior governmental experience.

As we shall see in Chapter 5, the 1973 oil price shock had a strong impact on the Brazilian economy, although the brunt would not be felt until the end of the decade—at the time of the selection of Geisel's successor, SNI chief Figueiredo. The Brazilian economic team decided to exploit Brazil's comparative advantage and continue to grow. Foreign borrowing escalated—but at relatively low rates of interest. Markets held up, and the trade balance was generally good. Brazilian exports continued to diversify. As Reis Velloso had provided the continuity from the Médici to the Geisel governments, so Simonsen would briefly serve as planning minister in the Figueiredo administration—and he quickly began to realize the dangers of rising inflation, a growing oil bill, and fast-rising debt levels. His effort in 1979 to dampen the economy met with strong resistance, and he was replaced by Antônio Delfim Netto, the miracle worker of the Costa e Silva and Médici periods.

Believing that economic, trade, and investment matters should be left to the technocrats, Geisel, Golbery, and their collaborators concentrated on the political liberalization process. The decision taken in the mid-1960s to allow direct elections for members of Congress and for municipal posts had posed no difficulty through the early 1970s. ARENA, the government party, was returned to office with large majorities. Some intimidation was involved, of course; many able candidates of the opposition had lost their political rights; many Brazilians actually believed that the government deserved their electoral support; and others became apathetic about voting specifically and about politics generally, and they chose to not participate.

But by the mid-1970s, with the first economic shock of the increase in petroleum prices and the emergence of societal pressures for liberalization, elections suddenly took on a different meaning, as manifested by the MDB's strong gains in 1974 in both the Senate and Chamber of Deputies. The results of the 1974 elections were viewed by many as a plebiscite on the 1964 Revolution—and the regime either had lost or had been taught a lesson, or both.

While the election results heartened civilian supporters of liberalization, they created problems for Geisel in dealing with the armed forces. The conservative viewpoint was that elections generally resulted in corruption and subversion. Geisel clearly thought otherwise, but he had to move with care. Using carrot-and-stick methods with both the armed forces and the opposition civilian forces, he tried to give something to both groups—without losing sight of his principal goal. Throughout 1975 and 1976, Geisel reacted by publicly cautioning those supporting liberalization to move with care. More concretely, he did not hesitate to use the powers of Institutional Act No. 5 to cancel the political rights of state and federal deputies, and senators charged with corruption or who challenged government, or committed other vague mistakes. The message was clear. If there was going to be liberalization, Geisel would orchestrate it. To counterbalance his military critics, the president moved military officers frequently, "exiling" those he believed were openly hostile to his plans and neutralizing those who appeared uncertain in their support.

In the 1972 municipal elections, ARENA had carried the day. This was not the case in 1976. While ARENA did well in the countryside, the MDB claimed a number of important urban successes. As a result, in mid-1977, Geisel took an opportunity to offer a carrot to the hard-line authoritarians. Congress had proven recalcitrant in providing the two-thirds majority required to pass a judicial reform bill; Geisel, without warning, recessed Congress. He then proceeded to promulgate, without political consultation, what became known as the "April package" of reforms, all of which were seen as regressive. The package canceled the planned direct elections of state governors in 1978; they would be selected indirectly by electoral colleges, the majority of which ARENA controlled. The new decree changed the pattern of voting in congressional elections and returned to the old rule, whereby the number of deputies was decided not by how many voters a state had but by how large the population was. This meant that in states with large populations but with small numbers of eligible literate voters, ARENA would do well. The *Lei Falcão* was extended to other elections. The law, first utilized in the November 1976 elections, excluded the use of radio and television in electoral campaigns, which again worked against the opposition candidates, who were the newer candidates in most cities and states and less well-known to the public. The term of the presidency was extended to six years, beginning with Geisel's successor. And a group of derisively termed "bionic" senators were created—each state was given a third senator, to be elected by the state assembly, thereby guaranteeing ARENA a solid majority in the federal Senate.

In January 1978, Geisel announced that SNI chief João Figueiredo was his choice for fifth military president of the Republic and that the civilian governor of Minas Gerais, Aureliano Chaves de Mendonça, had been selected as his running mate. Figueiredo was viewed by Geisel and Golbery as a supporter of authoritarian liberalization, even though he had close ties with the Médici conservatives in the armed forces and with political elites. Figueiredo came from a military family. His grandfather, father, and two brothers were army officers. His father, General Euclydes Figueiredo, was a near-legendary figure in the 1930s. He had been exiled in 1932 by President Vargas and imprisoned in 1937 when the Estado Novo was announced. A firm opponent of dictatorship, he had a profound impact on his son, and the father's commitment to democracy was a strong motivation in the new president's determination to continue and to hopefully conclude the liberalization process.

The opposition MDB leaders decided to contest the presidential election, although they knew that the electoral college, which would elect the next president, was controlled by ARENA. On December 1, 1977, meeting with members of ARENA, President Geisel made the surprise announcement that he was planning important institutional changes in the 1964 regime. The time had come, he stated, to move ahead with liberalization. The Institutional Acts were to be replaced with new legislation and new political parties, and other reforms were to be introduced in 1978. There were other indications that the process of liberalization was accelerating. In May 1978, the first massive strike since 1964 took place in the São Paulo industrial suburbs:

The stoppages in the auto industry in May 1978 opened up a new period for the working class in Brazil. After ten years of tight control, new parameters were established for workers and trade unions. Suddenly strikes became acceptable and the metalworkers in São Bernardo rose to national prominence.[10]

Both the private sector and the government responded hesitantly to this new challenge to the authoritarian regime—particularly given the economic importance of the region for the national economy. But as the strike mentality spread beyond São Bernardo to schools, hospitals, banks, and other public services, the government began to realize that it no longer controlled workers in Brazil as it had in previous decades. No one emerged satisfied from the messy negotiations that temporarily created a truce—but not trust. The unions prepared for the next round of wage negotiations in April 1979 and utilized the time to seek unity in the labor ranks and to set out a practical and just agenda of demands.

In June 1978, the progressive leadership of the São Paulo business community issued a manifesto in which it called for a return to democracy. The government decided to lift prior press censorship, which had been in force since 1964. In the same period, at the government's urging, Congress began to consider measures to liberalize the authoritarian regime. Among the most important were the abolition of the Institutional Acts; the restoration of habeas corpus; the return of political liberties, after 10 years, to those prosecuted under the provision of the Institutional Acts; limitations on the president's power to close Congress; and the creation of new political parties. It was made clear that Geisel, in return, would not accept any revision of the April 1977 package or any change in the application of the *Lei Falcão*, which regulated political use of radio and television in campaigns. Even with these changes, Congress remained relatively weak. It had no authority over the budget process and could modify neither the National Security Law nor the existing labor legislation, for example. After heated sessions in Congress, the legislation passed in September 1978, but only after the Presidential Palace implied a return to tighter controls if the president's proposals were not passed as proposed.

In October, the government submitted a new national security law to Congress that incorporated the basic security measures contained in the Institutional Acts. The National Security Law was a vital control mechanism for the process of authoritarian liberalization. It was intended to replace Institutional Act No. 5 and reassure skeptics on the Right that the liberalization was indeed controlled from the top. It became law in 1979.

After a spirited presidential campaign waged throughout Brazil, the ARENA-controlled electoral college convened on October 15, 1978, and, as expected, chose General João Figueiredo as President Geisel's successor. Figueiredo pledged himself to the process of liberalization. Coming shortly after the campaign and the decision of the electoral college, the congressional elections of November 15, 1978, further consolidated the process.

THE FIFTH GOVERNMENT OF THE MILITARY REPUBLIC: GENERAL JOÃO FIGUEIREDO (1979–1985)

João Figueiredo assumed the presidency at a difficult moment in Brazilian history. The economic fortunes of the country were poor, as we shall see in Chapter 5. The second oil price shock in 1979 and the consequent world recession badly hurt Brazil. The new planning minister, Mário Henrique Simonsen, attempted to halt policies of growth and spending, but he soon resigned in frustration. His replacement, Agriculture Minister Antônio Delfim Netto, sparked a national commitment to continued growth and expansion that would ultimately end in the debt crisis of 1982–1983.

Figueiredo also kept General Golbery as his chief political adviser. Senator Petrónio Portella, a wise and an experienced member of ARENA, received the post of minister of justice with instructions to work out the liberalization process. In his first months in office, Figueiredo was confronted with a series of challenges. Of these, two were most significant. One came from organized labor; a second emerged from the growing pressures for accelerated liberalization.

The Labor Unions

The May 1978 strike and its settlement had been the first experiment since 1964 with strikes and collective bargaining. The government had not interfered. The situation was different in 1979:

The May 1978 stoppages had created a new climate in which rank-and-file mobilizations were rife, and in the city of São Paulo the old union leadership had faced serious opposition during the annual wage-settlement negotiations in November 1978. The new leaders wanted to undermine the power of the pro-government elements in the unions even further. For the government, the annual negotiations would be a test of the degree to which democratization could be kept under control.[11]

At midnight, on March 13, 1979, two days before Figueiredo's inauguration, a massive strike erupted in the southern industrial belt of São Paulo, centered in the city of São Bernardo and the large auto plants. The metalworkers' union had refused to recognize the agreement negotiated a short time earlier between the manufacturers and the union leadership. Negotiations continued. Following a threat of government intervention, the union leaders agreed to put forward a proposal for a return to work, pending further negotiations over the following 45 days. During mass meetings of more than 90,000 workers, the compromise was rejected. The three opposing unions were then taken over by the Ministry of Labor.

To avert further polarization, a truce was arranged. The Ministry of Labor promised to withdraw from the unions in which it had intervened, and the workers agreed to return to work. Negotiations would continue for a new wage and work package. The final determination afforded neither party a clear victory, but it did accomplish the following:

The 1979 strike had shown that force would not resolve industrial relations problems if the workers could not be subdued. The encephalitic tendencies of corporatist trade unionism had made decapitation an effective remedy, but in São Bernardo the union's body—the organization and strength of its members in the plants—was developing rapidly.[12]

Pressures and Counterpressures to Liberalization

By mid-1980, the broad outlines of the regime's authoritarian liberalization were in place, and new parties were formed. Political amnesty had drawn exiled political leaders back to Brazil, and they were now actively involved in the new party structure. Habeas corpus had been restored, strengthening the integrity of the judicial system. Press freedom continued, and government censorship of radio and television diminished. The government was determined to restore direct elections for the country's governorships in November 1982, an important move to revitalize the federal system. The "bionic" senators were to disappear when their terms ended in 1986, thereby removing a point of embarrassment for the regime. The government also promised to consider revisions in the *Lei Falcão* and to review pressure to restore some congressional powers.

In April 1980, the government confronted organized labor in São Paulo once again. After massive strikes, the government intervened and arrested a large group of labor leaders, including Lula. The strike failed, but again the government was warned that labor militancy had become a fact of life in Brazil.

In September 1980, more than 1 million university students and 40,000 professors declared a nationwide strike that closed half of the country's universities. Their demand was for increased government spending on education and training. The government confronted a challenge in December 1980 with the publication of a nationalist manifesto in São Paulo, signed by a former government minister and high-ranking army officers. Societal pressures for political "decompression" were escalating.

The country was shocked in May 1981 by the explosion, outside of the Rio Center, a convention hall in Rio de Janeiro, of two bombs on the evening of a May Day concert for working-class Brazilians. An army sergeant died, and a security agency captain was badly wounded when the bombs exploded in their car. It was generally believed that the security agencies of the armed forces were involved in the tragic event. Figueiredo confronted a delicate, potentially serious situation. If he pushed for an investigation and a prosecution, he would create a direct challenge to the conservative members of the military leadership. If he ignored the incident, his public credibility was at stake. Political party leaders rallied around the president and met with him in Brasília. After a desultory investigation, the case was declared closed, although it was made clear in the press and informally in political circles that the Presidential Palace was divided over the government's response. The cautious decision to not confront the military was viewed as a judgment by Figueiredo about his level of support in the armed forces and his desire to continue to proceed with liberalization.

As a result of differences over the Rio Center incident and the strategy of the government in pursuing *abertura*, General Golbery resigned in August 1981. There were rumors of differences with Planning Minister Delfim Netto and also with SNI Chief General Octavio de Medeiros. The president acted quickly, calling Professor João Leitão de Abreu from the Supreme Court to take Golbery's place as head of the civilian household and chief political coordinator for the government. Many commentators noted that the Médici team was back in place with different jobs: Delfim in planning, Figueiredo as president, and Leitão as chief adviser to the president. All three had held high positions in the Médici government in the early 1970s.

In September, the second shock to the political system was the unexpected incapacitation of President Figueiredo, who suffered a heart attack. After a short period of doubt, it was decided to allow the civilian vice president, Aureliano Chaves, to become acting president in Figueiredo's absence. President Figueiredo returned to the palace in late 1981, determined to see through a crucial phase of the process of authoritarian liberalization—the national elections of November 1982. Taking firm control of the PDS, he initiated electoral reforms (called "counterreforms" by many in the opposition). As we saw in Chapter 2, the new reforms led to the fusion of the PP with the PMDB, further strengthening the principal opposition force in the liberalization process.

In June 1982, the government called for new amendments to the constitution—measures that increased the number of elected officials, restored the power of the Congress to call itself into session, and scheduled the presidential election for January 15, 1985 (moving it from October 1984). The reforms, which were seen as an additional effort to win votes for the PDS, were approved, despite objections from the opposition.

In an atmosphere more reminiscent of the annual Carnaval than of elections, Brazilians went to the polls on November 15, 1982. As shown in Chapter 2, the elections provided surprises for both the opposition and the government: the government party achieved a working plurality but fell short of an absolute majority. Efforts in 1983 to seek a dependable ally to create a majority were to prove unsuccessful.

The Political Implications of the Economic Crisis, 1982–1983

With the elections completed in November 1982, the Figueiredo administration turned to the pressing financial problems that Brazil confronted. As discussed in Chapter 5, the crisis over the Mexican foreign debt, which began in August 1982, and the uncertainty about Argentina's capacity to repay its foreign debt had a negative impact on Brazil's image in the international banking community. By December 1982, Brazil had agreed to negotiate with the International Monetary Fund as a prerequisite to receiving further loans from the private commercial banks.

As Congress organized in March 1983, the economic crisis and the deteriorating social conditions of millions of Brazilians who were jobless, hungry, and sick became a dominant theme in its debate. In addition, President Figueiredo's desire to postpone until 1984 a discussion of his successor was frustrated. As soon as the elections in November were over, the presidential race opened. With the social and economic difficulties confronting the government, 1983 was a year of intense national discussion about Brazil's future.

The Presidential Succession

With the counting of the November ballots barely completed, the immediate topic of conversation became the presidential succession.[13] The final selection of the president was to be indirect, by the 686-member electoral college, scheduled to meet in Brasília in January 1985. By June 1983, the government's plan for indirect elections faced a formidable challenge. Following on a little-noticed legislative initiative in March 1983, the leadership of the PMDB launched a nationwide campaign in favor of immediate direct elections (*Diretas Já*). Nurtured by the support of prominent opposition politicians, businessmen, students, average citizens, and leading show business personalities, the movement gathered national momentum.

In anticipation of a congressional vote in April 1984, which would decide the question, leaders of the *Diretas Já* campaign organized rallies in the major cities. In early April, a half million people turned out in Rio de Janeiro—Rio's largest political rally ever—followed by crowds of 200,000 in Goiânia and Pôrto Alegre. The major media—notably *TV-Globo*, which had prospered under military aegis and almost always touted the government line in its news coverage—resisted government arm-twisting and covered the events.

Though the *Diretas Já* movement ultimately failed in its effort to replace the electoral college with direct presidential elections, it did so by only 22 votes. Despite the strong-arm tactics of the government—including the imposition of a state of emergency in Brasília around the time of the vote—55 members of the government's PDS party voted for direct elections. Government forces, though winning the battle against *Diretas Já*, would subsequently lose the electoral war to keep one of their own in the *Planalto*.

Paulo Maluf, the former governor of São Paulo and a federal deputy, won the presidential nomination of the government-backed PDS, but not before his candidacy split the party. In early 1984, PDS Senator José Sarney and other members of the party's national committee abandoned the party in a dispute with Maluf. They subsequently formed the Liberal Front Party (PFL).

Meanwhile, the opposition had nominated PMDB Governor Tancredo Neves of Minas Gerais as its presidential candidate. Neves—a former federal deputy and government minister under Presidents Vargas and Kubitshcek and prime minister of the short-lived parliamentary government under President Goulart—was moderately left of center.

Neves, the consummate politician, assured military leaders that he had no intention of prosecuting military officials for human rights abuses committed during the Military Republic and harbored no desire to return to the politics that precipitated the 1964 coup. After a highly publicized meeting with the influential General Ernesto Geisel, Tancredo appeared to overcome whatever lingering opposition remained in the military. With Senator José Sarney as his running mate, Neves won the vote in the Electoral College, taking the presidency with 480 votes out of 686. It was left to Vice President-elect Sarney to assume the presidency and usher in the New Republic after Neves's tragic illness and death.

THE ARMED FORCES AND THE SARNEY GOVERNMENT

The transition from the Military Republic to a civilian regime was difficult. The incapacitation of Tancredo Neves on the eve of his inauguration presented the military government with a dilemma—should they allow Vice President-elect José Sarney to take office, or should they follow the strict letter of the existing constitution, which indicated that the "speaker of the house" should succeed? The issue was complicated, particularly because the outgoing chief executive, General Figueiredo, had developed a strong aversion to Sarney, who he considered a traitor for abandoning the military government to join the Neves forces. The leadership of the country's political elite and the military quickly decided to allow Sarney to assume the position of acting president. The expectation was that Neves, after his hospitalization, would become president. This did not happen. Sarney became the first civilian president of the New Republic. As a classic example of the political elite, he had been a full member of the patrimonial order throughout his career. Thus, not surprisingly, once ensconced

in the Presidential Palace, with weak support in Congress and among the political elite, and with little popular enthusiasm for his administration, he gravitated
to the armed forces for support. The army minister, a charismatic general, played
a key role as "tutor" throughout the Sarney government, as did the military
ministers, both in his government and at the head of the country's services.

Many observers were pessimistic that the transition would succeed in extri-
cating the military from politics. That pessimism appeared to be confirmed by
the strong role that the armed forces played during the deliberations of the
Constituent Assembly, which drafted the 1988 Constitution. They were the best
organized lobby in Congress. There were two clusters of interests, which the
armed forces were determined to protect. The first focused on their traditional
"moderating role," which the more populist elements in the assembly wanted
to eliminate. The military ultimately succeeded in protecting that prerogative.
The second was directly related to their patrimonial role. They opposed any
progressive commitment in the document to land reform; there was none at
the end. And they strongly supported a term of five years for Sarney; the populist position was in favor of no more than four years. Sarney received five
years.

Throughout the Sarney years, especially after the dramatic failure of the Cruzado Plan in late 1986, the military symbolized the institutional continuity of
the transition. Even though Sarney was highly unpopular and was generally
viewed as being inept, the military was adamant that the president was to remain
in office until 1990 to preclude new elections and political uncertainty. The
military ministers also made it clear time and again that they defended the
constitution—and the constitution gave them a privileged position in society
that they used without hesitation.

Unnoticed by most people, many developments in the late 1980s were emerging that would modify the traditional role of the military in Brazil. The first was
the combined impact of the election of Fernando Collor de Mello in 1989 and
the strong support he gave to regional economic integration—the common market of the South, Mercosur. The second was the end of the Cold War. And the
third was the arrival in power in 1995 of Fernando Henrique Cardoso, who
promulgated a new national defense doctrine. This policy is still evolving, but
it will nonetheless frame the next phase of civil-military relations and the role
of the armed forces, internally and externally, in the twenty-first century.

COLLOR DE MELLO AND NATIONAL SECURITY

Collor de Mello is best known, during his short, tempestuous administration,
for the bold opening of the Brazilian economy. But he should also be remembered for a number of initiatives that would impact strongly on the role of the
military in Brazil over time.

Collor de Mello continued his predecessor's commitment to regional integration, but he moved to hasten and deepen the process, the end result of which

was the historic *Treaty of Asunción*, signed by Argentina and Brazil in 1991, which laid the foundation for Mercosur, the regional customs union. It also provided a framework for civilian supremacy in regional security issues, though not widely noted at the time. Equally important, Collor made the risky decision to create a new Secretariat of Strategic Issues (SAE) in 1990. The SAE inherited, in part, the duties of the former Council of National Security and the infamous National Information Service (SNI). It was made clear that the role of the SAE was to directly provide advice and guidance for the civilian chief executive in determining Brazil's strategic and military priorities in the 1990s. This move was not popular with the armed forces, but they nevertheless acquiesced. Collor also made it clear that he would not rely on the military high command, as Sarney did, for political support; he also sharply reduced the positions and the role of the military in the Presidential Palace.

In Argentina, President Carlos Menem took office in July 1989 in the midst of a widespread economic crisis. He also confronted dangerous levels of military discontent over charges of human rights violations during Argentina's military regime (1976–1983). Collor de Mello was inaugurated in early 1990 with a similar economic problem and with a similar, yet more benign, expectation on the part of the Brazilian military that it would be expected to continue its tutelary role in the new administration. Both presidents wanted to destroy inflation, which bred social discontent and political instability and, simultaneously, as part of the process of reconstructing civil society, curb the political role of the military. They both agreed that one important mechanism to do so was to further regional integration between the two nations, which were traditional geopolitical rivals from the early days of independence.

Indeed, the adversarial position between the two militaries was a constant in the foreign policy and strategic thinking in both countries. The two new presidents understood that reducing internal instability robbed their militaries of a justification for defensive measures and, in the extreme, offensive military operations against the traditional adversary. One way to accomplish this was to reduce the military budget. Boldly, Menem cut armed forces spending dramatically; there was less to cut in Brazil, but Collor followed suit. As both economies opened, state corporations, in which the militaries had always played an important role for alleged defense purposes, played less of a role. New economic actors, not linked to the old military-civilian establishment, emerged. A free press played an important role in monitoring the commitment to democratic values of the new leadership in both militaries. While Menem's economic experiment was more successful at first than Collor's, there was room for discussion of a new strategic role in the Southern Cone for both countries. And Mercosur provided a justification for a broad range of consultations that would grow to include military meetings and exchanges.

The brief government of Itamar Franco (1992–1995) maintained the general lines of regional integration and cooperation begun under his predecessor. With the success of the Real Plan in 1993–1994, and the emergence of Fernando

Henrique Cardoso as the spokesman for reform in the 1994 campaign, it was possible to begin considering further steps to redefine civil-military relations after the election.

CARDOSO AND THE NATIONAL DEFENSE POLICY (PDN)

With the continued success of his antiinflation program, Cardoso set out in 1995 to address the important issue of civil-military relations in the post–Cold War era. The old justifications for a large and an intrusive military—communism and internal subversion—were irrelevant. But Cardoso was mindful of the important role of the armed forces in Brazilian history, their pride, and the importance of a rethinking of their strategic role at the end of the twentieth century. The SAE was reorganized and given a broad mandate to advise the president on strategic issues; to promote studies and plans and strategic projects, including the areas of economics and ecology; to define strategies of development; and to formulate a national strategic concept and assist in the functioning of the National Defense Council. It was made clear that the SAE was "a civilian organ, which exists and interacts with university professors, military from the three forces, scientists, diplomats, technicians from the Institute of National Economic Planning, etc."[14]

The continued economic and political success of Mercosur, in the context of a new world order after the fall of communism, allowed Brazil and Argentina to move quickly—in historical terms—to end the traditional and expensive rivalry. Speaking to the Argentine Congress in Buenos Aires in 1995, the minister of the SAE defined the bilateral relationship as a "strategic partnership." Two years later, the Rio Declaration formalized that understanding between the two countries and characterized the relationship as a "strategic alliance." That conceptual change—from wary rivals to strategic partners—allowed progress in a number of areas. In June 1997, both countries agreed to subscribe to the Nuclear Non-Proliferation Treaty, the Treaty of Tlatelolco, which guarantees a nuclear-free South America. Furthermore, both countries agreed to conventions that ban both biological and chemical weapons, and a series of strategic meetings were held bilaterally and with their immediate neighbors in the first Cardoso administration. In mid-1997, a Permanent Commission for Coordination was created by the presidents to address mutual defense matters.

In June 1998, President Cardoso signed both the Non-Proliferation Treaty and the Comprehensive Nuclear Test Ban Treaty during a visit to Brasília by UN Secretary General Kofi Annan. At the 14th Summit of the Presidents of Mercosur meeting in Ushuaia, Argentina, in July 1998, the leaders of all of the member countries declared the region a "zone of peace," free of weapons of mass destruction. And in a comparably important decision, the "Protocol of Ushuaia" declared that democracy was an indispensable prerequisite for membership in Mercosur.

Another component of the redefinition of the role of the military in the Southern Cone has been the strong support for participation in peace-keeping missions around the world. Both countries are advocates of this strategy. There is a strong possibility that Brazil will decide to create a new defense ministry to replace the existing separate army, navy, air force, and defense ministries. An important question is whether the president will feel sufficiently confident to appoint a civilian as the first Minister of Defense. Yet, surprisingly, military expenditures in Brazil have trended upward in recent years. In 1985, Brazil spent 0.8 percent of GDP on defense; in 1996, it was 2.1 percent.[15] In 1988, Brazil was ranked thirteenth in world military spending; in 1997, it had risen to tenth place, between Taiwan and South Korea, two countries with undoubtedly more acute security concerns.[16] The military's justification is that there are new challenges that need to be met. It argues that the traditional role of policing and securing frontiers is more complicated with the economic opening that makes borders more fluid and porous and drug trafficking and smuggling very appealing. Yet it is hard to see how the Brazilian military's recent purchases of over approximately 200 Belgian and U.S. tanks will assist in counternarcotics efforts.[17] A more cynical view would claim that Brazil's purchase of highly sophisticated weaponry has as much to do with international prestige than with any security threat. Nevertheless, how the second Cardoso administration deals with these pressures will determine the balance between the civilian government and the armed forces.

Upon reflection on that balance, the Cardoso administration issued a new National Defense Policy (PDN) in late 1996. The new policy has been called

the main innovation in the domain of civil-military relations which besides opening the way to the creation of a Ministry of Defense, serves as a guide for preparing the military in a manner that is attuned to the country's foreign policy. And both are geared to building a new prestige for Brazil in the international arena.[18]

President Cardoso, in his speech announcing the PDN, stated that the new policy was

anchored on a strategic posture that is of a deterring and defensive character, based on the following assumptions: borders and limits that are perfectly defined and internationally recognized; close relations with neighboring countries and with the international community; rejection of wars of conquest; the need to find peaceful solutions to controversies, using force only as a result to self-defense.[19]

There is still some ambivalence within the government about the emerging new role of the armed forces. President Cardoso did use the army to break up a strike by oil workers in order to regain control of oil refineries; the justification was that the strike would interrupt oil and gasoline distribution, incurring hardship for the majority of Brazilians. And in mid-1997, the president ordered the army to intervene in order to quell rebellious military police units, which had refused to follow the orders of the state governor. These events highlight the importance of reexamining the role of the state police and the possibility of creating, at the federal level, a National Guard that would replace army troops in missions involving internal order.

At the beginning of the second Cardoso administration in 1999, the issue of civil-military relations is normal, even quiescent. An important question for our consideration of the patrimonial order is whether the armed forces continue to have the desire for any type of involvement in internal affairs. The army minister, as recently as mid-1994, stated that the army must rise to its historic mission of "maintaining Brazil's unity, sovereignty, and territorial integrity."[20]

Does the maintenance of "unity" mean that a threat to national unity will require a new internal role for the military? The military and the church remain the two most respected institutions in Brazil, according to a 1997 poll by the *Wall Street Journal*—with the politicians in Congress being the least popular. Would an outburst of populism and irresponsible economic policy making require the armed forces to interpret their role in the PDN in favor of intervention? This is an important question. The answer is not clear, but we can assume that the military leadership is aware of this possibility in the future and is prepared, once again, to assume its historic role, if required. While there are few, if any, advocates for military intervention today, the traditional role of the armed forces in Brazil is woven into the fabric of the patrimonial society and, in time of crisis, cannot be overlooked or ignored.

NOTES

1. Thomas E. Skidmore, *The Politics of Military Rule in Brazil, 1964–85* (New York: Oxford University Press, 1988), p. 6.

2. Alfred Stepan, *Rethinking Military Politics: Brazil and the Southern Cone* (Princeton, N.J.: Princeton University Press, 1988), p. xiv.

3. Eliézer Rizzo de Oliveira, "Brazilian National Defense Policy and Civil-Military Relations in the Government of President Fernando Henrique Cardoso," in Donald E. Schulz, ed., *The Role of the Armed Forces in the Americas: Civil-Military Relations for the 21st Century* (Carlisle Barracks, Pa.: Strategic Studies Institute, 1998), p. 32.

4. Alfred Stepan, "Political Leadership and Regime Breakdown in Brazil," in Juan J. Linz and Alfred Stepan, eds., *The Breakdown of Democratic Regimes: Latin America* (Baltimore: Johns Hopkins University Press, 1978), p. 120.

5. June E. Hahner, *Civilian-Military Relations in Brazil, 1889–1898* (Columbia: University of South Carolina Press, 1969), p. 3.

6. Thomas E. Skidmore, *Politics in Brazil, 1930–1964* (New York: Oxford University Press, 1967).

7. Lourival Coutinho, *O General Góes depõe* . . . (Rio de Janeiro: Editora Coelho Branco, 1955), p. 496.

8. Stepan, "Political Leadership and Regime Breakdown in Brazil," p. 176.

9. For an excellent analysis of the Geisel government, see Walker de Goes, *O Brasil do General Geisel* (Rio de Janeiro: Editora Nova Fronteira, 1978).

10. John Humphrey, *Capitalist Control and Workers' Struggle in the Brazilian Auto Industry* (Princeton, N.J.: Princeton University Press, 1982), p. 160.

11. Ibid., p. 176.

12. Ibid., p. 198.

13. For a detailed account of the presidential succession, see Thomas E. Skidmore, *The Politics of Military Rule in Brazil, 1964–1985* (New York: Oxford University Press, 1988).

14. "Actividades da Secretaria de Assuntos Estratégicos (SAE)," *Parcerias Estraté- gicas* 1, no. 3 (June 1997), p. 217.

15. *The Military Balance* (London: The International Institute for Strategic Studies, 1997), p. 296.

16. *The Economist*, June 20, 1998, p. 120.

17. *The Military Balance*, p. 199.

18. Rizzo de Oliveira, "Brazilian National Defense Policy," pp. 33–34.

19. Ibid., p. 34.

20. Ibid., p. 48.

Chapter 5

The Brazilian Economy

The Brazilian economy in the 1990s began to benefit from strong leadership and realistic goals after decades of mismanagement. The new economic program, the Real Plan, which was created during the period in 1993–1994 by Fernando Henrique Cardoso and his team of professional economists, promises to modernize Brazil's financial and economic institutions. While Fernando Collor de Mello deserves credit for initiating the process, only with Cardoso's Real Plan did the appropriate "mix" of economics and politics come together to support sustainable institutional change. Much remains to be done, as we will see in this chapter. But the benefits of the Real Plan are nevertheless apparent to most Brazilians, and its success was in large part the reason for the reelection of President Cardoso in October 1998.

The necessity to do so became extremely urgent in mid-1998 with the dramatic volatility in the financial markets resulting from, first, the Asian currency crises in 1997 and, second, the collapse of the Russian ruble in mid-1998. A "contagion" effect quickly developed, in which reasonably healthy economies were seen by investors to be as weak as their Asian and Russian colleagues. Suddenly, in the summer of 1998, Brazil became the object of intense pressure from international investors who feared a devaluation of the *real*. Hoping to avoid any decisions that would impact negatively on the election outcome, the government postponed sending a package of fiscal reforms to Congress until November. The government also negotiated a support program with the IMF. But Congress refused to approve cost-cutting measures that could prove to be unpopular with the Brazilian public. Early in 1999, Governor Itamar Franco of Minas Gerais, the former president, declared a unilateral moratorium on the repayment of outstanding obligations to the federal government. Franco said that the state administration did not have the funds and that the prior agreement had to be renegotiated. Investors' confidence in the capacity of the Cardoso government to control its fiscal deficits collapsed. The Central Bank was forced to devalue the *real*. That opened a new chapter in the efforts of the government to manage a complex economy in a highly uncertain international setting.

The Real Plan needs to be examined against the recent history of economic development in Brazil. The import-substitution industrialization process of the post-1945 period expanded the role of the state in the economy and justified the accumulation of debt to cover current-account deficits. Economic growth was the highest priority of the Military Republic, installed in 1964. The twin goals of national security and national development required the transformation and modernization of the national economy. Brazil was heralded as a pacesetter in the Third World. Growth rates of more than 10 percent per year, combined with a rapid diversification of exports, impressed most observers. Only with the oil price increase in 1973, and more important, with the second shock in 1979, did the dark side of the miracle become all too apparent. The miracle had helped consolidate a swollen, apparently uncontrollable state sector. International borrowing left Brazil, when the debt crisis erupted in 1982, with the largest debt burden in the Third World. And the social disparities that plagued Brazilian society were aggravated by the military "miracle" as income distribution grew more unequal and poverty increased.[1]

The onset of civilian government offered the hope that there would be a redirection in economic policy. The Sarney administration (1985–1990) boldly announced the Cruzado Plan in early 1986—a heterodox shock program aimed at destroying inflation. A one-year unilateral moratorium on the foreign debt in 1987 severely frayed Brazil's credibility with the international financial community. A series of shock programs to contain inflation in the remaining years of the Sarney government also failed.

The election of Fernando Collor de Mello offered yet another opportunity to redirect the economy. The day following his inauguration, on March 15, 1990, his government promulgated another shock program that confiscated the better part of the nation's savings and undertook other unorthodox measures. While the president then proceeded to attempt to open and liberalize the economy, his plan failed too. By 1992–1993, the Brazilian economy was again imperiled by hyperinflation. With Collor's resignation, President Itamar Franco, lacking any economic expertise, finally moved Fernando Henrique Cardoso from the foreign ministry to the finance post in early 1993. Immediately, the new minister began preparations to announce the most far-reaching economic reform program since the failed Cruzado Plan. The early success in lowering inflation in 1994 provided a winning platform for Cardoso's bid for the presidency late that year. His first term in office (1995–1999) was spent in a valiant effort to reform the 1988 Constitution and thereby open the way for a broad set of modernization measures. Winning some and losing some in the first administration, the Cardoso team found itself in an emergency situation as the October 1998 election approached. When Congress refused to approve the fiscal reform package prepared by the government in late 1998, the situation further deteriorated. And, as in-dicated, the government was forced to devaluate the currency in early 1999.

This chapter provides a summary of the economic development of Brazil, although primary importance will be placed on the performance of the economy since 1964. Emphasis is given to the elements in the patrimonial order that still support the maintenance of outdated economic ideas. We also will explore the challenge posed by Cardoso and the Real Plan to the economic underpinnings of the traditional political elite and its reluctance to support change. Will the deep economic reforms prove to be the battering ram so long absent in previous, failed efforts to capitalize on Brazil's vast resource base? Or will the usual accommodations be possible, both to permit economic reform—imposed in large part by the relentless forces of globalization and competition—and to allow the political elite to remain the dominant force in the changing but enduring patri-monial regime?

EARLY ECONOMIC DEVELOPMENT

Brazil's economic development from the moment of discovery in 1500 to the twentieth century has been characterized by cycles. The first was that of sugar-cane cultivation, which began along the humid Northeastern coast in the 1520s and which firmly linked Brazil to world export markets. The sugar cycle required manpower not available in Portugal's new colony, and African slaves became the principal workers on the rich sugar plantations. Indeed, the *casa grande e senzala* (manor house and slave quarters) became the dominant symbols of Bra-zil's early history and the title of a famous book by Brazilian sociologist Gilberto Freyre.[2] Sugar exports created a wealthy, pampered plantation class and proved quite profitable for the mother country.

By the middle of the seventeenth century, the sugar boom had faded. Com-petition from the British, Dutch, and French colonies crowded out Brazilian production. While sugar did not disappear as an export crop in Brazil, it would never regain its earlier importance. Even so, its economic and social imprint is felt today. Many of the large landed estates continue to function, technologically backward and uncompetitive. The sugar estates help perpetuate a poor agricul-tural working class in an area of few other economic opportunities and reinforce a tradition of master–servant relations that precludes millions of citizens from being integrated into modern Brazil.

The second important cycle centered on the gold and diamond mines of what is now the state of Minas Gerais (general mines) in the Southeast. Gold mining began in the late 1600s and flourished well into the late 1700s, when Brazil accounted for about half of the world's gold production. The opportunities in the mining region attracted new settlers from all over Brazil and Europe. The mines stimulated subsidiary economic activity in agriculture and artisanry. Min-ing exports required a port, and Rio de Janeiro flourished in the seventeenth century as the shipping capital of the general mines region. The city would

become the capital of the colony in 1763 in recognition of its economic importance, as well as its value as a military base providing protection against other
European powers interested in Brazil.

By the end of the eighteenth century, mining had been exhausted. The end
of the colonial period was characterized by a minor boom in cotton and sugar
exports. Still a primitive economy by the early nineteenth century, Brazil underwent more rapid economic diversification with the arrival of the British and
the incorporation of Brazil into that country's mercantilism empire. Portugal,
long an economic and a diplomatic dependent of England, lost all control over
Brazil with the latter's independence in 1822. England quickly saw the advantages of a preferential place in Brazil's economic growth. British mercantilism
coincided with the emergence of a third and very significant cycle: coffee. From
modest beginnings in the early 1800s, it quickly grew to dominate Brazilian
exports, accounting for more than 60 percent of total exports by the end of the
nineteenth century.

Coffee plantations flourished in the areas north and west of Rio de Janeiro,
principally in the Paraíba Valley, until the 1870s, when the state of São Paulo
emerged as the coffee king of Brazil. With the arrival of the railroads in the
1860s, production was further stimulated. The abolition of slavery in 1888 attracted hundreds of thousands of European immigrants, many of whom went
directly to work on the coffee plantations.

Coffee cultivation concentrated wealth. The São Paulo planters quickly
emerged as the economic, social, and political leaders of republican Brazil. In
the absence of a tradition of small independent farmers, characteristic of the
United States, large landed estates dominated Brazil—first the sugar plantations
of the Northeast, then the coffee lands of São Paulo state.[3]

Early intermittent efforts at industrialization in the nineteenth century were
overwhelmed by the emphasis on export crops and the privileged position of
English manufactures in the Brazilian marketplace.[4] Only the textile industry
made any significant headway in the nineteenth and early twentieth centuries.
Between 1885 and 1905, cotton textile production increased about 10 times and
doubled again in the following decade. Textiles, combined with clothing, shoes,
and the food processing industries, made up 57 percent of the country's industrial production prior to World War I and more than 60 percent by 1920. This
early industrial growth was directly linked to the coffee economy. Coffee fortunes were invested in industrial operations. Immigrant families provided the
beginnings of a mass market for domestic products. Early infrastructure—railroads and power—stimulated local industry. In spite of these developments,
Brazil's economic profile in the 1920s had changed very little. Coffee accounted
for about 75 percent of national exports by the middle of the decade.

The depression of the 1930s led to a drastic curtailment of imports. Consumer
demand was maintained, in part, by the government's coffee support programs,
which bought coffee and destroyed whatever could not be sold or stored, thereby
stabilizing farm income and providing continued purchasing power for many

Brazilians. This artificial domestic demand stimulated early import-substitution industrialization in consumer goods production.

World War II introduced a period of increased output but not increased productive capacity. Little capital formation took place during this period, since capital goods were not available from traditional sources that were involved in the war effort. By 1945, Brazil's incipient industrial plant was fast approaching obsolescence. Werner Baer has accurately characterized the period prior to 1930 as one of industrial growth and not industrialization:

[Industrial growth] characterizes events until the end of the 1920s, during which time the growth of industry deepened mostly on agricultural exports, the leading sector. Also, despite the rapid growth of some industries, such a period of industrial growth is not accompanied by drastic structural changes in the economy. Industrialization, on the other hand, is present when industry becomes the leading growth sector of the economy and causes pronounced structural changes.[5]

During the depression years of the 1930s, Brazil entered a process of import-substitution industrialization. Unable to purchase needed manufactures abroad, a native industrial plant began to grow. By the end of the decade, Brazil was close to self-sufficiency in consumer goods, and it manufactured more than 80 percent of needed intermediate goods. Brazil's first efforts at economic planning also took place during the 1930s. A report by Otto Niemeyer in 1931 indicated the dependence of the Brazilian economy on the exportation of a few crops. The Cooke Mission visited Brazil in 1942 and 1943 and made a number of suggestions about priority areas of development, emphasizing the Southeast as the area best suited for rapid growth in the years ahead.[6]

POSTWAR ECONOMIC GROWTH

The Brazilian economy in 1945 was a simple one. Foreign trade was dominated by coffee, cocoa, sugar, cotton, and tobacco, exported primarily to United States and western European markets. The postwar prospects were not good for the Brazilian economy. Compared to manufactured exports worldwide, primary product exports were growing slowly. Moreover, Brazil's share in the world market dropped because of a policy of maintaining high prices for coffee, the country's main export, and increasing competition from agricultural producers elsewhere.

It soon became apparent that an alternative economic strategy was needed. Slowly, from 1945 to the mid-1950s, elements of an overall industrial plan evolved. Imports of capital goods increased dramatically immediately after the war, as Brazil used the reserves it had accumulated during the war to replace its aging physical plant. These reserves were quickly exhausted, however, and foreign-exchange controls were introduced to cope with the negative balance of payments. Government directives gradually came to favor those imports needed to create an industrial base. The amount of capital goods against consumer goods increased. In 1953, multiple exchange rates were introduced and, again, capital goods were favored. New legislation offered protection to new industrial enterprises. Foreign direct investment was encouraged. These policies were reinforced by a rigorous application of the "Law of Similars," which gave Brazilian firms preference over foreign firms in producing items for the domestic market.

A planning mentality accompanied government directives after 1945. Each government produced an overall economic development plan that intermittently served to guide investments and establish priorities. This process was aided by the work of the Joint Brazil–United States Economic Commission from 1951 to 1953. While the change of administrations in the United States following the election of Dwight Eisenhower in late 1952 mitigated the implementation of any lasting plan, one important by-product of this planning mentality was the creation of Brazil's National Bank for Economic Development. Contacts with the United States Economic Commission for Latin America in the mid-1950s exposed a generation of planners and economists to the then-prevailing doctrines of the commission. Of highest priority was rapid economic growth with a substantial role for the state as the engine of growth. The goal became an intrinsic part of the government of President Juscelino Kubitschek (1956–1961), who promised Brazil "Fifty Years of Progress in Five."

Kubitschek's planners emphasized energy, transportation, food supply, basic industries, and education. Bottlenecks to development were to be removed. Brazilians were to be trained to be efficient, modern industrial workers. Unnecessary imports were curtailed, and efforts were undertaken to diversify Brazil's exports. The Kubitschek government stimulated basic industrial production through programs of incentives for producers and investors. Brazil made impressive industrial gains in the 1950s but neglected important areas of the economy, such as agriculture. Inflation, which increased dangerously in the early 1960s, threatened the earlier gains. Rapid urban migration placed a strain on food production. A backward transportation system increased the cost of supplying the growing cities. New farm production came not from new investment and technology but from incorporating new lands into production.

Inflation and agricultural bottlenecks were accompanied by increasingly obvious social inequities in the Brazilian development model. Income distribution remained heavily unfavorable for the poor. Education and social services were of inferior quality. Balance-of-payments problems escalated, and Brazil's foreign debt grew. The import-substitution policies of the 1950s had neglected export promotion and diversification almost entirely. State enterprises had proliferated during the years following World War II, and they often became sinecures for overpaid and underworked state employees. While industry had come into its own in the 1950s as a priority goal of the government, it had not served to generate significant numbers of new jobs for entrants into the labor force.

Finally, these economic distortions and lags in the economy led to increasing social tension and political instability during the governments of Quadros (1961) and Goulart (1961–1964).[7] The failure to introduce basic social and political change in Brazilian society and the growing polarization of political opinion made sound and balanced economic decision making difficult, if not impossible. As the Goulart government attempted to appease its urban populist following with wage increases and efforts to hold down basic food prices, the landowners, industrialists, and more traditional elements of society began to withdraw their political support. Economic stagnation and widespread social malaise culminated in the Revolution of March 31, 1964.

While these distortions in Brazilian society and the economy were real, it should not be forgotten that the post-1945 period was one of important industrial expansion:

In the two decades following the War, Brazil experienced a very substantial process of import-substituting industrialization. From 1945 to 1962 industry grew at an average rate of 8.0 percent p.a. Industrial output grew nearly four times, and the share of industry in GDP increased from 20 percent to about 26 percent. Also, the ratio of manufactured imports to total supply of manufactured products dropped from 14 percent in 1945 to only 6 percent in 1964.[8]

So while a failure in regard to social development, the post-1945 progress did provide an essential platform on which the post-1964 program of economic growth could be constructed.

ECONOMIC PERFORMANCE DURING THE MILITARY REPUBLIC

The Castello Branco government (1964–1967) quickly moved to implement a stabilization program to correct the internal and external disequilibria of the postwar period. The expectation was that a draconian program of stabilization would yield high growth rates by the end of the decade.

The economic reforms, led by Planning Minister Roberto Campos and Finance Minister Octávio Bulhões, worked. While the years 1964–1967 had low rates of GDP growth (an average of 3.9 percent per annum) and of industrial expansion (3.6 percent per annum), inflation began to drop—from 87 percent in 1964 to 27 percent in 1967.[9] With the direction of economic affairs in the hands of Antonio Delfim Netto after 1967, and using the Campos–Bulhões stabilization program as a foundation, manufacturing grew impressively from 1967 to 1973, at an average rate of 12.9 percent per annum. The share of industry in GDP, which had remained constant at 26 percent between 1960 and 1967, jumped to 30 percent in 1972. Overall, the GDP grew at an average annual rate of about 11.5 percent, while the industry sector and the manufacturing industries expanded at rates of 13.2 percent and 13.9 percent, respectively.

The international environment—a period of rapid economic growth in the industrial world that opened markets for Brazilian exports—helped the industrialization strategy of the Military Republic. Total exports increased from $1.9 billion in 1968 to $6.2 billion in 1973, while manufacturing exports grew from $0.4 billion to $2.0 billion, reaching average annual growth rates of about 27 percent and 38 percent, respectively. As a result, the share of manufactured exports in total exports grew from 20.3 percent in 1968 to 32.4 percent in 1973. During the same time period, the share of total exports in GDP rose from 5.2 percent to 7.6 percent.

Brazil's economic expansion was directly related to higher levels of capital investment. Much of that investment came from state company expenditures, but a significant contribution was made by foreign capital. In Brazil, total investment in manufacturing increased by nearly four times between 1970 and 1979, growing at an average annual rate of about 15.5 percent in real terms. Significantly, the distribution of investment was highly concentrated in a small number of industries. The share of total investment of metallurgy, transport equipment, and chemical products added up to 47.3 percent in 1969, 62.2 percent in 1975, and 63.5 percent in 1979.

While foreign firms have a share in the assets of nearly all manufacturing activities, most have shown a decrease since the early 1980s. The increasing share held by private domestic firms is the result of specific measures adopted by the government in order to limit the increase of foreign participation in the economy. Summarizing the economic policy goals of the Military Republic, Werner Baer writes:

It was the vision of the new regime established in 1964 that the path of economic recovery lay in the control of inflation, the elimination of price distortions that had accumulated during the past, the modernization of capital markets that would lead to an increased accumulation of savings, the creation of a system of incentives to direct investments into areas and sectors deemed essential by the government, the attraction of foreign capital (both private and official) to finance the expansion of the country's productive capacity, and the use of public investment in infrastructural projects and in certain government owned heavy industries.[10]

To a remarkable degree, between 1964 and 1973, the government achieved many of these goals. Financial markets were reformed; there was a steady decline in the government budget deficit; a new capital market law increased the use of the stock market; and tax incentives were employed to influence the allocation of resources among regions and sectors given priority by the government. Infrastructure projects were begun, and a program to diversify Brazil's exports was undertaken.

The 1973 Oil Shock

As a result of the Arab–Israeli conflict in 1973, world oil prices rose precipitously in 1973–1974. Brazil, which imported more than 80 percent of its petroleum needs, was highly vulnerable. The new government of President Ernesto Geisel (1974–1979) had a long, complicated agenda it wished to accomplish during its five years in office. Of highest priority was the process of *abertura* (political liberalization). Also of importance was an increase in the standard of living of the working class, which had been deliberately suppressed in the preceding decade to finance the rapid diversification of the economy through forced savings and holding down real wages in the industrial sector. The introduction of measures that would slow the economy was unacceptable to the Geisel administration. The government decided to maintain the ambitious—and expensive—development goals of the Second National Development Plan (1975–1979), released in September 1974.

Within a year, it became clear that the financial burden of the import bill was growing rapidly. From 1973 to 1974, Brazil's import bill rose from $5.2 billion to $12.6 billion. The only way to meet Brazil's import expenses, from the government's perspective, was to borrow abroad. Eurodollars were plentiful in this period. Demand for loans was low in the industrial countries because of the oil-induced recession. By the end of 1977, Brazil's net debt had risen to $32 billion. Debt servicing required 51.2 percent of that year's exports. Few observers pointed out that 72 percent of the debt accumulated by the end of 1977 would be repayable by 1982.

The government took a lenient stand with regard to industrial pressure to raise prices in response to rising production costs that were linked to energy and labor costs. While price controls were in force throughout the 1970s, the enforcement agencies were lenient in allowing increased costs to be passed along through price adjustments. By the late 1970s, the government faced a serious inflationary spiral.

The government's interest in high levels of investment in public projects was an important factor, as were rising wages. The government's unwillingness to force the private sector to absorb increased costs further fueled inflation. The growing inflation also was fed by the indexation system in effect since the mid-1960s.

In spite of increasing inflation and the general decline in world economic conditions, the Brazilian economy had performed quite well during the 1970s.

In 1979, manufacturing accounted for 28.0 percent of Brazilian GDP, up from 26 percent in 1960, and the overall industrial sector accounted for 38 percent of GDP. These are very high figures for developing and industrialized countries' standards alike, reflecting a very advanced stage of industrialization of the economy. Brazil's share of manufacturing in GDP is only exceeded by 5 and equaled by 2 of the 76 developing countries for which data are presented in the 1981 World Development Report. Even more noticeable, only 4 of the 18 industrialized countries exceed Brazil's share of manufacturing in GDP.[11]

This was an impressive performance indeed. Equally important, in terms of the overall process of development, the share of industrial sector employment among the economically active population increased from 12.9 percent in 1960 to 23.2 percent in 1976. During this period, manufacturing was the main source of employment within the industrial sector; its share among the economically active population increased from 8.6 percent to 15.0 percent.

The Figueiredo Government

President Geisel's handpicked successor, General João Figueiredo, assumed the presidency on March 15, 1979. Mario Henrique Simonsen, Geisel's finance minister, received the position of planning minister; Antonio Delfim Netto, who had spent the Geisel years as Brazilian ambassador to France, was appointed agriculture minister.

There was a sense of both crisis and expectation surrounding the presidential inauguration. Figueiredo had promised to continue—indeed, to consolidate— the political liberalization process. At the same time, he had to address the challenges of an overheating economy and rising social expectations. Brazil's unions were striking for the first time since 1964. By 1979, servicing the foreign debt absorbed about 67 percent of export earnings. It was more frequently asked whether Brazil's productive capacity was to be totally subordinated to the private commercial banks and the outstanding foreign debt.

The government chose an uncertain economic course. Simonsen appeared to favor belt-tightening, but he was replaced by Delfim Netto in August 1979, who entered the Planning Ministry arguing that Brazil could grow out of its current difficulties. Ernane Galvêas, a former colleague of Delfim Netto, was named finance minister. By December 1979, Delfim Netto and his economic team realized that the growth-led model, so successful in the late 1960s, was not going to work a decade later. Suddenly, amid shrinking confidence in the government's plan, the economic leadership announced a "package" that, they argued, would solve Brazil's economic problems.

With hindsight, it is clear that 1980 was the year in which the economy began to unravel. The decisions made by the government in late 1979 and early 1980 were aimed at encouraging savings and exports and squeezing consumption and imports; they accomplished exactly the reverse. Brazilians did not believe the projected inflation figure of 45 percent (indeed, the figure would rise to 110 percent by the end of 1980), and they refused to save with an indexation of only 45 percent. Instead, they decided to spend whatever they had: land values soared, Rio stock market prices doubled in six months, and sales of household appliances rose by 21 percent in real terms during the 12 months ending in July 1980. The country's savings, which had averaged 20.2 percent of GDP during the period 1974–1978, fell to 16.9 percent in 1980.

By the end of 1980, Delfim Netto again changed course. The new measures led Brazil into a severe recession, of which 1983 was the third year. The prime goals of the government, since 1981, had been the control of inflation and the balance-of-payments deficit. The government was finally willing to concede that low or no growth was necessary to regain control of the inflationary economy.

THE BRAZILIAN DEBT CRISIS

Brazil's debt crisis did not occur in a vacuum.[12] The global economic recession that began in 1979 with the second oil price rise had severe implications for the Third World countries. World demand for Third World products fell drastically; commodity prices declined; high interest rates made borrowing expensive; and private commercial banks in the United States, western Europe, and Japan became increasingly reluctant to lend Third World countries more money.

In Latin America, Mexico and Argentina were clearly in serious difficulty by early 1982. The crisis erupted in the summer of 1982, when Mexico announced that it could not pay its outstanding bills. An emergency package was hastily put together by the private banks with the participation of the IMF and the U.S. government. Negotiations with Argentina were longer and more difficult. By the time private bankers and international banking officials gathered in Toronto in September for the meetings of the World Bank and the IMF, there was growing concern that a generalized debt crisis was emerging.

In September 1982, Brazil determined that it needed $3.6 billion in new loans to close its balance-of-payments gap in December 1982. It soon became obvious, given the mood in Toronto, that the money would not be forthcoming. The Brazilian situation was desperate, and the government had resorted to short-term loans and to drawing down its reserves in order to pay its bills. The short-term debt had risen from $8 billion at the end of 1981 to more than $14 billion in 1982; reserves had dropped from $7.5 billion to less than $3 billion. Brazil had hoped to demonstrate its creditworthiness to the world's bankers with a trade surplus in 1982 of $3 billion; world economic conditions allowed a surplus of less than $800 million.

As it became clear that new money was not readily available from the private commercial banks, Brazil faced the reality of having to enter into negotiations with the IMF to receive its approval for a Brazilian austerity program that would convince the private banks to resume lending. In late November and early December 1982, a number of important initiatives were undertaken. In a dramatic announcement during his trip to Brazil, President Ronald Reagan announced a $1.23 billion emergency loan to Brazil and expressed confidence in Brazil's capacity to manage its financial affairs. In addition, six private commercial banks in the United States agreed to lend Brazil $600 million. Finally, in mid-December, the industrialized countries' central banks approved a $1.23 billion emergency credit through the Bank for International Settlements in Basel. This loan decision was made in anticipation of a major loan by the IMF, which would be granted after careful negotiations with the government of Brazil. The IMF loan would be made conditional on the willingness of the 1,400 private commercial banks with outstanding loans in Brazil to continue lending.

There is little doubt that Brazil's financial situation was deeply affected by the private commercial banks' view of Mexico and Argentina. Prior to the crisis of mid-1982, Brazil had been borrowing about $17 billion each year in new money from the commercial banks for new projects and to meet payments on the existing debt. Before 1982, the private banks had gladly loaned Brazil additional funds. The country had a sound reputation and a solid record of performance in managing its financial affairs and in generating foreign exchange through exports. As the world economic climate deteriorated in 1981–1982, and as Mexico and Argentina created a panic mentality within the private banks, Brazil suffered.

Negotiations with the IMF were concluded in mid-December 1982 in Brasília. A $4.9 billion standby loan from the IMF was announced—if the private banks agreed to continue lending. In exchange for the financial support of the IMF and the banks, Brazil agreed to an austerity program.

At a dramatic meeting at the Plaza Hotel in New York City on December 20, 1982, the Brazilian economic team, in the presence of the IMF's managing director, announced the new program. A few days earlier, the IMF had accepted Brazil's letter of intent, which outlined these austerity measures. The IMF had made it clear that its financial support was contingent on the private banks' decision to continue lending. The Plaza Hotel meeting was meant to emphasize that understanding and to create the appropriate atmosphere for the new lending.

The plan that was presented to the banks called for a total of $9.6 billion for Brazil in 1983. By the time of the meeting, it was clear that Brazil's debt would soon add up to more than $90 billion, the largest of the Third World countries. The U.S. banks were particularly worried, because they held more than one-third of Brazil's debt.

By February 1983, it was clear that the December 1982 package was in trouble. The December 31, 1982, deadline for compliance had come and gone. A second call by the managing director of the IMF had not produced any significant results. The stumbling block was the fourth part of the package which, unlike the first three parts, required the approval of the smaller banks. They had little confidence in Brazil and refused to renew or increase lines of credit.

Brazil faced a dilemma. The IMF had stated that it would not approve its financial aid program until the private bankers agreed to provide continuing support. Moreover, the emergency loans of late 1982 were to be repaid from the IMF loan. Bankers began to realize in February 1983 that Brazil would need more money in 1983 and 1984 than it had requested. Failure to come to agreement on the December 1982 package would erode confidence in the way the private banks and the IMF had been cooperating.

Key to agreement with the banks was a large trade surplus that would earn the foreign exchange needed to service the outstanding debt. It became obvious to the government in early 1983 that the anticipated trade account improvement would not materialize without a swift change in incentives to export. Speculation against the cruzeiro was evident, in that export deliveries slowed and the surrender of export receipts was delayed. Consequently, the government decided in late February 1983 to devalue the currency by 30 percent against the dollar and to maintain the beneficial effect of this adjustment through further depreciation. Brazil's non-oil exports increased by 10 percent that year. Non-oil imports fell by 21 percent, precisely as much as planned.

In partial response to the devaluation and aware of the significance of Brazil to the international economic system, in March 1983, the IMF agreed to a $5.4 billion, three-year package. Brazil and the private banks also renewed their agreement on the first two of the four segments of the December 1982 proposal. The combined resources of the IMF and the banks amounted to the largest international rescue package yet put together for any Third World nation.

The cautious optimism of March had disappeared by May. The private banks and the IMF announced that the next disbursement, scheduled for May 31, would be withheld because the Brazilian government had not met the targets established for cutting spending. Brazil responded that higher than expected inflation had made it impossible to decrease the public deficit. The situation was made worse by the fact that Brazil was estimated to be more than $1 billion in arrears on scheduled payments on its existing debt.

By June, it was clear that the December 1982 program had failed. Moreover, the goal of achieving a $6 billion trade surplus was going to come not from new exports but from cutting needed imports. Indeed, during the first six months of 1983, exports rose only 6 percent in dollar terms, compared to the same period in 1982. The value of exports of industrial goods, Brazil's fastest-growing exports in recent years, declined. Imports (apart from oil) fell by nearly 30 percent in dollar terms in the first six months of 1983 from their level a year earlier. Brazilian businessmen began to express their concern that if the squeeze continued, bankruptcies would grow alarmingly, and the industrial base of the country would be severely eroded.

Negotiations opened among the IMF, the private banks, and Brazil in the summer of 1983. Meanwhile, pressure on the Brazilian government from domestic political and business groups to declare a moratorium increased. Members of the opposition parties, the government party, bankers, and independent businessmen urged the government to stop payments on outstanding debt.

Immediately before leaving Brazil for open-heart surgery in the United States, President João Figueiredo accepted the arguments of his economic ministers and convened a meeting of the National Security Council on July 31. Brazil was informed of a new law to be submitted to Congress that would restrict salary increases for the next two years to a level of 20 percent below the official cost-of-living figure. This action, Decree-Law 2045, was not subject to amendment by Congress and entered into effect immediately. Other steps were taken to respond to IMF conditions, including measures to control internal interest rates, rents, and new housing loans. It was not unnoticed that the president chose the

Security Council, which includes all military and civilian ministers, as the mechanism for the announcement. Clearly, widespread consultation within the Brazilian government had preceded the decision, and the armed forces were signaling that they supported the president's decision.

In August, Planning Minister Delfim Netto announced that Brazil had suspended payments on an estimated $7 billion to $8 billion of outstanding government-to-government debt, pending the outcome of its negotiations with the Paris Club, an informal group of Western creditor nations, on the rescheduling of amounts due in 1983 and 1984, estimated at $1.8 billion.

Shortly after an agreement was reached on a new letter of intent with the IMF, Brazilian political circles were shocked by the sudden resignation in early September of Central Bank President Carlos Geraldo Langoni, who refused to accept the austerity measures demanded by the IMF in its negotiations with the government. Langoni was replaced by the former secretary of finance of the state of São Paulo, Affonso Celso Pastore, a close associate of Planning Minister Delfim Netto. The IMF and Brazil then proceeded to agree on the conditions of the letter of intent, the most notable of which were bringing inflation down to 55 percent (from an estimated 200 percent in late 1983) by the end of 1984 and eliminating the public deficit by the end of 1984. In addition, the government pledged itself to the wage reductions imposed in July.

The year 1984 was good for the Brazilian economy. The trade surplus was high: $13.1 billion. Negotiations continued on rescheduling the debt, and Central Bank President Pastore appeared to achieve a breakthrough in the talks in early 1985 by agreeing to a 16-year rescheduling of some $54 billion of debt to mature during the period 1985–1991. It was widely understood that the agreement had the tacit blessing of the incoming government. The agreement would have spread the payments due up to 1991 over a 16-year period. The deal collapsed, however, when the IMF suddenly suspended its three-year, $4 billion program with Brazil. The IMF pointed to a flagrant breach of monetary targets, which had been agreed to by the Figueiredo government when it had negotiated the 1983 standby agreement with the IMF.

To many in the new civilian government, the collapse of the earlier negotiations was a blessing in disguise. The absence of a tough, formal IMF program in 1985 allowed the Sarney team to sort out its priorities and maintain its commitment to economic growth. After four years of austerity, the first civilian government since 1964 did not want to continue a program of economic recession merely to satisfy the country's foreign creditors and the international financial community. The initial months of the new government—during which President-elect Tancredo Neves died in April after a long illness—witnessed a struggle. On one side, Planning Minister João Sayad argued for growth with, if necessary, inflation; on the other, Neves's nephew, Finance Minister Francisco Dornelles, was committed to a program of orthodox adjustment and cooperation with the IMF.

President Sarney appointed a young university economist as his personal economic advisor. Luis Paulo Rosenberg would take the lead on debt negotiations and relations with the IMF. Negotiations with the advisory committee of commercial banks led that group to recommend in August that the remaining creditor institutions extend a freeze on the repayment of principal due in 1985 until January 17, 1986. The action was taken to give the talks with the IMF more time. The banks also decided to propose a third extension of $16 billion of interbank lines and trade facilities that were due to expire on August 31.

Suddenly, Sarney responded to the Sayad–Dornelles impasse over economic strategy. In late August, he dismissed Dornelles and the Central Bank president. The new finance minister was São Paulo businessman Dilson Funaro, then serving as president of the powerful National Democratic Bank. Fernão Bracher, an experienced veteran of economic policy making, was chosen to head the Central Bank. Funaro shared the Sayad position—growth over austerity—and he was known to take a jaundiced view of the IMF demand for adjustment. The new image was strengthened with the release of a ''Green Paper'' by the Planning Ministry that month, which argued that the greatest threat to national security was poverty, not subversion, and that the efforts of the Sarney government would be directed at raising the living standard of the majority of the population.

At the joint annual meeting of the IMF and the World Bank in Seoul, South Korea, in October 1985, U.S. Secretary of the Treasury James Baker announced the new U.S. initiative on debt that would become known as the Baker Plan. It called for continued adjustment efforts by the debtors and increased lending by both the commercial banks and the multilateral financial institutions. The Brazilian delegation, skeptical of the initiative, stated that it would seek an agreement with the creditor banks without an IMF austerity program—although it would welcome the ''approval'' of the IMF. The Brazilian position was that the economy was growing, reserves were increasing, and the trade surplus that year would be large—it appeared to be bargaining from a position of strength.

In December, Brazil reopened talks with its creditors in New York City. The delegation made it clear that it would not seek a standby loan from the IMF prior to reaching an agreement with the banks. As the negotiations carried over into early 1986, the Brazilians were euphoric. The 1985 trade surplus was $12.45 billion, the third largest in the world after Japan and West Germany. The country had grown at 8 percent in 1985, the highest growth rate in the world. Brazil was current on its interest payments to both the multilaterals and the commercial banks, but average inflation had reached 230 percent, and the public sector deficit was escalating dangerously.

THE CRUZADO PLAN

Committed to a policy of growth and distribution, the Brazilian economy in 1986 remained a prisoner of high inflation and a large public deficit. The Funaro team had begun to examine the issue of economic reform after taking office in 1985. Slowly, within the inner circle of the minister, there emerged a consensus to adopt an untried strategy—a "heterodox" shock package, not an orthodox one, as expected by the IMF. The concept was to destroy inflation, and in so doing, to consolidate the new democratic process. The team assumed that a sudden attack on the root causes of inflation would have widespread popular support, which proved to be correct in the early phase of the new plan.

By early 1986, high inflation rates had begun to erode the unity of the democratic coalition that had led the return to democracy. Unions were concerned about wages. The political Left had begun to grow in popularity as it called for more aggressive, populist measures to protect the working class. The Sarney inner circle took a deliberately political decision to confront inflation with an untried and unorthodox adjustment program that included:

• an across-the-board freeze on most retail and wholesale prices and utility rates;

• reform of Brazil's currency, with the new cruzado replacing the cruzeiro at 1:1,000 ratio;

• automatic salary increases whenever the yearly inflation rate surpassed 20 percent; and

• the fixing of a "stable" foreign exchange rate of 13.8 cruzados to 1 U.S. dollar.

The program worked, politically and economically, for a few months. Brazilian citizens took to the streets to check on prices and turned in to the police those found in violation of the price freeze. Consumer purchasing rapidly expanded in an inflation-free environment. The popularity of President Sarney, Minister Funaro, and the government skyrocketed; the Brazilian people believed that the new democratic regime had found a magic formula to eliminate inflation and financial uncertainty from the Brazilian economy.

The immediate results were impressive. The monthly inflation rate, as measured by the general price index, declined from +22 percent in February 1986 to −1 percent in March, rose to +.06 percent in April, declined to +0.3 percent in May, and rose to +0.5 percent in June. Meanwhile, economic activity accelerated rapidly. Real wages rose dramatically. Then, the warning signs appeared. The plan had eliminated the price mechanism as an allocator of resources. The longer the freeze lasted, the more serious the market distortions became.

While the authors of the Cruzado Plan agreed that the price freeze would have to be temporary, there was no consensus about how long it should last, since they could not predict how long it would take to reverse inflationary expectations. But as time passed, politics dominated economics. The popularity of Sarney, and of the plan, blinded the government to the need to make adjustments. The government calculus was that they would win the November 1986 congressional and gubernatorial elections with a large majority if they maintained the price freeze.

Predictably, there were widespread efforts to circumvent the freeze. Price-control evasion grew rapidly. Products of all kinds were suddenly in short supply, and long lines formed at the markets. Foodstuffs were scarce, as lower-income groups increased demand while producers reduced supply. To avoid raising prices, the government imported food and, by cutting some taxes and increasing subsidies, managed to increase supply. But the result was a soaring public deficit.

The Cruzado Plan was marked by rapid, excessive growth, much of it based on consumer spending. The public deficit was not trimmed, which might have been politically possible, given the overall popularity of the plan. Relatively low interest rates contributed to the overheating of the economy. The exchange rate was kept fixed far too long—the sharp increase in domestic demand and the de facto, if not fully measured, inflation after mid-March meant that the cruzado was increasingly overvalued. Clearly, the government resisted devaluation for so long because it feared reviving the inflation-devaluation-inflation cycle of the past.

In July, the government made a halfhearted effort to cope with some of the accumulated problems. Monetary policy was tightened. A 25 percent tax on international travel was imposed, and a compulsory savings scheme was put into effect. The goal of the "little Cruzado Plan" was to cool aggregate demand, capture savings, and promote investments. By mid-1986, the crisis was obvious in the external accounts. Net direct foreign investment fell sharply. Profit remittances and capital flight rose, one apparent sign of which was the rising "parallel" exchange market premium. Reserves plummeted.

The elections of November 15 gave the government and its supporters a tremendous victory, and the PMDB and PFL emerged as the big winners. Immediately after the elections, the government announced another dramatic adjustment program: Cruzado II. Its focus was a sharp realignment of "middle-class" consumer products and increases in taxes on them. Suddenly, a new reality emerged, and Brazilians discovered that the Sarney government had no magic formula to destroy inflation.

As a result of the new program, inflation revived. Wages rose, as the automatic trigger mechanism began to function. In the following months, inflation exploded and reached 25 percent in May 1987; by the middle of the year, the yearly inflation rate was well over 1,000 percent. Annualized short-term interest rates reached nearly 2,000 percent in early June. Even more significant, the international reserve position of the country had collapsed earlier in the year. The government had declared a unilateral moratorium on debt payments on February 20, 1987.[13]

THE DEBT MORATORIUM

Brazil, in March 1986, had reached an agreement with the private commercial banks to reschedule unpaid 1985 maturities and to roll over 1986 maturities into 1987. It had suspended debt service to the Paris Club creditors from June 1985 through April 1986; since the Paris Club refused to consider a multiyear rescheduling without an IMF agreement, relations worsened. In May 1986, at the height of euphoria about the Cruzado Plan, the Brazilian government resumed interest payments on its Paris Club debt. In January 1987, after the collapse of the plan, it received a rescheduling agreement from the Paris Club, with a promise to "enhance contacts" with the IMF. This meant that Brazil had to accept a series of IMF missions—contradicting the policy established in March 1985.

The unilateral moratorium of February 20 shocked the international financial community. The fear that the Brazilian decision would initiate a widespread default on outstanding debt in the Third World terrified the bankers. Obviously, Brazil hoped for a sign of solidarity, but its neighbors in Latin America, and its allies in the developing world, chose to ignore the old gesture. Other countries decided to continue "muddling through" negotiations with the banks. Planning Minister João Sayad resigned in March 1987, when it became clear that neither President Sarney nor Minister Funaro would accept his antiinflationary ideas.

THE BRESSER PLAN

Finally, in the face of almost unanimous criticism, Sarney named Luiz Carlos Bresser Pereira as the new finance minister in late April 1987. On his second day in office, he devalued the cruzado by 7.6 percent, over and above its established, regular daily devaluation. The devaluation was designed to boost the trade surplus, which had begun to lag badly. He indicated that he, too, would try a shock program, and on June 12, he announced the "Macroeconomic Consistency Plan," which froze prices for a maximum of three months, froze wages, and canceled the trigger mechanism for automatic wage increases. The new minister indicated that the government was willing to open conversations with the IMF.

But Bresser Pereira's plan failed too. With inflation again roaring out of control, he resigned in late December 1987. A principal reason was the public-sector deficit, estimated at close to 7 percent of the gross domestic product that year. Bresser's failure to reduce the deficit was directly related to President Sarney's need to use the public sector to supply jobs to members of Congress who were considering the length of his term of office. The Constituent Assembly, which had begun deliberations in early 1987, was at a crucial point, and the president's political fate hung in the balance. It was easier for him to lose his finance minister, and the hope of controlling inflation, than to risk seeing his term limited to four years, rather than the five-year term he wanted. Since his popularity was at an all-time low after the failure of the Cruzado Plan, the president needed to appease as many members of Congress as possible.

ANOTHER FINANCE MINISTER

Bresser Pereira was replaced by Maílson Ferreira da Nóbrega, the deputy finance minister; he was the fourth finance minister since March 1985. Maílson, as he was called in the press, stated that he would address the key issue of inflation—and seek a quick agreement with Brazil's foreign creditors. In April 1988, the new economic team revealed its plan. The third major economic reform since 1985 stipulated a two-month wage freeze for the nearly 8 million employees in the public sector; established incentives for early retirement; and increased an income tax surcharge for banks, among other measures. Estimates of 600 percent inflation for 1988 forced him to announce the new package.

But by mid-1988, the economy was in a deeper crisis, with investment at a halt, unemployment rising, inflation running at an annual rate of 600 percent, and growth not expected to reach 2 percent. In May, the government reduced its economic regulations and protectionist trade measures in an effort to stimulate the economy. In the only good news of the year, it was announced in late June that an agreement on debt rescheduling and new loan packages had been arranged with the country's creditor banks. The agreement formally ended the debt moratorium declared in February 1987. In August 1988, the IMF approved a $1.4 billion loan to Brazil that was scheduled to be disbursed in installments through February 9, 1990.

The new realities of formulating policy in a democratic context became clear in late 1988, when the Brazilian Congress, operating under the 1988 Constitution, attempted to increase rather than reduce government spending. The constitution gave the Congress substantial control over money matters. Throughout the deliberations of the Constituent Assembly, which acted as the national legislature for half of the day and as the constitution-drafting assembly the other half, economic nationalism dominated the debates. While Bresser Pereira and Ferreira da Nóbrega attempted to slow spending, Congress favored increased revenue flows to the states and municipalities. Under pressure from state corporation workers, Congress also opposed cuts in the public sector.

In November 1988, Brazilian business leaders, government officials, and trade union representatives signed a "social" pact, limiting wages and prices as part of a last-ditch effort to control annualized inflation of 1,000 percent. Valid for 60 days, the pact called for a limit on price increases for 94 basic items and state-sector services. But under relentless inflationary pressures, the pact collapsed at the end of the year.

In 1989, a year of presidential elections, the government drifted. The president announced a new, indefinite freeze on prices and wages and a devaluation of 17 percent in January 1989. He did so as the Finance Ministry announced that in 1988 inflation had reached 934 percent. The gross domestic product rose only 0.04 percent, and industrial production had fallen by 2.23 percent in 1988. The plan, called the "Summer Plan," was preceded by a set of new price increases. Public confidence in the government was at an all-time low.

By April, the government acknowledged that the Summer Plan had failed. It granted wage increases and reintroduced indexing mechanisms that had been canceled in January. The Sarney government, now a lame-duck administration, with new presidential elections scheduled for November and December, gave up talk of keeping inflation close to zero. The government said it hoped to hold the monthly rate to between 6 percent and 9 percent, or under 200 percent a year. But the federal deficit continued to grow throughout the year, and the credibility of the president and his administration sank ever lower. As the presidential campaign heated up, there were fears that President Sarney would be forced to step down prior to the scheduled inauguration of the new president in March 1990.

The 1989 elections offered Brazilians a clear-cut choice on economic strategies. One group of candidates favored liberalization and market economies; another group supported state intervention in the economy and a moratorium on the foreign debt. A field of 22 candidates contested the presidency in the first round of voting in November 1989; in the second round on December 17, a spokesman for market forces, Fernando Collor de Mello, confronted Luis Inácio da Silva ("Lula"), who supported a neo-Marxist economic program. Collor de Mello defeated Lula, and the country waited with anxious anticipation for some sign of his intentions concerning the economic future of the country.

THE COLLOR PLAN

January 1990 opened with the announcement that the inflation rate in 1989 had reached 1,765 percent. The January inflation rate was a record 56.1 percent; the February rate rose to 73 percent. As the Collor de Mello economic transition team studied various alternatives, the country braced for a new shock. It came the day after his inauguration, when the team promulgated the "Collor Plan." It called for:

- the creation of the fourth new currency in as many years, the cruzeiro, to replace the cruzado novo, with a conversion rate of 1:1;

- an 18-month freeze on a large part of savings and financial assets, announcing what was termed the largest liquidity squeeze in the history of the country;

- a 30-day wage and price freeze, to be followed by controls on future increases;

- a new wealth tax, a widening of the tax base to previously exempt sectors, and a tax on stock market transactions; and

- the compulsory purchase by financial institutions of nonnegotiable "privatization certificates" that could be converted into stock in companies taken public.

The package was all the more dramatic because it would be coordinated by the new economics minister, Zélia Cardoso de Mello, the first woman to hold that post in the country's history. A little-known economist from São Paulo with minimum experience, she had agreed to advise candidate Collor when the country's better-known economists ignored him.

With few options, the Brazilian Congress in April approved the central elements of the bold program. The president then proceeded to announce the opening of the Brazilian economy through trade liberalization, a commitment to the privatization of dozens of state companies, new foreign investment, and changes in the financial system. But on the foreign debt, the economics minister was obdurate—no negotiations unless they were carried out on Brazil's terms.

Ruling primarily by decree, the president slowly aroused the anger of Congress, which saw its role reduced to rubber-stamping presidential initiatives after the fact. In June, Collor suffered his first defeat when Congress rejected a measure to freeze wage increases. A week later, the Supreme Court ruled the measure unconstitutional.

In July, the president vetoed a law passed by Congress to reintroduce the indexation of wage increases to inflation. In August, a pro-government coalition narrowly voted down an attempt to override the president's veto. By September, the inflation rate hovered around 11 percent—it had been 82 percent when he took office in March. But the economy was moving into a serious recession, unemployment was rising, and consumption had dropped.

By December 1990, there were clear danger signs. Inflation had increased to 17 percent, the healthy trade surplus of the late 1980s had vanished, and the economy had shrunk by 4 percent—the worst performance in a decade. And the international banking community was wrestling over the terms for repayment of Brazil's $115 billion foreign debt. The president's confidence had been shaken in the November 25, 1990, elections for governors: opposition candidates were victorious in 10 of the 15 states that held elections, including São Paulo, the economic center of the country.

The year 1991 was one of disarray and confusion in the Brazilian economy. The economic figures from 1990 were very disappointing. Industrial activity had dropped 11 percent, the gross domestic product had contracted 4 percent, the harvest was down 21.2 percent, and the stock market had dropped 68 percent in value. Inflation had reached 1,800 percent for the year. It was clear that the Brazilian people were increasingly disillusioned with the Collor Plan. The president began that year with a new package of spending cuts, but there was little progress in cutting the public deficit or privatizing the many inefficient state companies that were subsidized by the federal administration. While presidential rhetoric was admirable, the Brazilian bureaucracy remained lethargic and sullenly opposed to the presidential goals.

To everyone's shock, the government suddenly announced a tough adjustment program in early February 1991. A freeze on prices and wages was imposed. The new measures included a 47 percent rise in fuel prices and increases of up to 71 percent in utility charges. The government was forced to act, as inflation reached 20 percent a month. The fifth austerity package introduced in less than five years was viewed as a confirmation of the failure of the Collor Plan.

On March 15, 1991, the first anniversary of his inauguration, the president announced a radical National Reconstruction Plan to promote growth and investment and to reduce the role of the state. The plan focused on stimulating growth through abolishing state monopolies in sectors such as ports, communications, and fuel; ending all agricultural and industrial subsidies; and ensuring equal treatment for foreign and national investment. It also introduced profit-sharing schemes for workers, supertaxes on the rich, compulsory retirement at age 60, and plans for 60,000 more public-sector dismissals in 1991.

A general strike called for in May by three of Brazil's largest labor unions was only partially successful but demonstrated the deepening rift between organized labor and the Collor administration. The business community and the administration were in open warfare over the appropriate economic strategy to pursue. Reacting to deepening skepticism, the president dismissed his economics minister in May. He appointed the Brazilian ambassador to the United States, Marcílio Marques Moreira, an experienced diplomat and banker. Moreira quickly replaced all of Zélia Cardoso de Mello's subordinates, promised to be more flexible in negotiations with Brazil's creditors, and vowed to continue the battle against inflation. But the new economic team had little success in achieving its modest goals in 1991.

On August 15, the government began to release the assets frozen in March 1990. The funds were scheduled to be returned in 13 monthly installments, and it was feared that, over time, the flow of new money would further escalate inflationary pressures in the economy. By the end of 1991, there was a growing consensus in Brazil that economic shock plans had not worked and that the country needed to find a long-term solution to its problems, based on some sort of "national understanding" among diverse social and political forces. But given the low prestige of the president and the hopelessly divided political leadership in Congress, it was unclear from where the needed leadership would come.

In spite of the president's efforts, by 1992, Brazil remained one of the world's most protected economies, with an average import tariff of 40 percent (compared to Argentina's 11.5 percent). Business still remained under the control of cartels and demonstrated little interest in cooperating with the government's economic stabilization efforts. Only at the end of 1991 did the first privatization process take place—with widespread protest and violence.[14] Collor changed his cabinet in early 1992, but within a few months a series of scandals erupted that would end his presidency in December of that year. Economic reform was on hold. Inflation continued, and popular discontent increased.

THE ORIGINS OF THE REAL PLAN

The new president, Itamar Franco, inherited a country in crisis. With no experience in economics or finance, Franco appointed and dismissed four finance ministers in a matter of months. Finally, he appointed Foreign Minister Fernando Henrique Cardoso, a PSDB senator from São Paulo, as his fifth finance chief. Quickly, Cardoso called together a young, professional group of economists and tasked them with devising a new, radical but workable economic plan for Brazil. Amidst great skepticism, the new program was implemented in late 1993. Critical to its success was the transparency with which it was discussed and put into place. Moreover, there were no gimmicks—no wage or price controls, no indexation schemes that actually nurtured inflation. This was not a shock program as the Cruzado and Collor plans had been—and failed. Nor were there any punitive measures, such as the seizure of financial assets early in 1990. In March 1994, the government announced a new "currency," the Unidade Real de Valor (URV), which was linked at a rate of 1:1 with the U.S. dollar. While not easy to translate from Portuguese, it roughly means the "real unit of value" to demonstrate to people that this was a brand-new initiative. The old currency continued to circulate, but price changes to accommodate inflation took place only in old currency terms; the assigned value of the URV remained unchanged. Gradually, prices in cruzeiros, the old currency, moved into alignment with the URV. What the team accomplished was to use the forces of the marketplace to create parity between two initially unequal currencies.

On July 1, 1994, the URV became the "*real*" at a 1-to-1 exchange rate with the U.S. dollar. But mindful of the workings of the Brazilian economy, the Cardoso team knew that fixing the *real* to the dollar—as was done in Argentina with the currency board system—would probably be too extreme. The pegging of the *real* to the dollar was significant, but it would be allowed to slowly depreciate in order to prevent the *real* from becoming overvalued. And the changes in value between the *real* and the U.S. dollar were always publicly announced by the Central Bank—no quick fixes or surprises. To many observers, the new plan did not look very different from the failed Cruzado Plan of 1986; indeed, many of the economists working with Cardoso in 1994 had been instrumental in designing the cruzado. But the critical difference in 1994 was the immediate emphasis given to the fiscal component of the undertaking.

The economic team prepared a balanced budget for 1994, and Congress approved it. Cardoso made it clear to the legislators that if the budget was not supported, the overall goals of the Real Plan would disintegrate. The balanced fiscal status allowed for the smooth implementation of the other aspects of the program throughout the year. With the sudden drop in inflation levels, Brazilians were able to plan ahead and not see their salaries disappear into an inflationary spiral. Cardoso's popularity soared in mid-1994, and he quickly passed other presidential contenders in the public opinion polls; in the October elections, he won an easy first-round majority. The inauguration on January 1, 1995, was the first in decades in which a new chief executive did not take office in the midst of deep economic malaise and a fiscal crisis.

THE CARDOSO GOVERNMENT AND THE
CONSOLIDATION OF THE REAL PLAN

The new administration—on the economic side—represented continuity with the team of economists that had developed the Real Plan during Cardoso's tenure as finance minister. Members of the team were quickly appointed to principal economic positions in the new government. As the team organized its plans, the still fragile *real* was momentarily endangered by the collapse of the Mexican peso in December 1994. The new government of President Ernesto Zedillo badly mishandled an adjustment to the peso's value, which rattled local and international investors, forcing a major devaluation. The uncertainty spread across Latin America and the emerging markets. The Cardoso team at first refused to consider any type of devaluation of the currency, but finally did so— clumsily, in March 1995. That decision resulted in a speculative attack on the currency, which caused an estimated loss of $6.3 billion in foreign reserves. But by the end of the week, a slow and credible devaluation had taken place, which helped avert the type of full-fledged crisis that was ravaging Mexico.

In a sign of troubles ahead, as the new government took office, it confronted a serious public-sector banking crisis that forced the Central Bank to intervene in the country's two largest state government-owned banks, Banespa in São Paulo and Banerj in Rio de Janeiro. Illiquidity at the two banks had forced the Central Bank to issue money in 1994 to keep them solvent. The main culprit was bad loans that had been made to the two state governments which they could not repay. The dilemma of the state banks had been a recurring problem in Brazil. Subject to strong political pressures from all political parties in power, the banks had become captive cash machines for campaigns, graft, and corruption. It was clear that the best way to deal with the situation was to privatize both entities—as well as the other banks in the states of the federation. But this was a highly political issue and would need the next few years to resolve.

It was assumed that the new government would immediately announce the next phase of its economic reform program. Inflation had settled down to 1 percent a month (from 6 percent in July 1994), and the cost of living was the most stable it had been in decades. In February, the government announced six proposals to change the 1988 Constitution. All were considered key in addressing the fiscal imbalance that was—and is—critical to the long-run success of the Real Plan. The changes proposed were to allow for foreign-owned companies to invest in mineral and oil extraction, removing a ban set in 1988, and for Brazilian subsidiaries of foreign companies to have the same legal status as Brazilian companies. Under the constitution, multinational units in Brazil were denied legal equality with Brazilian companies.

The goal of these reforms was to allow both private Brazilian and foreign companies to refine oil, distribute oil products, and participate in the maritime transport of oil—a "flexibilization" of the existing oil monopoly. Cardoso and his team were mindful of the strong, nationalist opposition that would erupt if they tried to privatize the state oil enterprise, Petrobrás. It harkened back to the days of Getúlio Vargas. Its union was large and politically strong. The best the new team thought it could accomplish was, therefore, a strategic relaxation of the old rules without running the risk of being accused of selling out Brazil to foreign petroleum interests.

They also proposed that both Brazilian and foreign companies be allowed to provide telephone and data transmission services under licence from the federal government. Under the constitution, only Telebras, the state company, and its subsidiaries were able to grant such licenses. This was another important opening of the economy—as the Real Plan introduced stability, interest by investors increased. New business meant a greater need for an efficient, modern telecommunications industry. Telebras had not provided those services. Competition was key in revitalizing this important sector.

Another amendment proposed that foreign companies should be allowed to compete in coastal shipping, an activity placed off-limits for foreign firms in the 1988 Constitution. And both foreign and Brazilian companies would be allowed to distribute natural gas to households and industry, a task reserved for Petrobrás.

While not shocking in many societies, the proposed constitutional changes were revolutionary in Brazil in 1995. The changes, if approved by Congress, would dramatically reduce government monopolies in telecommunications and oil, cracking for the first time the statist monolith erected in the 1940s and 1950s. The changes would accelerate a process of opening the Brazilian economy to foreign trade and investment, which had begun with the Collor privatizations and tariff reductions during the 1990–1992 period. This first batch of amendments to the statist 1988 Constitution was bold; but the government understood that the pace of change would be difficult and slow, given the resistance in public-sector unions, the leftist/nationalist opposition political parties, and much of the middle class long accustomed to the then-current structure of the economy. Additional changes in the social security system, the size of the public bureaucracy, and tax reform were proposed over the next few months.

Miscalculating its level of support in Congress, the administration suffered its first serious defeat in March, when a package of constitutional amendments aimed at restructuring the social security system was dismembered by a committee vote of 24 to 22, with eight of the "no" votes cast by alleged members of the multiparty coalition that sustained the government. Once again, the patrimonial interests of the political elite had outweighed the good sense of the new but untried Cardoso administration. Learning from the defeat, the economic team decided to postpone further discussion of social security reform—a highly volatile issue in Brazil. Emphasis would be given to the petroleum and telecommunications flexibilization process, which would attract the attention of foreign investors and strengthen Brazil's appeal as an attractive emerging market.

By mid-1995, the government was confronted with a new and an unpleasant reality—rising imports and a deteriorating current account deficit. Brazil was importing far more than it was exporting. Driven by low inflation, years of pent-up demand were causing Brazilians to consume significantly more than previous levels. The trade dilemma would haunt the administration throughout its four-year term of office. A quick fix would be to devalue the currency to promote exports, but that would undermine confidence in the Real Plan. The lack of fiscal discipline meant that the government was left only with monetary tools with which to manage the complex economy—and keeping interest rates high was one of the mechanisms chosen to keep domestic demand under control. One disturbing number appeared in 1995—the federal payroll had gone from $13.9 billion in 1992 to a projected $35 billion, and the payroll costs were a major factor behind a projected federal budget deficit in 1996 of $10 billion. That made fiscal reform even more imperative—but all fiscal changes had to be approved by Congress.

Cardoso made a highly successful and well-publicized state visit to the United States in May. During the same month, the presidential team pressured Congress for support, and progress was slowly achieved. The first important vote on the privatization of piped gas, then a state monopoly, passed in the lower house. Also in May, a committee voted to abolish the distinction between Brazilian and foreign-owned companies. With the change, foreign companies would be free to own mining companies in Brazil. The committee report also removed a federal "buy Brazilian" regulation that had denied foreign-owned companies equal access to government purchase contracts. In another important vote, an amendment was approved to allow private investment in the oil industry. And the first step was taken in the Chamber of Deputies to allow private companies more freedom in providing some telecommunications services in Brazil, including cellular phones, data transmission, and satellite communications. Foreign-owned sea and river transport between Brazilian ports would be allowed by an amendment that was voted by committee.

While these were welcome committee votes, the Cardoso government well understood that it was only the first step in the cumbersome constitutional reform process. The 1988 Constitution mandated that any amendment to the document receive two votes on separate occasions in each of the two houses of the legislature. Any changes to the amendment in either house had to be returned to the other chamber for another vote. Approval required three-fifths of the membership—not a simple majority—which meant that the government needed 308 votes in the Chamber each time it wanted a measure approved. The Senate was more Cardoso-friendly and normally supported the president; the Chamber was famous for its contentiousness. The enthusiasm of May 1995 soon gave way to frustration as the president's term of office ended with limited progress on some issues but with vital changes in social security and taxation unapproved.

In the most dramatic breakthrough in the initial reform process, the Chamber voted on June 7, 1995, to relax the state oil monopoly. The vote was taken in the midst of union opposition violence, with workers pushing their way into the Congress building, breaking windows, and shouting slogans against the vote. In the next few months, additional, positive votes in Congress moved the reform program forward, but at a snail's pace. The administration ended 1995, its first year in office, with price stability in place—but only with continued high interest rates, a controlled and an overvalued exchange rate, and favorable farm prices. One of the central problems confronting the federal government—overspending by mayors and governors—resulted in a spending deficit by December 1995 of

$12 billion. The trade numbers remained negative. But the stock market was resilient; foreign investors liked Brazil and its new government; the "tequila" effect of the Mexican peso devaluation had been overcome; and Cardoso's team received high marks for retaining investor confidence.

Early in 1996, the president recalled Congress to Brasília for a special legislative session. The hope was that quick action would be possible on tax, social security, and administrative reforms, but government efforts failed. Another try in March to gain support for social security changes met defeat once again. The pace of legislative action began to slow during mid-year with the looming municipal elections scheduled for October 3 (with a second round on November 15, in some cases). Given the centrality of local power elites in the Brazilian system, many members of Congress were more concerned about their showing and bases of support at home than in working with the president to move the reform agenda forward. The decision was taken by the president and his team to seek a constitutional amendment in 1996–1997 to allow Cardoso to seek a second four-year mandate, prohibited by the 1988 Constitution. Discussions took place, and a favorable vote occured in January 1997.

The municipal election results favored the PT and the PSDB parties but did little to shift the focus one way or the other in favor of constitutional change by the end of 1996. The year ended with promises of renewed effort in 1997 to convince Congress of the need to support institutional change. The federal budget and trade deficits (the latter was a worrisome $5.5 billion) continued to escalate as the administration found itself without the needed measures to control spending or to promote exports and dampen imports. Finally, accepting the reality of the deteriorating trade deficit numbers, the government, in April, issued a decree setting restrictions on import financing. The most important change required Brazilian importers buying goods on less than 180 days' credit to pay for their foreign exchange upon receiving the merchandise. The government's hope was that the measure would curtail imports significantly and help redress the trade deficit. Unfortunately, the measure was insufficient, and high deficits in the trade account continued into 1998.

In May, the government decided to try to attack the fiscal deficit by reducing payroll and pension expenditures. The initial, early favorable voting turned negative when the political implications of reform became clear. A basic problem for the government was that government job security for untrained labor constituted an important safety net for a significant part of the Brazilian working class—the elevator operators, messengers, coffee servers, chauffeurs, maintenance and security workers who make up the majority of employees in some government departments. Thomas Skidmore recently commented that

Brazil's swollen public payrolls and generous pension system are part of a broad social welfare net sprung from the expediency, in a patrimonial system, to make as many influential people and key groups—including constituencies, families and friends—as happy as possible.[15]

The government decision to target the poorest-paid workers was probably a poor tactical move. The Workers' Party and its allies were able to generate a good deal of sympathy in Congress for those who would be hurt by the proposed legislation. The government would have to wait for another 12 months before it was able to win support for civil service reform.

In May, the administration had an important breakthrough. The giant mining complex—Cia. Vale do Rio Doce (CVRD)—was finally sold to a consortium led by the Brazilian steel maker—National Steel Company (CSN). The consortium paid $3.15 billion for 41.7 percent of CVRD's ordinary shares—the largest ever in the history of privatization in South America. The sale went through after a week of battling injunctions in the courtroom and protestors in the streets. The opposition to the CVRD sale was mounted by the Catholic Church, the judiciary, the landless movement, a number of politicians, and the CVRD employees themselves.

The turbulent sale of the world's largest iron ore exporter allowed for a very significant reduction in the red ink of the Cardoso government's 1997 budget. The victory was important, because Congress accepted the government argument that the privatization was an essential part of an effort to modernize the government and make it more efficient in the delivery of social services. As a private company, CVRD would generate far more revenue for the government in tax payments than in profits, and its new owners are Brazilian, undercutting the argument of the opposition that Cardoso was "selling out" to the foreigners.

The Asian Crisis and the Brazilian Economy

Little noticed at the time, the government of Thailand devalued the *baht* on July 2, 1997, and allowed the currency to float. The Brazilian government appeared confident that there would be no repercussions at home. Indeed, the president rejected the comparison of Brazil to the Asian Tigers, the fast-growing countries of East Asia, when he stated that "we are not a tiger. We are a whale that moves slowly but firmly. We don't make feline jumps."[16] But what began as a decision in one country quickly spread to the region, and then to the emerging markets throughout the world. Brazil was potentially vulnerable, given the weak links in the Real Plan: an overvalued currency and a growing deficit in the current account. These were problems that Brazil shared—and still does—with many "booming" Third World economies that cheapen imports through overvalued currencies in order to promote industrial development and stabilize prices at the same time.

The Cardoso government, in 1997, had been slow to address the problem of the current account deficit, which records the net flow of goods, services, and unilateral transfers between Brazil and the rest of the world. What has traditionally saved Brazil from even greater vulnerability has been the continued strong flow of foreign investment, mostly through the privatization of government companies. The government authorities noted that, over the prior 12 months, direct foreign investment covered 47.3 percent of the current account deficit, and those numbers, they stated, should continue. But it was not yet clear how deep the Asian crisis would actually be. The Central Bank authorities were adamant that there would be no devaluation of the *real*. High reserves, foreign direct investment, investor confidence, and the slow but steady privatization process, they said, distinguished Brazil from other emerging markets.

As the crisis in Asia unfolded, all eyes were turned to the "numbers" in Brazil at the end of 1997. The good news was that inflation was negligible, indeed, almost nonexistent. But the July current account deficit widened. Privately, the monetary authorities began to monitor development in Asia with increasing care—and concern. Unemployment numbers in Brazil had been slowly climbing in 1997, creating another source of tension within the administration. And statistics from the University of São Paulo showed that the redistribution of income that marked the early days of the Real Plan had run its course. The gap between rich and poor, which narrowed after 1994, was widening again in 1997. It was reported that more than half of the urban population worked in service jobs, which generally pay less than factory work. By the end of 1997, the Brazilian reality was sobering—a falloff in consumption, which was the result of a combination of low salaries, high interest rates, rising unemployment, and overextended credit. While this scenario was not a surprise for the government—it reflected a deliberate policy to curb inflation and rein in the growing trade deficit—it was becoming clear that there were political implications that needed to be considered. Did the president want to face the voters in October 1998 with that set of economic realities? And with the added uncertainty of the Asian crisis, it was not clear which way the government would—or should—turn.

The environment worsened during the third week in October with a precipitous drop in the São Paulo stock market (Bovespa): it plunged 15 percent in one day, its biggest slide since 1990 and the fourth worst in its 107-year history. The problem was the pressure on the *real* and the expectation on the part of foreign holders of Brazilian equities that a currency crisis was inevitable. As the Bovespa index plummeted, investors seemed to bet on an imminent devaluation—the same recourse to which Thailand and its neighbors had resorted.

But the Cardoso administration was ready to react. Faced with a run on the *real*, the Central Bank tapped its foreign reserves, selling dollars to contain the *real* within its preestablished mini-band. The Bank also nearly doubled the prime rate and raised the interbank lending rate—a drastic move—but it stopped the bleeding. The sharp increase in interest rates meant that it became increasingly expensive for speculators to borrow *reals* in order to quickly sell them for foreign currency, betting that the Central Bank would be forced to devalue the *real*. Moreover, the higher short-term return on investments, which quickly brought capital back into Brazil, was enticing to even the most worried investors.

Cardoso put together a tough package of austerity measures, which he said Congress needed to approve immediately. It did. He moved to cut the budget and called on Congress to reignite the reform process with action on social security and civil service reform. In a crisis atmosphere, the legislature responded and passed the first of a meaningful set of civil service reforms in November. The legislation allowed the federal government, states, and municipalities to dismiss workers if the payroll costs exceeded 60 percent of existing revenues; job protection was dismantled for most civil service workers; the government was given wide authority to dismiss workers; and the single employment contract with identical job protections for all government employees, from street cleaners to university professors, was eliminated.

The Senate also passed the long-stalled extension of the Fiscal Stabilization Fund, which allowed the federal government to retain a portion of the revenues allocated to the states by the 1988 Constitution. On a state visit to England, Cardoso said that the government would speed up the fiscal reform process. And Congress agreed to the government initiative for an increase in income taxes. The government announced at year's end that a special session of Congress would be convened in early 1998 to consider urgent, additional reform measures.

1998: The End of the First Term of Office

The new year began positively with the federal Senate, as predicted, supporting the legislative initiatives approved in the Chamber on labor contracts and employment flexibility. In February, the Senate approved the measures relating to the streamlining of the federal bureaucracy. Finally, in February, the Chamber took the first positive step to consider fundamental changes to the social security system. There was a sense in the Planalto that things were finally going the president's way. It had taken a major financial crisis—the Asian flu—to move Congress to abandon its "do nothing" attitude that dominated the first three years of the Cardoso administration. The hope, early in 1998, was that the reform agenda could be finalized before the national elections in October.

The economic team received good news in late February, when Brazil received $543 million in a successful Eurobond offer, its first venture into the international market since the Asian crisis. Brazil found such strong demand that it raised its offering of 400 Euros to EUR500 million. Euro-denominated debt is a relatively new market that anticipates the yet-to-be-created currency of the European Union. Because the market is new, those who agree to pay back their debts in Euros receive slightly lower interest rates than they would through borrowing in the traditional Eurodollar market. Brazil was the first Third World country to contract debt in the new European currency, which demonstrated continued confidence in the country's ability to manage its affairs. The success in the Euro market was matched by a strong inflow of dollars in the first quarter of 1998. The net inflow in February, for example, was a record $5.15 billion, which helped lift the country's international reserves to $58 billion.

The downside for the economy was the public deficit. The government failed to meet any of its targets for 1997. The nominal deficit was equivalent to 5.9 percent of the GDP, overshooting the target of 5 percent. The primary deficit, which does not count inflation or debt payments, was supposed to show a surplus of 1.5 percent in 1997, but instead it posted a deficit of 0.7 percent, the worst since 1991. Once again, the principal culprits were the state and city governments, which spent more than they earned, the social security system, which continued to be a massive drain on federal government revenues, and the combined interest payments of the federal government, states, cities, and government companies on debt and bonds.

Finally, the alarm bells went off in Brasília when the January 1998 unemployment figures were released in March. The government-run Brazilian Institute of Geography and Statistics (IBGE) reported that the jobless rate zoomed from 4.8 percent in December to 7.3 percent in January, the highest in 13 years. The numbers would climb throughout the year as the economy slowed down because of the high interest rates and the poor export performance of many companies. And, as many observers commented, Brazil was being impacted by the high-tech revolution and industrial restructuring that was taking place. The new marketplace was not creating additional jobs. It was reported that between 1989 and 1997, for every 10 percent jump in investments, there was only a 2 percent increase in jobs. This is a problem that most developing countries confront, but the numbers were sobering for Brazil; one economist reported that since 1990, Brazilian industry has reduced its employees by 35 percent, while the service sector has exhausted its capacity to absorb them.

By mid-year, the deficit remained the principal Achilles' heel of the administration. As the reporting authorities released monthly numbers, the public-sector deficit widened. This growing deficit continued to put pressure on the *real* to appreciate, something that would surely worsen an already glaring current account deficit. So while it was obvious that making major reductions in the deficit would be close to impossible, the government nevertheless took an alternative—yet still dramatic—step to reassure markets and investors. The Central Bank announced a widening of the mini-band, in which the dollar trades against the *real*. The immediate effect was that the Central Bank would have less pressure to intervene in the market to keep the rate within the band. The change, it was argued, would boost confidence in Brazil because it reduced the chance of speculation. The *real* would be less vulnerable to the attacks witnessed in the Asian crisis, as the wider band would raise the risk for the short-term investor or speculator.

Another welcome effect was the possibility of a decline in interest rates. Having raised the prime lending rate to a crushing 43 percent in October to protect the *real* against the Asian crisis, there was growing pressure to lower the rates, if feasible. But given the country's delicate fiscal situation, it was a process that needed careful coordination. That became a reality with one of the most impressive victories to date for the Cardoso economic modernization program. Yet, as one should come to expect when observing the Brazilian economy, this bold move by Cardoso would prove to be only a temporary fix, as the protracted crisis in Asia and new currency troubles in Russia would put tremendous pressure on the Brazilian economy in 1998.

The Privatization of Telebras

Telecommunications, throughout the developing world, has become a critical bellwether for long-term modernization. Without access to modern communications technology, no country can expect to compete in the twenty-first century. In Brazil, Telebras, the giant telephone holding company, had become one of the ''sacred cows'' of those who favored the retention of state controls on the economy and, by extension, the patrimonial state. The Cardoso administration had long wanted to move to privatize the industry, but fierce political opposition resulted in a delay. Finally, in 1998, it was announced that the breakup and sale of the company would take place on July 29. If successful, the sale would constitute the largest privatization in Latin America, to date.

In preparing for the auction, the government broke the holding company into three fixed phone systems, eight cellular concessions, and one long-distance company, and it created an independent regulatory agency, Anatel, to monitor the telecommunications industry. It was announced that the successful completion of the first phase of the privatization would be followed by a second auction of so-called mirror licenses for competing companies. In 2002, the industry will be opened to even broader competition.

As soon as the date was announced, the auction became part of the 1998 electoral campaign. Lula called for an audit of the process, by which the Telebras minimum price was set, and vowed to scrutinize any contracts awarded by the government if he was elected president. His vice presidential running mate, Leonel Brizola, stated that he would revoke any privatization of the phone companies. As the date approached, the opposition launched an avalanche of lawsuits. The trade union for the workers in the industry said that it would initiate up to 100 legal actions against the auction. The PT also said it would follow suit. The Cardoso administration, aware of both the domestic and the international importance of this issue, had more than 200 lawyers ready to appeal if any injunctions were awarded by the courts. It was clear that the opposition refused to accept the government's justification for the auction—it was crucial to the maintenance of economic stability and to the confidence of international investors in their ability to work with Brazil as a reliable partner.

Walking through a series of legal land mines, the auction took place on July 29, 1998. There was a great deal of violence in the streets surrounding the building where the auction took place, and legal battles were waged until the night before the auction occurred. Riot police clashed with thousands of protestors—students, labor unionists, and members of the MST—who accused the government of selling the national patrimony to foreign interests. But the government emerged the victor. The sale of Telebras brought $18.9 billion—a premium of 63.6 percent over the minimum price—reinforcing that even theretofore skeptical international investors are convinced that Brazil is committed to economic reform.

Following the successful auction, the government immediately set a timetable for the sale of licenses to compete with the fixed-service telephone companies it sold on July 29. This was another important step in opening a critical industry to new capital and technology, which will update basic services for the average Brazilian and provide an incentive for greater investment in Brazil, since investors will be able to count on services such as faxes, the Internet, and other vital operations that are needed to be competitive in today's global economy. The auction also gave the Cardoso administration breathing space to deal with the fiscal deficit until it was able to reinitiate the fiscal reform process in 1999.

An important result of the successful auction was the government's decision to cut basic interest rates by 1.25 percentage points. The Central Bank reduced the basic interest rate (which had been up to 43 percent in October 1997) from 21 percent to 19.75 percent, which provided another positive sign to investors and reinforced confidence in the government's handling of the economy in the midst of the ongoing Asian crisis. Politically, it was a crucial breakthrough in the election year in which a defeat for the government might have hurt the possibility of Cardoso's reelection. And, also critical, it was another important loss for the regressive forces that continue to support the patrimonial state. The cutback in state employees and the resulting modernization of telecommunications should make a major contribution to a more efficient Brazilian state and greater employment opportunities as a result of new investment in the economy.

Contagion Strikes Again

As the presidential campaign came to an end in 1998, it was noted in the press that

the tough talk of last year has disappeared, and the promises of Civil Service and Social Security changes that backed the fiscal-stabilization program four years ago remain half-done. Though Brazil is still vulnerable to the strains and threats from emerging markets half a world away, the federal government in Brasília has ceased moves to cut spending.

Of the 51 austerity measures, only those that involved raising revenue were enacted, while layoffs and other cost-cutting measures were either watered down or abandoned. Even the crackdown on fraudulent pensioners has collapsed.[17]

In hindsight, even with the reforms implemented in October 1997, it was obvious that a financial crisis was brewing. The financial markets once again were highly volatile by mid-1998. The Asian crisis did not appear to be improving; efforts to reflate the Japanese economy had apparently failed; the Russian ruble had collapsed; and the deficit numbers in Brazil continued to grow. In May and June 1998, there were sharp drops in the Bovespa, but it recovered.

In July, the Central Bank of Brazil attempted to roll over or extend a portion of Brazilian government debt by auctioning off fixed-rate bills, which it had been doing since 1994. The commercial banks would do so only at a risk premium—a higher rate of interest. The government refused to do so. An important rating agency in the United States downgraded the outlook for Brazil from "stable" to "negative" in the same month.

In August, as a result of contagion and investors' nervousness, the Bovespa fell 19.2 percent in the first 18 days of the month. It was estimated that $3.6 billion left Brazil—$1 billion alone on August 18. The situation continued to deteriorate throughout August and September. As the joint meetings of the IMF and the World Bank approached in Washington, D.C., the finance ministers of Latin America called for the international financial community to help protect their currencies from further contagion and instability. They argued, correctly, that they had done far more to modernize their economies than either the Russians or the Southeast Asians.

U.S. Secretary of the Treasury Robert Rubin indicated publicly in September that Brazil was the main focus of American concerns in Latin America. President Bill Clinton delivered a speech in which he called for a major overhaul of the international financial "architecture," and he urged support for Brazil. In response to the clamor for action by his administration, President Cardoso spoke to the country in late October and pledged to cut $7 billion in spending from the deficit-ridden federal budget in 1999. The president did not spell out the details in the speech, but pressure built for him to do so quickly. A few days later, the government introduced a three-year, $80 billion package of spending cuts and tax increases in an effort to restore the country's credibility in world markets and prepare the way for a rescue program by the IMF and the international financial community. The plan called for $23.5 billion in savings in 1999, with about $11 billion coming from tax increases and $7 billion from spending cuts. The rest was to come from pension and fundamental financial reforms. Part of the plan sought to set up mechanisms to limit the spending of Brazil's states and municipalities.

In preparation for the announcement of the government fiscal program, the IMF and the international financial community prepared a $41.5 billion "safety net" for Brazil. The approval of the changes in the social security system, which was voted in by Congress in early November 1998, was the first positive step in gaining political support for the fiscal package. But that was the last good news for the Cardoso government. The remainder of the package stalled in Congress in December 1998 and January 1999. With investors increasingly nervous, a sudden political shock precipitated a financial crisis. Governor Itamar Franco of the state of Minas Gerais declared a unilateral moratorium on debt repayments to the federal government. A number of other opposition governors momentarily appeared to be prepared to follow suit, although they ultimately negotiated a truce with the Cardoso government. Franco acted for a number of reasons. He had inherited a heavily indebted state government, leaving him little leeway for public works programs and other projects. The Real Plan had been formulated during his presidency—indeed, he had appointed Cardoso as finance minister. He believed that his role in the creation of the Plan had been ignored, and he saw himself as a strong candidate to recapture the presidency in the next election in 2002.

Combined with the lack of action in Congress and with large outflows of funds from Brazil in January, the Central Bank was forced to abandon its crawling peg in favor of a floating exchange rate on January 13. The currency immediately plunged and the *real* lost more than 40 percent of its value against the dollar in a matter of days. The crisis produced by the devaluation forced Congress to react and the fiscal reform package, long delayed, was finally approved. The government reopened negotiations with the IMF, which ultimately approved new targets and indicated its support for the government's plans.

In February, President Cardoso appointed a new head of the Central Bank, Arminio Fraga, with long experience as an investment banker on Wall Street. The decision quickly restored credibility to the Bank and bolstered investor confidence in the medium-term outlook for the economy. Within a few months of the devaluation, Fraga was able to begin to reduce interest rates from their high of 45 percent in small increments, which further began to help restore confidence in the management of the economy.

The country fell into recession soon after the devaluation as surging interest rates throttled investment and consumer demand. While the devaluation helped Brazilian exporters compete in world markets, it quickly resulted in a drop in imports which hurt multinational corporations operating in Brazil. The expectation was that the recession would last through year-end but that a return to growth was feasible in 2000 if the new team succeeded in stabilizing the currency and controlling inflation. The Central Bank developed a strategy that made controlling inflation in 1999 the principal policy goal. The Real Plan had in large part been viewed as a success because it had driven inflation down to single digits. The Bank expected that inflation would return to single numbers at the end of 2000; it targeted an inflation rate of under 20 percent. The inflation target was critical because any pass through from the devaluation to the prices of goods and services could result in runaway inflation. A perception that the government had lost the battle against inflation would unleash pressures for a reindexation of the economy, which was the source of Brazil's troubles in the 1970s and 1980s.

The Real Plan in Perspective

Against the background of the last few decades, the Real Plan stands as a radical and thus far successful economic stabilization effort by Brazil's first modern government. The plan did what no other plan had done—it apparently destroyed hyperinflation, which had become a state of mind for the average Brazilian. But the fiscal imbalances remained unstable, and a number of factors brought the first phase of the Real Plan to an abrupt end. Investor confidence collapsed in the context of growing financial contagion from the crises in Asia and Russia. Brazil's inability to demonstrate forceful action to cut the deficits unnerved investors, who began withdrawing large amounts of money from the country in late 1998 and into 1999. The precipitate action of Governor Itamar Franco and his unilateral moratorium on debt repayment was the final blow.

The devaluation of January 1999 and the new leadership at the Central Bank, combined with congressional approval of the fiscal reform program in early 1999, offers hope that the economy will adjust in 1999 and return to a pattern of growth early in the next century. But this will require continued vigilance by the monetary authorities. Public spending must continue to be reduced. The federal government will need to work with the mayors and governors to control spending at the local and state levels. A commitment to continued privatization of state companies is important, and the battle against inflation must continue to receive highest priority.

The key challenge for the second Cardoso administration is continued fiscal reform. An important question is whether continued fiscal reform will further weaken the patrimonial order. Unfortunately, no one predicts that this government will be totally successful in achieving its fiscal goals. There will be sufficient resistance in Congress and at the state and municipal levels to do so, thus a leaner—perhaps meaner—political elite will seek to build a new means of access and influence in the structure of the patrimonial state. Only when the social reform phase has been implemented—still a distant goal—will there begin to be a redistribution not only of income but of political power and influence. The economic and financial reforms are merely prerequisites for societal change. Until that is done, the narrow-minded political elite will survive and prosper under new conditions, perhaps, but will still be immune to reform—unless forced to react as it did during the October–November 1997 Asian crisis and, again, in 1999 with the contagion effect from Russia and Asia. Will it do the minimum it thinks is necessary, and then return to its traditional posture of delaying reform and postponing a serious discussion of deeper institutional change?

NOTES

1. For an excellent analysis of Brazil's economic development, see Werner Baer, *The Brazilian Economy: Growth and Development*, 5th ed. (Westport, Conn.: Praeger, 1999).

2. Gilberto Freyre, *The Masters and the Slaves* (New York: Alfred A. Knopf, 1964).

3. Celso Furtado, trans. by Ricardo W. De Aguiar and Eric Charles Dyrsdale, *The Economic Growth of Brazil: A Survey from Colonial to Modern Times* (Berkeley and Los Angeles: University of California Press, 1963), provides an excellent overview.

4. Richard Graham, *Britain and the Onset of Modernization in Brazil, 1850–1914* (New York: Cambridge University Press, 1968), offers a fascinating view of English involvement.

5. Baer, *The Brazilian Economy*, p. 39.

6. For a more detailed discussion of the Niemeyer report and the Cooke Mission, see Werner Baer, *Industrialization and Economic Development in Brazil* (Homewood, Ill.: Richard D. Irwin, Inc., 1965), pp. 31–33.

7. See Werner Baer and Isaac Kerstenetzky, "The Brazilian Economy," in Riordan Roett, ed., *Brazil in the Sixties* (Nashville, Tenn.: Vanderbilt University Press, 1972).

8. World Bank, *Brazil: Industrial Policies and Manufacturing Exports* (Washington, D.C.: World Bank, 1983), p. 2.

9. Ibid.

10. Baer, *The Brazilian Economy*, p. 75.

11. World Bank, *Brazil: Industrial Policies and Manufacturing Exports*, p. 8.

12. For an overview of the evolution of the debt crisis in Latin America, see Riordan Roett, "The Debt Crisis: Economics and Politics," in John D. Martz, ed., *United States Policy in Latin America: A Quarter Century of Crisis and Challenge, 1961–1986* (Lincoln: University of Nebraska Press, 1988).

13. For a comparison of Argentina, Brazil, and Mexico in the debt crisis, see Robert R. Kaufman, "Stabilization and Adjustment in Argentina, Brazil, and Mexico," in Joan M. Nelson, ed., *Economic Crisis and Policy Choice: The Politics of Adjustment in the Third World* (Princeton, N.J.: Princeton University Press, 1990).

14. See Julia Preston, "Brazil Begins Sale of Firms Owned by Government," *Washington Post*, October 25, 1991, p. F1; and Nathaniel C. Nash, "Amid Latin Growth, Brazil Falters," *New York Times*, September 28, 1991, p. A35.

15. *Brazil Watch*, May 5–19, 1997, p. 6.

16. *Brazil Watch*, July 28–August 11, 1997, p. 1.

17. Diana Jean Schemo, "Brazil's Economic Half-Steps," *New York Times*, August 1, 1998, p. B1.

Chapter 6

Brazilian Foreign Policy

Brazilian foreign policy has evolved rapidly in recent decades. The years following World War II witnessed an early continuation of a "special relationship" with the United States. But the seeds of discord also were apparent and, by the early 1960s, Brazil sought to enunciate an autonomous foreign policy under Presidents Quadros and Goulart. Briefly, with President Castello Branco in 1964, the special relationship reemerged as the guiding principle of policy. A definitive shift took place in the late 1960s toward a more aggressive, nationalist concern for defending and projecting Brazil's international interests. This shift paralleled, and resulted from, the appearance of the economic miracle and the expansion of the world economy. Brazil saw the South or developing world as an important area for trade and as an arena in which it could play a leadership role.

With the second petroleum crisis in 1979 and the onset of the international debt crisis in 1982, foreign policy was again redefined. This time, economics and finance, rather than traditional diplomacy and geopolitics, governed Brazil's international relations. And, in the 1980s, the foreign policy agenda was expanded suddenly to include issues seldom considered relevant in prior decades: the environment, regional economic integration, and indigenous affairs. Following the transition to a civilian regime in 1985, a historical development—Mercosur—refocused Brazil's strategic thinking, both economically and politically. The creation of Mercosur, the common market of South America, would be the predominant theme in the international relations of Brazil and of the region. The election of Fernando Henrique Cardoso in 1994, who had served as foreign minister and was well-known outside of Brazil, provided a natural entry into international circles. Cardoso has maintained strong support for Mercosur, but he has also articulated a more complex set of goals for Brazil's role in the world. In this chapter we will briefly consider the evolution of Brazilian foreign policy. After an overview of policy prior to the Revolution of 1964, we will examine the international relations of the Military Republic as it moved from a concern with the Third World and nationalist issues to a growing sense of urgency about problems of debt and trade. Finally, we will see that the restoration of democracy in 1985 resulted in another redefinition of foreign policy that has provided a significant redefinition of Brazil's interests in South America and in the post–Cold War world.

FROM INDEPENDENCE TO 1964

Following independence from Portugal in 1822, the foreign policy of the Brazilian Empire had three principal foci: Portugal, because of the strong cultural and historical ties with the mother country; England, due to the privileged position in trade and commerce with Brazil, inherited from Portugal; and Argentina, as a result of traditional Brazilian concern with a balance of power in the Río de la Plata area.

Unlike Portugal, independent Brazil quickly established a pattern of intervention in Río de la Plata affairs. Brazil's concern led to the creation of Uruguay as a buffer state between Brazil and Argentina. As a result of the geopolitical maneuvering in the region at the time of the wars of independence, Paraguay withdrew into almost total isolation. Brazil's concern with the River Plate area led to its deep involvement in the War of the Triple Alliance from 1865 to 1870, when it joined Argentina and Uruguay in subduing Paraguay in an effort to restore what it thought to be an advantageous balance in the subregion. The European emphasis in Brazilian foreign policy was reflected in the trade statistics of the era: England provided more than 50 percent of Brazil's imports.

With the overthrow of the Empire in 1889, Brazilian foreign policy underwent a significant modification. The move away from the traditional alliance with England, which paralleled a shift from sugar to coffee as the mainstay of the economy, and a redistribution of internal political power from the Northeast to the Southeast (particularly the states of São Paulo and Minas Gerais), was the master plan of the baron of Rio Branco. Foreign minister during four administrations (1902–1912), the baron emphasized three policies during his tenure: (1) the settlement of outstanding territorial boundary disputes with Spanish American neighbors, which eliminated the need for conflict; (2) the maintenance of equilibrium with Argentina in the Río de la Plata area; and (3) the beginnings of an "unwritten alliance" or special relationship with the United States. That the United States received the latter policy favorably was in part due to Argentina's hostility to U.S. foreign policy and to the nationalist and independent stance in hemispheric affairs assumed by the government in Buenos Aires.

Because of the growing militarization of Argentina, Brazil's neighbor and rival, and the fragility of world affairs (which in 1914 resulted in World War I), Brazilian elites became increasingly preoccupied with their security on the continent after Rio Branco's death in 1912. Following the world war, Brazil felt increasingly isolated as the 1920s opened. Without strong allies on the South American continent, Brazil had to look outward. The United States was an obvious choice, given the clear directions established by Rio Branco in the creation of the "unwritten alliance," and Brazil worked assiduously in the 1920s to link its interests to those of the United States. Another obvious option in the 1920s became the League of Nations—the imaginative, if doomed, effort by U.S. President Woodrow Wilson and his European allies to structure the postwar period in such a way as to avoid a repetition of the slaughter of the "Great War." Brazil was the only country in South America to have declared war on the Central Powers, and thereby received the right to send a delegation to the Paris Peace Conference. It was selected to sit on the first Council of the League of Nations, the only country in the Western Hemisphere to receive that honor. Reelection came in 1922. As Stanley Hilton observed:

The 1920s offered, in the form of a League of Nations, what seemed to be a unique opportunity for bolstering Brazil's international status through the political endorsements of the great powers. Understandably, then, Brazilian foreign policy had (until 1926) a trans-Atlantic or European thrust, in addition to its traditional continental projection.[1]

Brazil had hoped to gain a permanent seat on the Council of the League of Nations and openly campaigned for such recognition. In 1926, the country was denied permanent status and angrily withdrew from the Geneva-based organization. Ties with the United States, which had earlier rejected membership in the League, intensified. President-elect Herbert Hoover visited Brazil in 1928, and President-elect Júlio Prestes returned the visit in 1920. With the overthrow of the Old Republic in November 1930, the personalities changed, but the basic lines of Brazilian foreign policy endured.

The 1930s were for Brazil a period of diplomatic maneuvering and scrambling for economic opportunities. The world financial collapse created serious development problems for the new regime of Getúlio Vargas (1930–1945). Trade became increasingly linked with national defense during the 1930s, and new markets were sought for traditional exports in order to purchase armaments. Industrialization also became a national goal, and crucial imports could be paid for only if Brazil exported in order to earn foreign exchange. Brazil's drive for autonomy in trade relations led to a parting of the ways with the United States in the mid-1930s. For example, the United States supported Ethiopia in its struggle against invasion by Mussolini's Italy; meanwhile, Brazil sought to sell to Italy and rejected the League of Nations appeal for sanctions against it.

Brazil demonstrated strong sympathy for the nationalist forces of General Francisco Franco in the Spanish Civil War and sought to establish commercial and trade ties with the regime of Adolf Hitler in Berlin. Vargas maneuvered with skill, attempting to assure the United States that their friendship remained untainted by Brazil's ties with the Italians and Germans. But a neutral United

States was unable to offer help to Brazil in one important area: the purchase of weapons. The military high command, keenly aware of the continuing arms buildup in Argentina and the deterioration of world politics that would inevitably lead to another world war, lobbied intensely in the mid- and late 1930s for new weapons. By 1936, Germany had provided 23 percent of Brazil's total arms imports and had purchased 13 percent of that country's exports.

A breakthrough came in the mid-1930s, when the decision was made to use blocked currency, earned by the sale of surplus raw materials, to buy weapons in Europe. Scarce foreign exchange would not need to be spent, further burdening the country's balance of payments.[2] Brazil contracted to buy submarines, delivered in early 1938, from Italy, and artillery from German producers, the first of which arrived in early 1939. These emerging commercial ties were strongly aided by the large Italian and German colonies in Brazil that were sympathetic to stronger links with the mother countries. In addition, the United States was unable to provide real alternatives to the lure of Italian and German arms until World War II broke out in September 1939. When the trade blockade was imposed by Great Britain against the Axis powers, Brazilian trade with Germany declined precipitously and finally ended completely when President Vargas broke diplomatic relations with the Axis powers in January 1942 and Brazil entered the war on the side of the Allies.

In exchange for its support in the war, Brazil received arms and ships from the United States, as well as financial support for a steel plant at Volta Redonda, outside of Rio de Janeiro. The Volta Redonda plant was a crucial symbol to Brazil of its success in industrializing the country. As a sign of Brazil's importance to the Allied war effort, President Franklin D. Roosevelt stopped in Natal, on the Northeast coast (the site of important U.S. air bases during the war), to confer with President Vargas on his way to the Casablanca Conference in January 1943. Brazil, in turn, sent an expeditionary force in July 1944 to fight in Italy against the Axis powers.

Though fearful of a strong, armed Argentina to its south, and of its general weakness in an increasingly militarized world, Brazil has always believed that it would eventually attain great power status in the international system. That theme was emphasized, for example, in a memorandum drafted for Getúlio Vargas by Oswaldo Aranha, his foreign minister, in preparation for the 1943 meeting with Roosevelt, as explained by Frank McCann:

Aranha saw Brazil and the United States as "cosmic and universal" nations, whose futures could only be continental and worldwide. Realistically he knew that Brazil was still "a weak country economically and militarily," but he had no doubt that with a capital and population which would come from the country's natural growth, or would flow to it after the war, it would be "inevitably one of the great economic and political powers of the world"—it already was second in the Americas.[3]

The end of World War II coincided with the bloodless overthrow of President Vargas in late 1945. His democratically elected successor and former war minister, General Eurico Dutra, supported the U.S. initiative to create the United Nations (UN) and to create the inter-American security system. At the UN, the United States supported Brazil in its bid for a permanent seat on the Security Council; that initiative failed, but Brazil was elected to one of the nonpermanent seats in January 1946. The keystone of the inter-American system, the Rio Treaty, was signed in Rio de Janeiro in partial recognition of Brazil's role in World War II and its strong support, after 1945, for U.S. foreign policy in the Cold War. Brazil and the United States signed the first Latin American military assistance agreement after the termination of the war.

The strong relationship between the United States and Brazil sharply contrasted with the ties between both of these countries and Argentina. The Buenos Aires government did not declare war until March 1945, and then only to be eligible to attend the organizational meeting of the UN. Argentine "neutrality" during the war had been viewed by both Washington and Rio de Janeiro as sympathy with the Axis cause. With the election of Juan D. Perón as president of Argentina in 1946, relations between the United States and Argentina deteriorated at the political level, in comparison to the apparent goodwill that existed between Brazil and the United States.

Much of the goodwill, on Brazil's part, led to an expectation of economic help from the United States after the conclusion of the war. In addition, Brazil saw itself as an important outpost in South America against the militaristic impulses of the Perón government in Buenos Aires. As before the war, the Brazilian military high command urged, without great success, that Dutra secure arms support from the United States. That lack of response from the United States was repeated in the area of economic assistance. As U.S. attention turned to western European recovery and strategic concerns in Asia, little time or money was left for the Western Hemisphere. Increasingly, Washington told Brazil and other Latin American states that private capital was the key to their development, and that the government should do everything possible to attract multinational corporations to invest. The Joint Brazil–United States Technical Mission, established in 1948, endorsed that recipe for economic growth.

Stung by the apparent insensitivity of the American government, the Brazilians refused to support the U.S. war effort against North Korea and China in the 1950s. The recommendations regarding Brazilian economic development and the appropriate role of the United States contained in the report of the 1950 Joint Brazil–United States Commission for Economic Development went unheeded in Washington following President Eisenhower's inauguration in 1953. The new American president stressed the role of private capital in all of his references to Latin America and the Third World. Confronted with the insensitivity of the United States, Brazilian policy makers began to believe that "national strategy toward the United States and Spanish America had been counterproductive and that the only way Brazil could acquire the requisite bargaining strength vis-à-vis Washington would be to ally itself with its Spanish-speaking neighbors."[4]

With the overthrow of the government of General Fulgencio Batista in Cuba in January 1959, U.S. concern with the hemisphere increased dramatically. A fear of Communist subversion now characterized U.S. policy in the region. Reluctantly, the United States agreed to the creation of the Inter-American Development Bank in 1959. During President Eisenhower's visit to Latin America in 1960, President Kubitschek urged him to consider social and economic development aid; Eisenhower replied that the real menace was Communist subversion and that private capital needed to be attracted in order to resolve development issues.

The ongoing frustration in Brazil with U.S. unwillingness to respond to Latin American initiatives motivated Kubitschek's successor, Jânio Quadros (1961), to declare an openly independent foreign policy for Brazil. In an article written before, but published in *Foreign Affairs* after, his resignation in August 1961, the chief executive declared:

The interest shown in the position of Brazil in international affairs is in itself proof of the presence of a new force on the world stage. Obviously my country did not appear by magic, nor is it giving itself momentarily to a more or less felicitous exhibition of publicity seeking. When I refer to a ''new force,'' I am not alluding to a military one, but to the fact that a nation, heretofore almost unknown, is prepared to bring to bear on the play of world pressures the economic and human potential it represents, and the knowledge reaped from experience that we have a right to believe is of positive value.[5]

He proceeded to defend Brazil's ties with the Third World, the nation's need to control foreign investment, and Brazil's independence: ''Not being members of any bloc, not even the neutralist bloc, we preserve our absolute freedom to make our own decisions in specific cases and in the light of peaceful suggestions at one with our nature and history.''[6]

Quadros's sudden resignation opened a short, conflict-ridden period in which the Brazilian political system appeared to serve domestic interests. Vice President João Goulart, who succeeded Quadros in September under a hastily arranged parliamentary system, was viewed with great suspicion by many in the armed forces, the middle class, and the more conservative groups in Brazil. He had served as President Vargas's labor minister in the early 1950s, and he had actively supported the nationalist thrust of Vargas's policy. This sympathy for the labor movement and nationalist forces in general led the new president to quickly seek basic reforms in Brazil's economic and social structure. His support for the Alliance for Progress diminished rapidly as the U.S. presence in Brazil increased in 1962 and 1963. Of great importance to the United States was Brazil's refusal to support its position with regard to Cuba. Determined to defend the independent foreign policy position, the Brazilian delegation led the opposition to that of the United States at the eighth meeting of consultation of foreign ministers, held at Punta del Este, Uruguay, in January 1962. Self-determination and nonintervention were the key concepts used by Brazil to oppose the expulsion of Castro's Cuba from the Organization of American States. Six states (Brazil, Argentina, Chile, Mexico, Bolivia, and Ecuador) voted against the resolution, although the measure received the necessary two-thirds majority required for passage.

In November 1963, at the meeting of the Inter-American Economic and Social Council in São Paulo, Brazil's hostility to the United States was apparent. Little reference was made to the Alliance for Progress by the Brazilians. The host delegation called for a common Latin American policy against the industrialized world in preparation for the first meeting of the newly established United Nations Conference on Trade and Development, scheduled for 1964. At Brazil's urging, the São Paulo meeting established the Special Commission for Latin American Coordination (CECLA), which did not include the United States, to coordinate Latin American development policies and to establish a Latin American bargaining position vis-à-vis the industrial world, particularly the United States.

Other areas of friction emerged. Goulart's attitude toward the Soviet Union did not coincide with that of the Kennedy and Johnson administrations. The Brazilian government supported and practiced coexistence. Brazil strongly endorsed Third World efforts to seek disarmament agreements and joined the United Nations Disarmament Conference. Increasingly, Brazil's foreign policy demonstrated a sympathy for the basic tenets of the nonaligned states: anticolonialism, coexistence with the Soviet bloc nations, ideological pluralism in the Third World (best demonstrated by Brazil's support for the regime of Fidel Castro), and a radical restructuring of economic relations between North and South.

THE CASTELLO BRANCO PERIOD (1964–1967)

The military intervention of March 31, 1964, and the overthrow of the Goulart regime dramatically changed the course of Brazilian foreign policy. The government of General Humberto Castello Branco openly endorsed U.S. foreign policy goals. Diplomatic relations with Cuba were broken in May 1964. In the crisis that accompanied U.S. intervention in the Dominican Republic in April 1965, the Brazilians agreed to contribute troops to the Inter-American peace-keeping force and to provide the commanding officer. The government revised the nationalist 1962 Profits Remittance Law in order to favor foreign investors in Brazil. In February 1965, the government negotiated an investment guarantee agreement for multinational corporations. In return for strong support for U.S. interests, U.S. foreign aid increased dramatically. Aid between November 1961 and March 1964 amounted to $128 million; between April 1964 and June 1966, $563 million. In addition to official aid, international financial support and direct private investment returned to Brazil with the blessing of the U.S. government. Indeed, from 1964 to 1967, Brazil ranked behind only India, Pakistan, and South Vietnam in net official aid receipts.

Ironically, the strong support of the United States for Brazilian economic recovery and diversification contributed to the next stage of U.S.–Brazilian relations: a slow but perceptible parting of the ways. What had appeared a permanent reassertion of the special relationship or alliance between Brasília and Washington did not survive the Castello Branco government. Albert Fishlow observed:

The economic miracle that followed, instead of ratifying this new alliance, progressively eroded it. Up to the oil crisis of 1973–74, two factors predominated. First, successful Brazilian integration into the world economy actually weakened official ties to the United States. Second, a changing Brazilian leadership found a continued junior role both unnecessary and undesirable.[7]

The Brazilian economic miracle of the late 1960s was not the only factor that contributed to a reassertion of Brazil's search for an independent foreign policy. The nature of the Costa e Silva government (1967–1969) also was an important factor. While Castello Branco and his ministers were generally supportive of close ties with the United States, the Costa e Silva group was more wary of Washington's preeminent role in the hemisphere. The Castello Branco group had close ties to the United States, which resulted in part from the experiences of World War II and the creation of the Superior War College (ESG) in Brazil in 1949. The Costa e Silva ministers were from another wing of the Brazilian armed forces, one given less to theory and more to practice. They thought of themselves as action-oriented planners and implementors.

THE COSTA E SILVA (1967–1969) AND MÉDICI (1969–1974) GOVERNMENTS

The dynamics of institutional politics in the Brazilian armed forces led to the selection of General Arthur da Costa e Silva as the Military Republic's second chief executive (1967–1969). The contextual linkages between internal development and external policy were redefined in an abrupt, little-understood manner. With Costa e Silva, the authoritarian nationalists rose to prominence in Brazil, displacing the "Sorbonne" contingent, so called because of their intellectual approach to problem solving. The new group represented a victory for what was at times a position of strident economic nationalism, a questioning of the role of appropriateness of foreign capital in the national economy, a reluctance to return decision making to civilian politicians, and a deep concern about national security that focused on the occupation and colonization of the national territory. Brazil's natural resources must not be given over to foreign exploitation. International communism must be opposed at all costs. With regard to the United States, the authoritarian nationalists were not afraid to confront that country—if Brazil's interests so demanded. The nationalist officer group was less identified with the ESG, had less exposure to the Expeditionary Force experience, and had fewer contacts outside of Brazil. Among the best-known advocates of this position were General Alfonso Augusto de Albuquerque Lima, Costa e Silva's Minister of the Interior, and General Emílio Garrastazú Médici, director of the National Intelligence Service (SNI); the latter would succeed Costa e Silva in 1969.

The election of Richard Nixon in November 1968 and the mesmerization of the United States with the Vietnam War set the tone of American foreign policy for the early 1970s. Henry Kissinger's well-known aversion to the Third World, and his preoccupation with ending the war and rebalancing relations with China and the Soviet Union, dominated U.S. policy making. A policy of "benign neglect" settled over U.S.–Latin American affairs. While Nixon would state, during Médici's visit to the United States in the early 1970s, that as went Brazil, so would go Latin America, American policy did little either to assist or to deflect that observation. Not until the very end of the Kissinger era would Brazil emerge again as America's preferred "chum" in the hemisphere. The Republicans took few policy initiatives with regard to Latin America that affected Brazil. Private capital was warmly encouraged to take advantage of the Brazilian miracle, and investment soared. Americans, on the rare occasions when they thought about Brazil—the world soccer championship in 1970 was one exception—were vague about the nature of the society or why it was important or unimportant to the United States.

Thus the perception complacently continued in Washington that the unwritten alliance remain in place. While the Brazilians did nothing publicly to dispel that notion in the minds of the Republicans, events in Brazil qualitatively transformed that country's view of its role in world affairs. The most obvious manifestation of the change came with the economic model of export-led growth inspired by Antônio Delfim Netto's leadership from 1967 to 1974. Building on the effectiveness of Roberto Campos's stabilization program (1964–1967), Delfim Netto turned to a two-pronged policy of making Brazil very attractive for foreign capital and generating high levels of exports—both traditional and industrial, and agro-industrial. The economy grew at rates not seen in decades: 10 percent and 12 percent a year. Brazilian products penetrated the markets of both the Third World and industrialized countries. Suddenly, Brazil's economic role in world affairs was no longer a laughing matter:

Accelerated expansion of world trade and more aggressive Brazilian export promotion policies combined in the late 1960s and early 1970s to stimulate a rapid growth of Brazilian exports. . . . A 27 percent annual average export growth between 1968 and 1973 brought in its wake diversification both in sales and purchases. A decline in the dominant position of the United States was inevitable.[8]

The internal concomitant of the external drive was a growing concern with development. The authoritarian nationalists' view of Brazil required social change, government- and military-directed, to guarantee future social and political stability. Venal politicians were incompetent to direct that change; a suspicious eye fell on foreign capital, seen as exploitative, as well as on the underdeveloped regions of Brazil, such as the Northeast and the Amazon Valley. These areas required immediate and effective government attention if they were to not become areas of potential subversion in the future.

The Costa e Silva presidency ended abruptly with the incapacitation of the president in August 1969. An intricate process of military consultation took place, and the director of the SNI, General Médici (1969–1974), emerged the victor in the presidential sweepstakes. Médici, the most conservative of Brazil's military presidents, presided over a socially and politically closed society but over the most dynamic period of economic growth and external expansion in Brazil's postwar history.

National integration, when linked to the national security concern of the new government, led to a developmental emphasis on the Amazon. The city of Manaus was defined as a "free zone" to stimulate industrial development in the Amazon. SUDAM (Superintendency for the Development of the Amazon), modeled on SUDENE in the Northeast, was created. Project Rondon took urban youths into the Amazon to work on social and economic community problems. The culmination of this urge to integrate the Amazon into Brazil—*integrar para não entregar* (integrate, so as not to hand over)—was the construction of the Transamazon Highway.

The National Integration Plan emerged in June 1970. The *Transamazônica*, about 3,200 miles long (about 5,100 kilometers), would run from the coast westward to link with the road system of Peru; the second major highway would run north from Cuiabá in Mato Grosso to Santarém on the Amazon. There also would be spur roads to Boa Vista, near Guyana and Venezuela. Construction began with worldwide fanfare. The reaction in Spanish America was less favorable.

In part, Brazil began to distance itself from the United States in response to the suspicions of the authoritarian nationalists about U.S. foreign capital and the ill-advised unequal partnership between the two countries. A strong and an assertive Brazil, at home and abroad, would take second place to no one. Equally important, Brazil suddenly found itself in an economic position to assume a stronger role in world affairs.

As official bilateral assistance declined—American legislation defined Brazil as a middle-income country and therefore ineligible for further public economic assistance—billions of dollars in private resources were available; and lending from the World Bank and the Inter-American Development Bank also increased. West Germany and Japan became important customers and investors in Brazil.

The surge of autonomy was well represented by former foreign minister and then incumbent Brazilian ambassador to the United States, João Augusto de Araújo Castro, in an address to the Brazilian National War College in 1971, when he stated that it was inadmissible that the great powers freeze the international system before Brazil had achieved its rightful place. That theme was echoed by Ambassador Pio Correa, former secretary general of the Foreign Ministry, in 1973:

Driven by an irresistible vocation, Brazil is today launched on the conquest of external markers. Its interests, therefore, not only cross frontiers, but establish roots in foreign lands. We cannot refuse a destiny that, already marked by greatness, imposes responsibilities and tasks of world scope on us.[9]

Brazil refused to sign the 1968 Treaty of Nonproliferation of Nuclear Weapons. In 1967, it had rejected pressure to sign the Tlatelolco Treaty that prohibited nuclear weapons in Latin America. President Médici unilaterally declared Brazil's claim to a 200-mile territorial sea in the early 1970s. Brazil had strongly endorsed the 1969 "Consensus of Viña del Mar," adopted at a meeting of CECLA in May 1969 and presented to the Nixon administration as a Latin American blueprint for economic and social change in the hemisphere. But while visiting Brasília in 1973, Secretary of State William Rogers commented that there were no problems between the two countries.

Brazil's policy in Africa, which had been generally supportive of U.S. goals, shifted with the visit of Foreign Minister Mário Gibson Barbosa to nine black African countries in 1972 and, in 1973, to Kenya. At the United Nations, in early 1974, Brazil moved away from its support of Portugal's position, and with the April 1974 Revolution in Lisbon, the break with the past was complete. Brazil became the first country to recognize the MPLA (Popular Movement for the Liberation of Angola) government in Angola as independent, in clear contrast to Washington's antipathy to that regime.

The oil crisis of 1973–1974 dramatically exposed the trends that had begun in the late 1960s. Postwar U.S. economic hegemony ended with the oil price increases. The resulting global recession dramatically highlighted America's interdependence on economic allies; balance of payment problems and the 1971 devaluation of the dollar (repeated in 1973) made the United States vulnerable. Washington's vulnerability was matched by Brasília. In a moment of crisis, amid a slow but an inexorable drift, Brazil suddenly understood that the United States could be of little help in its dilemma. As Brazil's post-1974 strategy emphasized guaranteed energy sources and markets for export, the United States emerged not as an ally—written or unwritten—but as an antagonist.

In July 1974, the U.S. government notified Brazil that it could not guarantee the processing of nuclear fuel for Brazilian reactors—reactors under construction by Westinghouse, an American firm. What had been a "guarantee" became a "conditional" commitment. The nuclear option ranked high in Brazil's alternative energy sources at that time. During the same year, U.S. countervailing duties were applied to Brazilian exports to the United States.

The Brazilian response was quick. In May 1975, it signed a comprehensive nuclear power agreement with West Germany. An umbrella document, the agreement provided for a large number of commercial contracts between the two countries. Germany received a promise of secure uranium supplies. A heavy components facility was to be built in Brazil with German technology. Nuclebrás, the Brazilian nuclear agency, undertook to construct a pilot fuel-element fabrication plant.[10]

THE GEISEL ADMINISTRATION (1974–1979)

In response to a sudden realization that things were not, from the perspective of Latin America, as they should be with Brazil, the Ford administration attempted to fashion a new policy. Brazil was urged to assume a moderate leadership role within the Group of 77 (developing countries) and the advocates of a New International Economic Order. Brazil's growth prominence in the Third World was belatedly recognized in Washington, though Washington failed to understand Brazil's unwillingness to shift from dependence on the United States to a sheepdog for the nonaligned movement. Efforts to work out bilateral disagreements encountered the flinty demeanor of Brazil's new Foreign Minister, Antônio Azeredo da Silveira, who adhered to the independent foreign policy of his predecessor but gave greater weight to strengthening Brazil's ties with western Europe, particularly with West Germany (where he had served as ambassador).

The capstone of Henry Kissinger's efforts to involve Brazil in his campaign to deal with the New International Economic Order demands of the Third World, and to recreate the unwritten alliance between the two states, was the "special relationship" established during the February 1976 visit of the secretary of state to Brasília. Azeredo da Silveira graciously accepted the consultative mechanism that lay at the heart of the agreement, but he did not change Brazil's foreign policy.

The Carter administration took office in January 1977 with two strikes against the chances of forging a positive relationship with Brazil. Candidate Carter had singled out Brazil during the campaign as a violator of human rights. After the election, Vice President-elect Walter Mondale, in a preinauguration trip to Western Europe, publicly tried to dissuade the West German government from implementing the nuclear agreement with Brazil. After the inauguration in January 1981, a State Department report on worldwide violations of human rights appeared. The report had been prepared by the previous administration, in response to congressional legislation that required the monitoring of human rights in those countries receiving assistance from the United States. While the report was mild compared to those delivered in other countries, the Brazilian government found it unacceptable, and it unilaterally broke the military agreement that had been in effect between the two countries since the end of World War II. For the remainder of the Carter years, relations between Brasília and Washington were correct but cool.

Barely noticed at the opening of the Geisel government in 1974 was an important decision: to turn toward the Western Hemisphere in a general realignment of Brazil's foreign policy. The African card had been played by Gibson Barbosa during the Médici government in 1972 and 1973; it would continue, successfully, and rise again in public prominence after the inauguration of President João Figueiredo in March 1979. While Figueiredo would make Latin American diplomacy the hallmark of his government's foreign policy, Geisel and Silveira undertook the preparatory work. In an effort to build a bridge to the Andean Pact nations, Figueiredo met with the president of Peru at the border. President Geisel undertook a state visit to Mexico in 1978.

The most dramatic initiative of the hemispheric policy was that begun in November 1976, when Brazil proposed a treaty to establish an integrated physical infrastructure for the Amazon Basin. While the early 1970s had seen national integration focus on highways and airports, the mid-1970s, more realistically, looked to regional cooperation. Sixty-three percent of the Amazon Basin is within Brazilian territory. Since the earlier initiatives had not resolved the question of integration, a multilateral effort might prove more successful. Fear of Guyana's becoming a permanent staging base for Cuban troops and material moving to Africa also may have prompted the undertaking. The long-standing antipathy between Caracas and Brasília helped spur the effort to find a common ground of cooperation with Venezuela. The countries bordering the Amazon Basin met in Brasília in March 1977.

After rounds of negotiations, the treaty was signed in Brasília on July 3, 1978, by the eight countries sharing the Amazon Basin. It was ratified by all of the countries and took effect on August 3, 1980. The treaty represented an important effort by Brazil to multilateralize its diplomacy and its economic and resource policies in South America.

FOREIGN POLICY DURING THE TRANSITION TO DEMOCRACY

With the end of the Geisel administration, although it was not recognized at the time, an era was terminated. The economic miracle was running out of steam. The world economy was about to experience the most severe recession since the Great Depression of the 1930s. Regional conflict in Central America and the South Atlantic heralded a new period in inter-American relations. And, at the end of the 1980s, the collapse of the Soviet Union and the international Communist movement would have important implications for Latin America generally and Brazil specifically.

The selection of the head of the National Intelligence Service as President Geisel's successor was a controversial decision. Figueiredo's reputation as intelligence chief had been that of a dour bureaucrat. Surprisingly, he turned into a popular campaigner and easily won the indirect vote in the electoral college in 1978. Figueiredo, like Geisel, represented an effort to blend different schools and loyalties in the army. He had worked closely with the Médici group but had close ties to the Geisel–Castello Branco wing of the armed forces. He was viewed as being hardworking, dedicated, and sympathetic to the Geisel process of *abertura*. While attempting to continue the general lines of the Geisel foreign policy after 1979, the new government would find itself increasingly constrained because of Brazil's precarious economic and financial plight and by the general downturn in the world economy. The opportunities of the 1970s in both diplomacy and trade and in investment quickly evaporated.

The 1980s brought a number of surprises for Brazilian foreign policy. The first was the "lost decade" of the international debt crisis that began in 1982. The second was a continued and deepening emphasis on regional economic integration. The third was the emergence of a new regional diplomacy, accompanied by a dramatic political realignment of Brazil's relations with its neighbors. The fourth important set of policy questions concerned the environment, Brazil's indigenous population, and related social issues.

REGIONAL ECONOMIC INTEGRATION

The dramatic downturn in the world economy in the 1980s created an environment for reconsidering existing economic strategies. The old concept of going it alone was not feasible. In an increasingly competitive world economy, countries were forced to seek partners. For Brazil, the countries of the Southern Cone were an obvious target of opportunity. The rethinking of economic strategy coincided with the restoration of democracy in Argentina (1983) and in Brazil (1985). It is doubtful that much progress would have been possible if one or both states had remained under military rule. The rapprochement that began in the Figueiredo government was welcome but not sufficient to overcome old rivalries and security concerns between Brazil and Argentina.

The two new democratic regimes began to seek similar answers to the economic development problems. Both adopted heterodox economic shock programs—Argentina in 1985 and Brazil in 1986. While both programs ultimately failed, the moves were preceded by months of consultations between economists in both countries. The two presidents, Raúl Alfonsín and José Sarney, developed a close relationship and spoke frequently about a wide range of foreign policy issues.

In what is now viewed as a historic turning point, President Sarney visited Argentina in late July 1986. He and his Argentine counterpart signed a 12-point protocol aimed at creating a regional common market by 1999—the Argentine–Brazilian Program for Integration and Economic Cooperation (PICAB). In December, President Alfonsín traveled to Brasília, and the two chief executives initiated 20 economic agreements and finalized the general strategy that had been discussed in Buenos Aires in July. President Julio María Sanguinetti of Uruguay joined his fellow presidents at the meeting and indicated his country's strong interest in immediately joining in the regional integration program.

Presidents Alfonsín and Sarney, in November 1988, signed the Treaty on Integration and Economic Cooperation, the goal of which was to transform Argentina and Brazil into a customs union by 1999. Both the PICAB and the 1988 Treaty were highly significant. For the first time since independence, more than 150 years ago, the two countries put aside their mutual suspicions and committed themselves to a deepening of their relations—economic and political. The two agreements fostered an immediate increase in bilateral trade. Measures were initiated to facilitate the movement of goods among the four countries. Most important, the PICAB included a program designed to encourage cooperation in the nuclear energy and aeronautics fields which have contributed to a sharp reduction in the tensions between the militaries in the two countries. This may well be the most important contribution of PICAB. With the drop in military suspicion, budgets could be redirected to civilian enterprises; and, given the important institutional role of the armed forces in both nations, military compliance with regional integration goals was essential.

But the integration process faltered in the next few years. Both countries saw their heterodox economic adjustment programs fail. Presidents Alfonsín and Sarney found their popularity quickly disappearing, and they spent most of their time in political skirmishes. While Sarney completed his term of office peacefully in March 1990, Alfonsín was forced to transfer power to his Peronist successor, Carlos Menem, six months early as a result of the economic chaos in Argentina.

A potentially important event took place on June 27, 1990, which spurred a renewal of interest in integration throughout the hemisphere. President George Bush announced the creation of the ''Enterprise for the Americas Initiative.''[11] This was a new and bold effort by the United States to support the movement underway in the region to liberalize the economies, adopt outward-looking economic models, and spur trade and investment. The initiative was generally seen as the most important U.S. proposal since the Alliance for Progress of President John F. Kennedy in 1961—and perhaps since the Good Neighbor Policy of President Franklin D. Roosevelt in the 1930s. Unfortunately, the initiative would soon lose momentum because of the intervention of world events such as the Gulf War and related security issues. Yet another opportunity for a Latin American–U.S. partnership was lost.

In the spirit of the Bush initiative and the recent decision to negotiate a North American free trade arrangement among Mexico, Canada, and the United States (which would become the North American Free Trade Agreement—NAFTA), the newly elected presidents of Argentina and Brazil signed the ''Act of Buenos Aires'' on July 6, 1990, to reignite the economic integration movement. They decided to hasten the integration process and set December 31, 1994, as the new date for the common market to come into effect. This was the founding document for what would become Mercosur. They also decided to proceed to create a free trade zone by the end of 1995—following the setting up of the common market at the end of 1994. In September, nine working groups were formed to clear the way for progressive tariff reductions and to unify policy on matters ranging from weights and measures to farm and transportation.

Events moved quickly thereafter. A meeting in February 1991 in Buenos Aires drafted the Southern Cone Common Market Treaty and reconfirmed the target date of December 31, 1994. The goals were—and are—ambitious. The market will do away with trade barriers among the four countries, establish a common external tariff, create an identical trade policy toward nonmember countries, and coordinate agricultural, industrial, monetary, financial, and transportation policies. In addition, the countries were committed to developing a common position to deal with subsidies, dumping, and other unfair trade practices. A program of gradual reduction of import tariffs was created until most rates reached zero in December 1994.

It also was decided that the same treatment must be given to products from all of the member countries, which applies to all taxes that will be levied. The Treaty of Asunción was signed by the presidents of the four countries in the Paraguayan capital on March 26, 1991, which formally launched the new integration initiative. The small, administrative headquarters of the new organization, South American Common Market (Mercosur), is in Montevideo, Uruguay.

The first summit meeting of the four Mercosur presidents was held in Uruguay in December 1991. Although they were duly proud of the progress made thus far, it was clear that the weakest area of the agreement remained macroeconomic integration. While only 4.2 percent of Brazil's total exports were earmarked for Mercosur partners, the common market represented 14.7 percent of Argentina, 35 percent of Uruguay, and 39.6 percent of Paraguay at the time of the signing of the Treaty of Asunción. However, intraregional trade has grown substantially throughout the decade.

In spite of strong skepticism both within and without Mercosur, the union has prospered (see Table 6.1). It has survived the Mexican peso devaluation in 1994, and it appears to have weathered the Asian currency crises of 1997–1998. Mercosur has seen presidents come and go, and appears to be widely supported in all four countries, both by the general population and the political elite. The agreement has resulted in important physical infrastructure goals and a number of complementarities in trade and investment across the market.

The Free Trade Area of the Americas (FTAA)

A third initiative in regional integration began in late 1994 (the first was Mercosur, and the second was NAFTA) when President Bill Clinton called for a summit of the democratic presidents of the Americas in Miami in December 1994 to establish a plan for hemisphere-wide economic integration. In particular, the Brazilians were reluctant to see Mercosur absorbed by the U.S. plan. In the planning sessions prior to the Miami meeting, Brazil carved out an important role for Mercosur in future negotiations. While this annoyed the American negotiators, it was supported by Brazil's regional allies. The "dream" of Miami— a free trade area throughout the Americas by 2005—was dealt one setback with the Mexican peso devaluation soon after the summit adjourned, creating many

Table 6.1
Intra-Mercosur Trade (1990–1997)

Year	Intra-Mercosur Trade (Millions of U.S.$)
1990	4,127
1991	5,103
1992	7,214
1993	10,027
1994	12,049
1995	14,384
1996	16,770
1997	20,280

Source: "Mercosur 2000: Crecimiento económico y nuevas oportunidades para la inversión," *Centro de Economía Internacional*, Secretariat of International Economic Relations, Government of Argentina, 1998.

months of financial uncertainty. Another drawback was the inability, in succeeding years, for Clinton to gain "fast track" authority from Congress to negotiate comprehensive trade agreements. Fast track, which all recent presidents have been given, allows the executive branch to negotiate an agreement and then ask Congress to vote yes or no—but with no amendments or changes. This allows the president to tell those with whom he is negotiating that the agreement, as signed, will either pass or fail without modification. Generally, Congress has backed the White House on trade arrangements.

But the 1990s were different. Many in Congress did not think that NAFTA was working very well, and the fact that it had been approved under fast track authorization made many members wary of giving Clinton fast track for further trade negotiations. Globalization had made many American workers fearful that their jobs would be exported to low-wage neighbors in South America. The labor unions became strong opponents of fast track, mainly since they thought that the inability to amend the treaty once it had been negotiated would make it virtually impossible for their concerns to be integrated into any final agreement. And the environmental groups wanted special safeguards in any future agreements. The two parties in Congress could not agree on appropriate language, and President Clinton withdrew his request in November 1997.

The participants in the Miami Summit had decided that a second Summit of the Americas would be scheduled for April 1998 in Santiago, Chile. Between Miami and Santiago, the principal negotiations would take place to allow the heads of state in Santiago to initiate the FTAA negotiations with the goal of completing the agreement by 2005. This did not happen, mainly because Clinton did not have fast track. The Miami vision for hemispheric integration also was hindered by the Mercosur countries' call for a slower, more nuanced integration process. This forceful stance by the South American nations rattled Washington, as it became quite evident that the United States was not going to be able to completely dictate the course of integration. Moreover, seeing that the United States might be lagging behind in regard to trade negotiations, the countries of Mercosur have developed a renewed interest in greater economic and social integration with the European Union (EU). In short, a new reality began to take shape in the hemisphere—a division between the North and the South; it was not a hostile separation, but a realistic belief that "North America" was emerging as an important actor, as was South America. The United States would be the dominant player in the North, and it was assumed that Brazil would play that role in the South.

But the United States did not accept this interpretation and clung to the U.S.-led Miami vision. However, during the long and tedious negotiations between Miami and Santiago, Mercosur was able to defend its position. The final co-chairs of the trade negotiations within the FTAA framework will be Brazil and the United States, which means that compromise and give-and-take will be required to arrive at a final agreement. No one country will have a veto or the power to force others to accept unwanted requirements or goals.

Mercosur: Broadening or Deepening?

An important structural issue for Mercosur is when—and whether—it should "broaden" (invite other countries to become members) and/or "deepen" (create supranational institutions that will make common decisions for all of the members). Much has been written about both aspects of the integration process, but it is generally believed that to maintain the credibility of the integration process, progress needs to be made in both areas. Mercosur reached that turning point in the late 1990s.

The broadening issue has received the most attention. A general assumption at the Miami Summit in 1994 was that Chile would quickly become the fourth member of NAFTA. That has not happened, because the U.S. president did not receive authority to negotiate a fast track agreement with the Chilean government. As time went on, the Chileans became more impressed with the option that Mercosur offered. Since the early 1990s, Chilean trade with its Southern Cone neighbors has grown a great deal, and Chilean businessmen have begun to invest throughout the region. In response to these new realities, and in the absence of a NAFTA option, Chile and Mercosur signed an associate member agreement in June 1996. Associate membership means that Chile will participate only in Mercosur's intraregional free trade scheme and not the projects's customs union. The Chileans have less interest in the customs union because it would mean having to drop their own 11 percent across-the-board external tariff and adopt the higher Common External Tariff (CET) of Mercosur.

The second country to sit down with Mercosur and negotiate a similar arrangement was Bolivia. The trade accord Bolivia signed with Mercosur in December 1996 fell short of the full membership status it had originally sought, but it is similar to the status of Chile. The other members of the Andean Pact—Peru, Ecuador, Colombia, and Venezuela—are in different stages of discussions with Mercosur regarding associate member status. The belief is that Mercosur will continue to broaden in the twenty-first century. If indeed we are seeing the reconfiguration of the Americas into a Northern sphere of Canada, the United States, Mexico, and possibly Central America and the Caribbean, then a Southern region would logically fall into place with Mercosur as its driving force.

The question of broadening is related to deepening, in that many observers believe new institutional arrangements are needed very soon for the existing membership of Mercosur and certainly if new full members are contemplated in a few years. Deliberately seeking to avoid the large, cumbersome bureaucracy in Brussels of the EU, the Mercosur members have opted for minimal institutionalization. The Treaty of Asunción provided for three institutional bodies that were to be replaced by January 1, 1995: the Common Market Council and the Common Market Group to oversee the administration and implementation of the process during the so-called transition from November 1991 to December 1994, and the secretariat in Montevideo.

The Protocol of Ouro Preto (Brazil), which was signed in December 1994 and came into full force one year later, implemented a new institutional framework. The protocol retained the original bodies and added three new ones. The Protocol also is important because it gave Mercosur a juridical personality under international law, which allows Mercosur to negotiate agreements with other countries, trade blocs, and international organizations. The three decision-making bodies created at Ouro Preto were the Mercosur Trade Commission, the Joint Parliamentary Commission, and the Socio-Economic Advisory Forum. The Common Market Council, the highest body of authority, is made up of ministers of foreign relations and ministers of economy. The presidency of the council rotates among the chief representatives of the four member countries for a six-month period. The council meets as often as is needed but must meet once every six months. At least once during the six-month period, the presidents of each of the four member countries must attend. In practice, the presidents have been very attentive and rarely miss a meeting. The Common Market Group is a support entity for the council, and it proposes policies for the consideration of the presidents. It also oversees the activities of 11 technical working groups.

The Mercosur Trade Commission, a new creation of Ouro Preto, assists the Common Market Group, particularly in areas that will help the smooth functioning of the customs union. It proposes common trade policies for the members. The Joint Parliamentary Commission is another new creation, the main duty of which is to ensure that decisions issued by Mercosur's institutional bodies are adopted expeditiously by the legislatures in each member state. Members of the legislatures in each country are chosen on a rotating basis for membership in the commission. The Socio-Economic Advisory Forum is another interesting addition, designed to represent the interests and opinions of groups in society that are impacted by the integration process—business and labor are important participants. The forum makes recommendations to the Common Market Group on how to improve shortcomings and strengthen the integration process.

While it is somewhat easier to make decisions regarding broadening, the deepening process is more controversial. To "deepen" means to authorize institutions that function above the control of the nation-state to make binding decisions. Mercosur has been reluctant to do so. The result has been a concentration of decision making in the presidents at their council meetings every six months. It also means that the three smaller members are mindful of the important role Brazil plays in the economics of the customs union, as well as in the diplomacy of Mercosur. In addition, all directives and resolutions must first be ratified by the respective countries. This procedure is time-consuming and prevents the rapid resolution of the many asymmetries that currently exist among the members. Another issue is that policy needs to be reached among the presidents by consensus, and each member has only one vote. In the future, there may be a need for a weighted voting system as well as decision-making bodies that can act independently and whose declarations will have the impact of law in all of the member countries, as happens today in the EU.

Mercosur has proven a timely and exciting development in South America. It has opened, for the first time, possibilities for collective investment in roads, ports, railroads, airports, pipelines, and the sharing of natural resources. Chile's membership means that the markets of Asia are within reach. Physical integration will bring social and, ultimately, some forms of political collaboration and integration. And other world actors, such as the EU, have taken note of the progress of Mercosur and have signed a series of agreements that reaches across the economic and financial, foreign policy, environmental, and social areas. A summit between the political leadership of the EU and Mercosur was held in June 1999 in Brazil.

While the economics of Mercosur are impressive in terms of trade and investment, the common market must be seen as an important step in stabilizing political democracy in the region. As a result of a coup d'état scare in Paraguay in 1996, the presidents quickly passed a resolution stipulating that membership in Mercosur was open only to democratic states. We have mentioned the downgrading of military competition as an important result of Mercosur. And, increasingly, companies are looking at Mercosur as one market, not as "four plus two," four full members and two associate members. There is talk of a Mercosur currency. But these developments will need to be based on a harmonization of economic fundamentals, which has yet to be achieved. And it will require some movement to create institutions for the resolution of disputes, for example. But the progress of Mercosur since the Treaty of Asunción is impressive. For the first time since independence, a successful subregional integration scheme has a strong chance of succeeding. And it has begun to play an important role in changing civil-military relations and guaranteeing democracy in the area. The

January 1999 devaluation of the Brazilian currency, as discussed in Chapter 5, had an immediate, negative impact on trade relations among the members of Mercosur. Brazilian exports became much cheaper after the devaluation. The recession in Brazil in 1999 reduced demand for exports from its neighbors in Mercosur. The expectation is that a return to growth in late 1999 or early 2000 in Brazil will restore the dynamism of the customs union in the Southern Cone.

REGIONAL DIPLOMACY

Another new—and challenging—development has been the emergence of a pattern of consultation and diplomatic cooperation in Latin America. This is a direct result of the restoration of civilian, democratic governments in all of the countries, as well as of the rapidly changing global environment in which the region must adjust quickly to new opportunities and challenges. As noted, the willingness of Brazil to seek deeper ties with its regional neighbors was an important change that accompanied the restoration of civilian government in 1985; as discussed, the creation of Mercosur, and the binds it created with Argentina, Paraguay, Uruguay, Chile, and Bolivia, is the most important.

But Brazil's participation has taken various other forms, signaling a willingness to commit itself to being an important actor in the region. During the 1980s, the government joined its neighbors in seeking a political solution to the devastating debt crisis that had erupted in 1982. Brazil attended a summit meeting of regional presidents in Quito in January 1984 and signed a "Declaration of Quito" and a "Plan of Action" that called for help in easing the burden of the crisis to save democracy and to protect the poor in Latin America. Brazil was present at the formation of the Cartagena Group in that Colombian city in June 1984 (which resulted from the meeting in Quito). President Figueiredo had joined his colleagues from Argentina, Colombia, and Mexico in May 1984 when they issued a joint letter, addressed to the Group of Seven (G-7) leading industrial powers, calling for immediate relief from the debt burden.[12]

The finance and foreign ministers of the Cartagena Group met throughout 1984 and 1985 without reaching agreement on a common debt strategy. The Latin American presidents attempted to enlist the support of the G-7 countries to relieve the region's debt burden, but appeals to the G-7 annual summits were to no avail. When U.S. Secretary of State James Baker announced the "Baker Plan" at the annual meeting of the World Bank and the IMF in Seoul, South Korea, in October 1985, the Cartagena Group welcomed it as a positive step, but an insufficient one to resolve the issue. While the Baker Plan provided little, if any, debt relief, it did begin to depoliticize the debate. Another initiative by Baker in June 1987, which expanded the possibilities for debt relief, further quieted the confrontational approach of the Latin American countries adopted in Quito and Cartagena.

Brazil chose to break ranks on the debt issue in early 1987, when it declared a unilateral moratorium on its debt. That dramatic move was not followed by any of its neighbors, and Brazil became increasingly isolated on the debt issue. The other countries had opted for a policy of negotiation and incremental adjustment. Although the Cartagena Group disappeared within two years of its creation, it had served to bring the Latin American governments together to address a common problem.

Another such initiative in which Brazil was involved in the 1980s was the crisis in Central America. The governments of Colombia, Mexico, Panama, and Venezuela had organized the Contadora Group in January 1983 and drafted a peace proposal for the Central American conflicts. That effort was strenuously opposed by the government of President Reagan. But the Contadora Group persisted in seeking a peaceful solution to the conflicts in El Salvador and Nicaragua. In July 1985, at the inauguration of President Alan García in Lima, Peru, a "support group," composed of Argentina, Brazil, Peru, and Uruguay, was formed to bolster the Contadora process. Brazil and the other members of the support group met in Cartagena in August with the four members of the Contadora Group to discuss common strategy.

As the wars in Central America continued, the support group and the Contadora nations met again in January 1987 and sent a diplomatic mission to Central America. The mission met with the presidents of Costa Rica, Nicaragua, Guatemala, Honduras, and El Salvador, but it was not able to report any progress. At the first summit meeting of the Latin American presidents, held in Acapulco, Mexico, in November 1987, the eight countries of Contadora and the support group issued a communiqué that called for a pacific solution to the Central American crisis. But the Reagan administration remained adamantly opposed to interference in its strategy for the region, which was the elimination of Marxist movements.

Only with the election of President George Bush in November 1988 did U.S. policy change. In the following year, the president and the Democratic Party leadership in Congress agreed to support democratic elections in Nicaragua and to seek a negotiated settlement to the civil war in El Salvador. The first was accomplished with the inauguration of Violeta Chamorro as Nicaraguan president on April 25, 1990, following her defeat of the Sandinista candidate in the campaign. The government of El Salvador and the main guerrilla insurgency group, the Faribundo Martí National Liberation Front (FMLN), agreed to a peace accord in the early 1990s, which finally put an end to that tragic conflict.

While Brazil did not play an important role in the Contadora process, its willingness to participate indicated that the Sarney government did not want to be excluded from an important regional initiative. It was another demonstration that Brazil was now a bona fide member of the Latin American community of nations, and that it was willing to risk the displeasure of the U.S. government on a policy issue of highest importance to Washington.

A third initiative was the evolution in the 1980s of what is now known as the Group of Rio. This initiative originated at a meeting of the Group of Eight—Contadora and the support group of nations—in Rio de Janeiro in December

1986. The foreign ministers drafted a "Permanent Mechanism of Political Consultation and Cooperation" that was to create a permanent forum for the discussion of the entire agenda of multilateral concerns of the countries. At a subsequent meeting of the foreign ministers in August 1987, it was announced that the heads of state would hold a summit meeting in Mexico in November. At the Acapulco summit, the heads of state issued a document entitled "Acapulco Commitment to Peace, Development, and Democracy." That document was the first panoramic statement about international and development issues by the Group of Eight.

With the meeting held in Rio de Janeiro, Brazil assumed the role of secretariat for the Group of Eight. That responsibility gave Brasília a leading role in setting the agenda for future meetings and serving as a catalyst for the group. A second summit meeting was held in Uruguay in October 1988. At that meeting, the Group of Eight numbered seven. Panama was not invited because General Manuel Noriega had overthrown the democratically elected president of that country. At the Uruguay meeting, the presidents decided to designate the group as the Rio Group, which would act as a counterpart to the Paris Club (representing major industrialized creditor nations). The purpose of the Rio Group was to produce a concrete proposal for debt relief for Latin America. The summit dealt with a wide range of issues, including the debt, and the drop in international prices for the region's agricultural and mineral exports. The Rio Group finance ministers met in Rio de Janeiro in December 1988 and called for a presidential summit, with the main industrial countries to seek a cut in the region's debt burden. The Brazilian finance minister acted as spokesman for the group throughout the meeting and was very much in evidence as its coordinator. In response, President-elect George Bush stated that he would undertake a broad review of the debt strategy of the United States in January 1989. U.S. Treasury Secretary Nicholas Brady announced the Brady Plan in March 1989. That was followed by intensive negotiations between Mexico and its creditor banks, which led to a historic agreement for that country in early 1990.

At the next summit meeting—the entity was now called the Group of Rio—in Caracas, Venezuela, in October 1990, the seven presidents (Panama was still excluded) endorsed the Bush Enterprise for the Americas Initiative and called for a revamping of the Organization of American States and the Latin American Integration Association. In December 1990, the Rio Group foreign ministers held a historic meeting in Rome with their EU counterparts. A declaration was negotiated and signed—the "Declaration of Rome"—which aimed to create a more regular series of political contacts and deeper cooperation in trade, economic development, and science and technology.

It is clear that the Rio Group—which now consists of 14 members—is an important landmark in Latin American diplomacy. Brazil has been a consistent supporter of that process and is identified with it symbolically because it carried the name of Rio. The Rio Group holds an annual meeting each year, at which a wide range of multilateral issues is discussed. The meetings often are employed to defuse contentious political issues, as it was made clear at the eleventh meeting, held in Paraguay in August 1997. At that encounter, the presidents of Argentina and Brazil diplomatically resolved a growing dispute over a Latin American seat on the Security Council of the United Nations. There are various proposals under discussion, many of which call for an expansion of the council to include representatives of the Third World; Argentina and Brazil are the two logical candidates from South America. Prior to the Paraguay meeting, government bureaucrats had exchanged pointed statements defending their country's position and candidacy. The two presidents refused to allow the diplomatic dispute to impact on either the Paraguay Summit (1997) or on the broader goal of strengthening Mercosur.

Brazil has been an active participant in other regional initiatives. We have mentioned the "democratic" initiative in Mercosur. At the time of the national elections in Paraguay, in 1998, Brazil publicly reiterated its strong support for a democratic outcome, or the democracy clause would come into play. In the border conflict between Ecuador and Peru, which erupted in 1995, Brazil was one of four "guarantors" of a cease-fire that had originally been negotiated in the early 1940s. Along with Argentina, the United States, and Chile, Brazil actively sought to reinstate the cease-fire when conflict broke out again, and it has sought to find a permanent solution to the Andean border dispute. Brazil has been an active participant in the annual Ibero-American Summits, which bring together the heads of state of the Latin American countries with those of Spain and Portugal. This has been a useful way of reestablishing ties between Europe and the region which, historically, were very strong. The Ibero-American Summits are a useful backdrop to the negotiations underway between Mercosur and the EU over closer ties in a variety of areas, ranging from trade and investment to the environment, drug trafficking, and social questions.

Brazil has assumed an important leadership role in an area that has long been controversial in South America—nuclear weapons. During the Cold War, there was a great deal of diplomatic concern about limiting the spread of the deadly weapons to the Third World. In the early 1960s, Brazil proposed that Latin America be made a nuclear-free zone. In 1961, Brazil formally proposed this in a draft resolution to the UN General Assembly. Following the Cuban missile crisis in 1962, Brazil led a group of five Latin American presidents, which again urged the UN to act. The Assembly approved the concept of a nuclear-free zone in November 1963. A meeting was held in Mexico City in 1965 to draft an agreement. The Treaty for the Prohibition of Nuclear Weapons in Latin America was signed on February 14, 1967, in the Tlatelolco section of Mexico City— hence the agreement is called the "Tlatelolco Treaty." While a majority of the countries in the region moved to ratify the treaty, Argentina and Brazil did not. Argentina had signed but had not ratified the document; Brazil and Chile ratified it, but with the reservation that the treaty would not enter into force for them until all other eligible states had ratified it (that is, Argentina). This issue became an increasing point of contention in the Southern Cone and between the United States and Argentina and Brazil.

During the military dictatorships, there was little room to maneuver, since the armed forces naturally defended their right to develop a nuclear capability, if needed, for strategic defense purposes. Brazil's interest in developing a nuclear capability during the Military Republic was paralleled by the development of a large and competitive arms industry. The Brazilian military created a wide range of weapons and aircraft that was in high demand in the Third World, called "tropical technology." By the end of the military dictatorship, Brazil had become the world's sixth largest arms exporter. In the Sarney government, Brazil rose to the position of the fifth most important exporter of arms. It had more than 40 nations as customers, with sales estimated in 1986 at $1.5 billion.

President Collor de Mello entered office and moved quickly to dampen the military appetite for arms manufacturing and nuclear research. He closed down existing secret facilities and publicly endorsed the nonproliferation regime. In November 1990, Argentina and Brazil formally renounced the manufacture of nuclear weapons. Other agreements followed in the 1990s to reduce the level of tension in the Southern Cone and to bring those countries into compliance with regional and international norms of behavior—the most important have been the dismantling of the Condor 2 ballistic missile project, the ratification of the Tlatelolco Treaty, and the adherence to the Missile Technology Control Regime (MTCR). All of these undertakings have reduced the friction between the United States and Argentina and Brazil, as well as between the two regional leaders.

Brazil has been an active player in the Organization of American States (OAS) in recent years, as well as in the various pre-Mercosur trade agreements negotiated in the 1960s and 1970s. It has agreed to take part in UN peacekeeping missions as part of its growing international responsibilities. The Brazilian government was very active in the negotiations leading to the creation of the World Trade Organization (WTO). All of these initiatives represent part of the response of the Brazilian government, especially the administration of President Cardoso, to meet the new realities of world politics at the end of the century. As discussed in the chapter on the armed forces, Cardoso's new national defense policy has set the parameters for both redefining the role of the military but also of Brazil's foreign relations for the twenty-first century. The Brazilian foreign minister summarized the framework within which Brazil seeks to define its role in world affairs in an address to the Superior War College:

A democratic revolution swept the world, starting in Latin America, and nowadays the huge majority of people live under democratic regimes. . . . An economic revolution took place, based on the exhaustion of the more closed models that prevailed in the 50s through the 70s, and today the vast majority of people live in economic systems based on market freedom. . . . We also had a revolution in the behavior of states, with the growing universalization of the rules of political coexistence in areas such as nonproliferation of weapons of mass destruction and environmental protection. . . . It seems that the path to isolation, autarchy, to options outside the mainstream of international relations is definitely closed. . . . There is a clear and intolerable cost for marginality and xenophobic behavior. . . . Democracy, economic freedom and participation in economic and commercial mechanisms and the universal systems that regulate relations between states became the standards.[13]

THE AMAZON AND THE ENVIRONMENT

The Amazon holds an almost mystical fascination for Brazilians.[14] Although it was not systematically explored or settled until the late twentieth century, it attracted numerous anthropological and botanical study groups from Europe and the United States in the nineteenth century. It also was a favorite on the world tours of European aristocrats and adventurers. The region enjoyed international fame during the short-lived rubber boom prior to World War I, when the rubber barons built the famous opera house in Manaus. President Theodore Roosevelt visited the region in 1912 and was fascinated by the variety of the flora and fauna.

But few Brazilians knew much about the Amazon. It was not until Getúlio Vargas took power in 1930 that the Brazilian armed forces began to think of the Amazon in geopolitical and defense terms. Concerned about the vastness of the territory and its vulnerability, given the relative backwardness of the country, they feared it might easily become prey to its neighbors or to foreign invaders. The events of World War II diverted military thinking from the Amazon, and again it was almost forgotten during the decades following the war.

It was only after the military intervention in 1964 that the Amazon Basin achieved political and economic importance. There were a number of reasons for this. The strategic importance of the region reappeared in military thinking. A military regime that based its right to rule on the dual propositions of national security and national development saw the Amazon through both prisms. The Brazilian state finally had the financial resources to secure the area through emigration and settlement. It also could think about the integration of the region into Brazil—finally. The building of the Transamazon Highway in the 1970s served all of those purposes. There were strong domestic economic interests too. The need for foreign exchange and the expanding international market for food-stuffs led inexorably to the introduction of agro-industry—large, mechanized farms that produced for export. Land was always an attraction in the Amazon, and significant numbers of Brazilian speculators saw the possibility of get-rich-quick schemes; others wanted the land for cultivation. Whatever the motivation, there soon was an escalation of violence, as small landholders or squatters were forced off of the land. Their cause was taken up by the Roman Catholic Church in the 1970s.

The Amazon also served, in the eyes of Brasília planners, as a "safety valve" for the poverty-ridden Northeast. Social and agrarian crises might be amenable to resolution by fostering the movement of large numbers of people into the open spaces of the Amazon. That began a rapid escalation of internal migration that quickly resulted in the introduction of slash-and-burn agriculture. By the late 1970s, there were permanent brush fires in the region, their smoke often rising thousands of feet through much of the year. The rain forest and the woodlands had begun to disappear. The government's road-building program in the 1970s made it possible for more people to move further into the region, thereby introducing greater destruction of the environment.

The Military Republic had ambitious development goals. The Amazon provided important hydroelectric potential. Large dams were constructed, with incalculable damage to the ecological balance of the region, as rivers and lakes were dammed up to produce electricity for the rapidly growing industrial base in the southern part of the country. These projects of the Brazilian miracle were often funded with money from the international banks as well as from the multinational corporations.

With the onset of the political transition in the late 1970s and early 1980s, environmental issues suddenly surfaced in Brazil, and those issues rose to the top of the international agenda as well. Scientists and ecologists were forming impressive alliances that began to lobby for the Brazilian government to stop the destruction of the region, which they argued was an ''international resource.'' The governments of the industrial countries were pressured by scientists and environmental groups, and they began to pressure the Sarney administration to develop a program to protect the environment. At this point, the fate of the remaining Indian tribes in the region converged with the concerns over the ecology, damage to the ozone layer, and the disappearance of the flora and fauna.

As Andrew Hurrell has pointed out, at the point that pressures were building within and outside of Brazil for the government to respond, the Brazilian state was in a weak position to respond.[15] Strong lobbies had developed to represent domestic economic and commercial interests that were active in the Amazon. They were able, for example, to veto the inclusion of land reform in the 1988 Constitution. The military, in the late 1990s, ''rediscovered'' the Amazon. Some officers resented the interference in Brazil's internal affairs by outside groups. Others argued that there was an emerging ''plot'' on the part of the industrial countries to ''occupy'' the Amazon for their own purposes. And still others saw the issue in geopolitical terms—ecological arguments blunted the goals of defense and military strategy.

The Sarney years (1985–1990) were ones of resentment and conflict in Brazil over the Amazon. Sarney lashed out at domestic and international critics of his government's unwillingness—or inability—to prevent further devastation of the Amazon Valley. Finally, unable to resist the growing outcry, on October 12, 1988, the president announced a set of measures that were aimed to check the rapid destruction of the rain forests. In a television speech that came across as defensive, he announced the suspension of the government's subsidies—including tax cuts, loans, and other measures—that had been used to support agricultural expansion in the rain forests. He also announced a complete ban on the export of logs. Cattle raising was to be severely controlled and would be outlawed in the woodlands along the Atlantic Coast. It became known as the "Our Nature" (*Nossa Natureza*) environmental program.

But the measures were seen as insufficient and unlikely to be rigorously enforced. As the debate continued, the murder of an environmentalist and a labor organizer brought new international attention to the Amazon and marked a turning point in the history of Amazonian development. On December 22, 1988, Francisco ("Chico") Mendes Filho was shot to death in his home in Xapurí in the state of Acre. Mendes Filho had been an outspoken opponent of the destruction of the rain forests. He had been the president of the Xapurí rural workers union, an organization of itinerant rubber tappers. In that capacity, he had become a major thorn in the side of the local landowners and commercial interests. He received the United Nations Global 500 ecology prize in 1987 for his pioneering work in the region.

Mendes was an instant celebrity, both in Brazil and in international environment circles. Lively and intense, he communicated a sense of urgency about the need to control the degradation of the forests. He had been instrumental in persuading the Inter-American Development Bank to halt funding for a project to extend a major highway, BR-364, into Acre, and he had helped persuade Brazil to set aside 5 million acres of rain forests as reserves. It was quickly determined that he had been murdered by local landowners, who thought that they could do so with impunity—the law of the frontier.

In late January 1989, three U.S. senators made a highly publicized visit to the Amazon rain forest. They discovered a plan for the construction of a paved road from Acre to Pucallpa in Peru and then over the Andes to Lima. The road was to be financed by Japanese banks. The beneficiaries were to be exporters of nuts, timber, and other products to Japan. Both the World Bank and the Inter-American Development Bank had refused to pay for the Acre-to-Peru road, under a new policy of not helping projects that would damage the rain forest. The three senators urged the Japanese government to pressure the banks to withdraw, and they took their protests to the Japanese Embassy in Washington, D.C., when they returned.

As the level of indignation rose in Brazil over foreign meddling in the internal affairs of the country, the Sarney government received strong support from its neighbors. In March 1989, the Amazon Pact members met and denounced "foreign meddling" on the issue of preserving the rain forest. The pact members gave their full support to the Brazilian position and stated that they "reject any foreign interference over member countries' actions or policies in Amazônia."[16] At almost the same time, Prime Minister Margaret Thatcher, speaking in London at an international conference on the ozone layer, condemned deforestation in the Amazon.

Indicating the close link between military security and the government's resentment over outside interference, one of the ranking military ministers in the Sarney government addressed the governors of northern Brazilian states in March in Manaus. The message from the general was clear: "Brazil refuses to be deterred from the task of incorporating [the Amazon region] into the world economy and exploiting its resources."[17]

To further reinforce Brazil's position, President Sarney rejected an invitation to attend an international environment conference at The Hague in March, on the grounds that Brazil had been singled out for unfair criticism because of its failure to protect the rain forest. The original invitation from President François Mitterand to Sarney had been accepted; the Brazilian president changed his mind after a meeting with the chiefs of the army and the military intelligence service in Brasília. The president said, "We are masters of our destiny and will not permit any interference in our territory."[18]

International pressure escalated in April 1989, when a group of Latin American intellectuals called on Sarney to put an immediate halt to "massive deforestation" and other "acts of barbarism" in the rain forest. In a statement issued in Mexico City, the group accused Brazil of carrying out "a policy of ecocide and ethnocide."[19] The document was signed by 28 of the region's leading novelists, painters, poets, and actors from nine countries. No Brazilians appeared on the list.

Reacting to the growing international outcry, Sarney announced a $100 million, five-year program to zone the 1.9 million-square-mile (almost 5 million-square-kilometer) forest basin for economic and ecological use. Financed in part by the UN Food and Agriculture Organization, the program targeted the "rational sting of economic activities" and "the environmental monitoring of these activities."[20] The Sarney speech was marked by a strongly nationalist tone. The president raised Brazil's centuries' old battle cry: *A Amazônia é nossa* (the Amazon is ours).[21] As Sarney's term was winding down, the following editorial in the *New York Times* stated:

Mr. Sarney's government, due to leave office in six months, presides over an irreparable ecological catastrophe, destroying the richest assemblage of plants and animals created in the planet's history. The Government pleads economic necessity; yet its projects are inherently uneconomic. It ignores alternative approaches that would provide income while preserving the forests. It encourages a desolation that will, unless the next government is wiser, become an enduring monument to the limits of human wisdom.[22]

Collor de Mello and the Environment

The rain forest was one of many issues discussed in the 1989 presidential campaign in Brazil. Fernando Collor de Mello, the ultimate victor in the December balloting, had a reputation of being a nationalist regarding the Amazon. In his first press conference as president-elect, he stated, "I think every one of us, every country, should clean up his own house." He continued, "Brazil can't be put in the defendant's dock as the cause of today's environmental prob-lems."[23] It was pointed out that the president-elect had strong ties to the con-servative landowning elite in the North, which had supported his campaign. The turbulent year of 1989 ended on a positive note for Brazilian environmentalists. A rancher and his son were convicted in the murder of Chico Mendes and both received 19-year sentences.

President Fernando Collor de Mello, following his inauguration on March 15, 1990, announced a series of measures that confounded his critics. He appointed a world-famous environmentalist as the new secretary for the environment; cre-ated a new working group to review environmental zoning in the Amazon; nominated a new research director for the Brazilian Institute for the Environment and Renewable Natural Resources (IBAMA), the principal agency for over-seeing Amazon policy; set up the Research Center for Tropical Forest to study the problem of sustainable development in the Amazon; replaced in the territory of Roraima the governor who had opposed attempts to limit gold miners' en-croachment on Indian lands; established environmental departments in all of the major government ministries; and made the historic decision to impose an ef-fective system of income tax on agricultural land.

These actions by the new president were widely seen as an effort to reimpose Brasília's control over the Amazon, which had been severely weakened in the Sarney years. It also was frank recognition that the image of Brazil had been damaged by the growing international outcry over the destruction of the rain forest. The constant public criticism of government policy by ecologists and scientists had begun to interfere with negotiations over multilateral loans, trade and investment possibilities, and Brazil's role in international relations. Collor's desire to collaborate closely with the industrialized countries, and not with the Third World, which had been the traditional stance of the Foreign Ministry, also motivated this shift.

During 1990, many symbolic steps were taken to demonstrate that the new government was serious. In March, in an effort to protect the last Stone Age tribe—the Yanomami—in the country from devastation, the president ordered the dynamiting of all illegal landing strips built by gold miners in the northern Amazon. By ordering the destruction of the strips, the president hoped to block the miners from returning to the tribe's mineral-rich lands. The mining opera-tions severely damaged the environment, and the miners brought diseases against which the Indians had no natural immunity.

The new government intermittently continued its environmental emphasis dur-ing its first two years in office. It suspended many government subsidies that had encouraged deforestation; imposed more controls on forest burning, includ-ing higher fines; carried out the demarcation of Indian reserves from some tribes; and adopted an activist role in international environmental negotiations in planning for the June 1992 United Nations Conference on Environment and Development, which was held in Brazil.

At the end of 1991, there was firm evidence of a slowdown in the rate of deforestation. The Brazilian government figures showed a drop of 65 percent in the number of fires. The total area deforested in 1990 was 27 percent lower than in 1989. But progress was slow. The government lacked the financial resources to undertake a more vigorous program. The collapse of the Collor Plan left little revenue to be used in the fight to preserve the rain forest. There were sharp differences of opinion within the government over ecological issues. The military continued to oppose selling out the Amazon to foreign interests and to defend Brazil's right to develop—or to not develop—the Amazon. Economic interests continued to fight for special privileges.

A hopeful note was struck in November 1991, when the president overrode mining interests and military protests and reserved a stretch of Amazon rain forest as a homeland for the Yanomami Indians. The new reserve, coupled with a slightly smaller area across the border in Venezuela, was meant to allow the Yanomami to roam freely over 68,331 square miles (almost 178,000 quare kilometers) of Amazon wilderness—an area the size of Portugal. And in December 1991, an ambitious $1.5 billion project to save the rain forest was announced. Called the Amazonian Pilot Project, it will be funded by the G-7, the European Community, and the World Bank. The Brazilian government had submitted the plan to the London economic summit in June 1991, but interest waned with the complicated international agenda the industrial countries confronted. But pressure by Collor de Mello finally resulted in what appeared to be a breakthrough agreement between First and Third World countries to cooperate on a major environmental program.[24]

An important turning point took place in 1992 in Brazil with the convening of the United Nations Conference on Environment and Development in Rio de Janeiro—the "Rio Conference," as it was called. A principal outcome of the conference was "Agenda 21," an action plan for the 1990s and the twenty-first century, which elaborated strategies and integrated program measures to halt and reverse the effects of the environmental degradation and to promote environmentally sound and sustainable development in all countries. The Rio Conference gave the Brazilian government the opportunity to take the spotlight and to appear sympathetic to the environmental concerns after many years of international criticism. Unfortunately, the strong support for the Rio Conference of the Collor de Mello government evaporated shortly after the close of the meeting. By December 1992, the president had resigned from office, and the Franco administration took office.

From 1993 onward, the global implications of Agenda 21 and the general recommendations of the Rio Conference have been dwarfed by the complicated interplay in the Amazon of national economic interests, the sharp increase in concern about the indigenous people, and the continued absence of land reform. None of these issues are easy to resolve, although the public commitment of the Cardoso administration to do so is clear. Whether change can occur remains to be seen in the president's second term of office.

Old Problems, New Governments

It is important to understand that the Amazon is a vast, poorly explored area of South America. But in recent years, its mineral wealth and uninhabited space have attracted adventurers, explorers, and landless peasants. One of the most difficult problems for the government has been the constant invasion of thousands of miners, drawn to the gold discoveries of the mid-1990s. Tragically, many of the gold discoveries were made on land reserved for the Yanomami Indians.

The approximately 20,000 surviving Yanomami, who live along the border of the Brazil-Venezuela frontier, have been heavily impacted by imported diseases and pollution that have crippled their hunting and fishing. Continual efforts by the government to protect the Yanomami have met with fierce opposition. When the government decided, as a result of the Rio Conference, to decree a Yanomami reserve that would encompass a 37,000-mile area, straddling the Amazonas and Roraima states, local politicians and mining groups ignored the decree. And the plight of the Yanomami has dominated international press headlines, embarrassing the government.

Part of the difficulty is that the 1988 Constitution stipulated that all indigenous lands were to be demarcated by October 1993, but that goal has never been met. The government's Indian foundation—Funai—has been relatively helpless in achieving the demarcation objective because of politics. Indigenous people are poorly represented in Congress, and demarcating land in poorer regions is fiercely opposed by local politicians, whose interests in mineral or timber extraction income are worthless if an area is declared Indian land. The military establishment also resists the government's wishes by opposing the ceding of the control of land along Brazil's borders for reasons of security. And even when the land has been demarcated, the areas have been invaded, usually by farmers, wildcat gold miners, or loggers. The presence of the federal government is quite weak in these regions. And local authorities, especially local police, refuse to become involved when invasions are backed by local political leaders.

Another problem on the Brazilian frontier is that of the landless farm laborers who often invade unoccupied or underutilized lands to settle and farm. This issue became increasingly serious in 1995, during President Cardoso's first year in office, when a series of shoot-outs between the police and landless farm laborers resulted in the death of 10 people in the state of Rondônia. It was just the latest of a long succession of rural battles, but it created a public outcry in Brazil and received widespread international press coverage. The violence on Brazil's ''frontier'' has already brought the Roman Catholic Church, acting through its land commission (CPT), into growing conflict with the government, as the CPT attempts to protect and represent the landless peasants.

The land disputes are linked to the country's unequal land ownership. The richest 1 percent of landowners control 44 percent of arable land, while more than half of Brazilian farmers scrape by on less than 3 percent of the land.[25] Among the poor, most families have plots of less than 25 acres, sometimes barely enough to support themselves. The government land reform institute—Incra—like Funai, the Indian institute—is poorly funded and staffed. Both suffer from the strong opposition of local landowners, their supporters among the police and political elite, and the concern of the federal government of alienating political support in Congress for its program of reform.

Throughout the first Cardoso administration, the international repercussions of the violence escalated. The government was confronted with an ongoing series of media reports denouncing the inequality and brutality on the frontier. Reporters wrote about slavery in the Amazon among rural laborers, the deforestation of the Amazon forest due to fires and logging, the brutal murders of poor farmers by local guns-for-hire, and the grinding poverty of millions of Brazilian peasants with no other alternative to survive than occupying unused lands. The movement in favor of the landless has gained new strength in Brazil, and it has captured increased international media attention with the creation of the *Movimento dos Trabalhadores Rurais Sem Terra* (Movement of Landless Rural Workers, or MST). The MST has become a vocal, well-organized protest movement that has gained the support of the Roman Catholic Church, nongovernmental and human rights groups, and an increasing number of average Brazilians, who are now well aware of the injustice on the frontier.

As a result of the pressure, the Cardoso government in 1998 hastily announced that it would set aside 62 million acres of Amazon rain forest for conservation. This would put 10 percent of the Brazilian Amazon under governmental protection. While few doubt the good intentions of the president and his supporters in Brasília, the government confronts a centuries' old tradition of impunity on the frontier, poorly registered titles to land, disdain for the surviving Indian population, and weak central government institutions in the Amazon Valley.

The foreign policy implications of the complicated situation in the Amazon are obvious. The Brazilian government must defend Brazil from foreign criticism. But, increasingly, it is obvious that the inability to address the complex issues of indigenous rights, frontier justice, land reform, land titles, illegal logging and mining activities, and deforestation has created a negative international image for the country. However, the internal realities remain in place. Implacable opposition by local and state interests to any reform stymie the Cardoso government's capacity to make anything other than symbolic gestures. These complex issues—internal and external—remain a high priority for the second administration of Fernando Henrique Cardoso. But, realistically, it is understood in Brasília that at least a generation of change in attitudes and actions will be needed before substantive progress is possible. Meanwhile, the tensions created by international criticism and the internal pressures to do nothing place the federal government in an almost untenable position.

The dilemma of the Amazon demonstrates how the patrimonial order remains resilient. While the government in Brasília issues decrees and reorganizes the bureaucracy, mining and agro-industrial activities continue. The devastation of the rain forest has not been stopped. A coalition of landed and industrial interests, working with the support of the armed forces and elements of the federal bureaucracy, has been able to slow much of the positive work of the Collor de Mello government. Members of Congress, dependent on the support of the patrimonial order to retain their seats, have done little to help the president. The twenty-first century will undoubtedly witness an escalation in the concern of the military and its allies in Brazil to freeze the environmental policy of the government in the Amazon. And the concern of the international environmental lobbies will grow. Opposition within Brazil to protecting the environment will continue and is bound to clash with international pressure, especially if multilateral funding is made available. The international community will want results; the groups opposed to foreign intervention will argue that the new funds are little more than disguised efforts to control Brazil's use of its own resources. Yet, no matter how these dynamics evolve, what is certain is that the Amazon's complex problems will require equally complex—and unique—solutions. As journalist Thomas Friedman pointed out during a visit to a rain forest near the city of Una, saving the environment in the future will require the collaboration of many groups of Brazilian civil society:

The only way to save the rain forest today is with this sort of collaboration: environmentalists who can create jobs, high-tech entrepreneurs ready to use their enormous leverage in today's world to promote the environment, groups like Conservation International that can get corporate sponsors to kick in, and local officials ready to adapt. Without more coalitions like this, the only rain forest your kids will ever see will indeed be the Rainforest Cafe.[26]

CONCLUSION

As we approach the twenty-first century, Brazilian foreign policy has matured. Traditional regional rivalries—military and political—have begun to disappear. Brazil is deeply committed to regional and continental economic integration. The progressive economic reform program of the Cardoso government will provide a strong foundation for Brazil's new role in world affairs, both in interregional relations, such as with the EU, and in multilateral terms, as in the WTO and other international organizations. The weak spot remains the internal social and economic inconsistencies that prevent Brazil from achieving "developed" status. As President Cardoso has said, Brazil is not an underdeveloped country, it is an unjust one. That remains true today and may well characterize Brazil for some years to come. But it is clear that the president and his advisors are aware of the price that is paid by not responding to the international demand, and the growing internal support, for meaningful reforms. During the next century, as the major economic reforms are completed, a space may finally open for the government to begin the long-overlooked issues of land reform and social justice.

NOTES

1. Stanley E. Hilton, "Brazil and the Post-Versailles World: Elite Images and Foreign Policy Strategy, 1919–1929," *Journal of Latin American Studies* 12, no. 2 (November 1980): 351.

2. I am indebted to Stanley E. Hilton's excellent analysis in *Brazil and the Great Powers, 1930–1939: The Politics of Trade Rivalry* (Austin and London: University of Texas Press, 1975).

3. Frank D. McCann, Jr., *The Brazilian-American Alliance, 1937–1945* (Princeton, N.J.: Princeton University Press, 1973), pp. 304–305.

4. Stanley E. Hilton, "The United States, Brazil and the Cold War," *Journal of American History* 68, no. 3 (December 1981): 620.

5. Jânio Quadros, "Brazil's New Foreign Policy," *Foreign Affairs* 40, no. 1 (October 1961): 19.

6. Ibid., p. 26.

7. Albert Fishlow, "Flying Down to Rio: Perspectives on United States–Brazil Relations," *Foreign Affairs* 57, no. 2 (Winter 1978/1979): 394.

8. Ibid.

9. Quoted in Ronald M. Schneider, *Brazil: Foreign Policy of a Future World Power* (Boulder, Colo.: Westview Press, 1976), p. 43.

10. For a discussion on the agreement, see William W. Lowrance, "Nuclear Futures for Sale: To Brazil from West Germany, 1975," *International Security* 1, no. 2 (Fall 1976): 147–166.

11. For two views of the initiative, see Roger B. Porter, "The Enterprise for the Americas Initiative: A New Approach," *Journal of Interamerican Studies and World Affairs* 32, no. 4 (Winter 1990): 1–12; and Sidney Weintraub, "The New U.S. Initiative Toward Latin America," *Journal of Interamerican Studies and World Affairs* 33, no. 1 (Spring 1991).

12. For background on the debt crisis in the 1980s, see Riordan Roett, "The Debt Crisis: Economics and Politics," in John D. Martz, ed., *United States Policy in Latin America: A Quarter Century of Crisis and Challenge, 1961–1986* (Lincoln: University of Nebraska Press, 1988).

13. Eliézer Rizzo de Oliveira, "Brazilian National Defense Policy and Civil-Military Relations in the Government of President Fernando Henrique Cardoso," in Donald E. Schulz, ed., *The Role of the Armed Forces in the Americas: Civil-Military Relations for the 21st Century* (Carlisle Barracks, Pa.: Strategic Studies Institute, 1998), p. 44.

14. Roger D. Stone, *Dreams of Amazônia* (New York: Viking Penguin, 1985), provides a fascinating overview of the history of the Amazon.

15. Andrew Hurrell, "The Politics of Amazonian Deforestation," *Journal of Latin American Studies* 23, pt. 1 (February 1991): 197–215.

16. Mac Margolis, "Amazon Nations Back Brazil on Rain Forest," *Washington Post*, March 9, 1989, p. A32.

17. Ibid.

18. Richard House, "Brazil Declines Invitation to Conference on Ecology: Sarney Fears Amazon Will Be Singled Out," *Washington Post*, March 4, 1989, p. A20.

19. Larry Rohter, "Latin Intellectuals Urge Brazil to Save Amazon Rain Forest," *New York Times*, April 5, 1989, p. A14.

20. James Brooke, "Brazil Announces Plan to Protect the Amazon," *New York Times*, April 7, 1989, p. A5.

21. Ibid.

22. "Forest Murder: Ours and Theirs," *New York Times*, September 20, 1989, p. A26.

23. James Brooke, "Brazil's New Chief Raises Doubts on Amazon," *New York Times*, December 25, 1989, p. A5.

24. Christina Lamb, "Talks Raise Hopes for Amazonian Rainforest Project," *Financial Times*, December 9, 1991, p. 4.

25. Diana Jean Schemo, "The Dispossessed," *New York Times Magazine*, April 20, 1997, p. 42.

26. Thomas L. Friedman, "The Little Rain Forest That Could," *New York Times*, July 28, 1998, p. A19.

Chapter 7

Challenges for the Next Century: The Social Agenda in Brazil

In earlier chapters, we referred to the "social duality" that characterizes Brazil—historically and today. And we argued that the maintenance—deliberate or not—of a large portion of the population in poverty has at least two dimensions. First, it holds back Brazil's economic progress. Brazil severely lacks enough of the educated and competitive workers that a global economy requires. To be sure, it has many university-educated managers, but this is outweighed by countless more poor, unskilled workers and many others who either cannot find work or are part of the invisible, informal economy. What the country lacks is a critical, intermediary group of skilled workers who are able to understand the new world of the Internet, technology, computers, and those developments that are increasingly commonplace in the industrial countries and in those societies making rapid progress in the improvement of living standards.

Second, whether on purpose or not, the political elites, for centuries, have ignored the need to provide minimal standards of education and nutrition for a majority of the population. Brazil is, in President Cardoso's words, not an underdeveloped country—it is an unjust society. Why? A country of conquest, Brazil's Portuguese settlers had little interest in the welfare of the few indigenous peoples they found upon their arrival. More significant, of course, was the long period of slavery and exploitation that characterized the Brazilian economy and society until abolition in 1889—one of the last nation-states to take that step. Following abolition, the poor black population either remained on the estates as poorly paid, marginal wage employees or drifted into the cities where they became a permanent lower class.

The late industrialization process in Brazil meant that skilled workers were not in demand until well after World War II. And the growth of Brazilian industry in the decades after 1945 was accompanied by the emergence of political populism—playing to the incipient urban working class for electoral support. Some benefitted from exaggerated workers' rights, which all too often were quickly undercut by inflation and incompetent fiscal governance. The majority of the marginal urban poor and all of the rural poor were left to fend for themselves.

The challenge for the Cardoso government is to scale back the inflated retirement rights and other perquisites of the few to identify a strategy to include the many. There is no doubt that the reformist government of Cardoso would like to accomplish that goal. Why is it improbable that it will happen in the short term? Because the still influential political elites, long accustomed to the machiavellian rules of the patrimonial society, have neither the social consciousness nor the political interest in reallocating resources to address the issues of poverty and malnutrition in Brazil. Poor people are manipulable people. They are insufficiently housed, educated, or nutritioned to become active members of society. And those who dominate the political elite in Brazil are at times well served and well satisfied with that state of affairs. But the elite is neither stupid nor suicidal; as we have seen, it has allowed sufficient "trickle down" to the poor to avoid social chaos that would severely challenge the patrimonial regime. The urban poor are better off than the rural poor. The industrial working class is better off than the marginal population in the city slums. Indeed, there is a pecking order. The potentially dangerous are targets of populism and, at times, of well-meaning welfarism.

As the World Bank, the Inter-American Development Bank, and other international organizations point out, Brazil ranks scandalously low on the social scale for a country of its size, wealth, and industrial power. It is difficult to find any other reasonable interpretation of this state of affairs than the existence of a cynical, self-satisfied elite that now sees the best bet for its survival in continuing this state of affairs. If the bureaucratic patrimonial state, behind which it has hidden for so many decades, is beginning to crumble—and it is not yet certain that this is so—the elite will retreat to a second line of defense, and that will be the continuation of poverty and marginalization for the majority of Brazilians.

What is the reality for the majority of Brazilians today? For most of Brazil's history as an industrializing country, the most recognizable emblem of poverty has been the *favela*, the urban shanty town inhabited by squatters. With dwellings cobbled together from scraps of wood, leftover bricks, and metal sheeting, the *favela* is a community improvised with the remnants of more fortunate urban dwellers. As such, it is a constant reminder of the gulf between the rich and poor.

In Rio de Janeiro, São Paulo, and other cities, poor people have occupied the space the government gives them or have appropriated the land abandoned by the more affluent, often near garbage dumps and industrial cites. Though many *favelas* have, over time, acquired electricity and potable water, few have adequate sanitation or other public services. They remain painfully impoverished and, with a growing drug culture, increasingly violent.[1]

Sadly, today the *favelas* are no longer home to Brazil's most destitute, as an increasing number of Brazilians could not afford to live even in a *favela*. To the degree that there were improvements in the slums, their original occupants encountered greater difficulty in staying there. Many had to leave because their salaries would not cover the cost of electricity or water—the very conveniences that constituted an "improvement" in their standard of living. Economic growth—during the "economic miracle" and even in the troubled years of the debt crisis—had brought social gains. But they were short-lived or nonexistent for those at the lower end of the social ladder. In recent years, however, the plight of the marginalized poor has begun to improve somewhat as newly found price stability and the Cardoso administration's relatively committed social agenda have finally provided a glimmer of hope.

While the situation of the urban poor is desperate, that of the rural poor is often beyond imagination. While Brazil ranks poorly by international standards on many social indices, within Brazil the Northeast region is even far behind national standards. As we shall see in this chapter, the Northeast is a classic case study of the ability of the political elites to ward off social and political change in their own interests—and of the weakness of the central authorities to counteract the concerted effort, over decades, of the regional leaders to preserve a clientelistic, manipulative political system that has been at the heart of the patrimonial order in the Northeast since early colonization. In this chapter, we look at the social infrastructure of Brazil—with an emphasis on the millions of poor—with an eye toward identifying unfinished business: the social agenda for Brazilian leaders in the next century.

POSTWAR IMPROVEMENTS

Setting aside for the moment the more recent history of Brazil's poor, we find a pattern of steady and substantial improvement in the social conditions in the years following World War II. Consumer technology found its way into Brazilian homes with a vengeance. While only 15.6 of Brazilian households had running water in 1950, by 1988, fully 71 percent were so equipped. Only 26.1 percent of Brazilian homes had refrigerators in 1970, while by 1988 the proportion had grown to 69 percent. By 1988, television sets could be found in 72 percent of Brazilian homes and automobiles in nearly one-third of Brazilian households.[2] Likewise, government programs to improve the education and health of the masses have reached ever-greater numbers in the postwar era, thus the abysmal conditions in which poor Brazilians live must be viewed within the context of several decades of social improvement. As one study summarizes: "The access of the population to essential social services like education, basic

Table 7.1
Human Development Index Ranking for Selected Latin American Countries*

Chile	30
Costa Rica	33
Argentina	36
Uruguay	37
Panama	45
Venezuela	47
Colombia	51
Brazil	**68**
Ecuador	72
Cuba	86

*The Human Development Index was created by the United Nations Development Programme to provide a statistically integrated way to compare levels of human development among countries. A smaller ranking number indicates a higher level of human development.
Source: United Nations Human Development Report 1997.

sanitation and health services has improved significantly in recent decades. Nevertheless, the improvement has not been sufficient to reduce the regional inequalities, and, in absolute numbers, the population lacking assistance is great."[3]

That the absolute numbers of the Brazilian poor remain so great is a testament not only to the tripling of the Brazilian population in the postwar era (from 52 million in 1950 to some 172 million by 2000) but also to the limited capacity and desire of the patrimonial regime to respond adequately to that population growth. The essence of this halfhearted response is made especially plain when Brazil's human development is measured against that of other countries (see Table 7.1).

While the regime has maintained a level of development for the lower classes sufficient to prevent wholesale social upheaval, the economic and technological improvements since World War II have been enjoyed mainly by elites. As Hélio Jaguaribe and his colleagues point out:

Brazilian society is characterized by the major discrepancy between its economic and social indicators. The former, ranking Brazil as the eighth largest economic power in the western world, approximate those of the industrialized countries of Europe while social indicators more closely approximate those of the least developed countries in the African and Asian world. Nearly one-third of Brazilian families live in misery and nearly one-fourth in abject poverty; that is, nearly 65 percent of the population, including those without income, find themselves in the part of the social spectrum which extends from the most absolute misery to a level of severe poverty.[4]

As the *abertura* reached full bloom in 1985, the cry of Brazil's disadvantaged became louder and more articulate. The social inequities still extant with the coming of civilian democratic rule and those aggravated by a political system in transition from authoritarianism to republican government became more visible and undeniable. By the government's own admission, income became ever more concentrated in the hands of the richest Brazilians in the last years of military rule and the early years of the New Republic: "In the 1980s, the considerable reduction in the rate of growth ended up increasing the specter of poverty and an aggravated inflationary process acted to worsen the distributive profile even further."[5] By 1985, the government acknowledged that "the poorest 50 percent of the population received only 13 percent of total income and the richest 10 percent, almost 50 percent of total income."[6]

While this distributive profile certainly reflects the ultimate failure of the military regime's development blueprint, the patrimonial regime under civilian rulers in the late 1980s and 1990s has not done much better. Until recently, the leaders of the New Republic had been unable to make any substantial progress in the social sphere. The debt crisis of the 1980s may be somewhat to blame. However, it also is clear that the elites guiding the patrimonial regime have worked no more energetically in recent years than they did previously to promote a more equitable, efficient distribution of public resources. As a United Nations report pointed out in 1990:

Brazil failed to achieve satisfactory human development despite high incomes, rapid growth and substantial government spending on the social sectors . . . public resources did not reach the poor or improve the basic dimensions of human development. Substantial public subsidies were provided for "private" goods, usually consumed by the better-off sections of society, while "public" goods and services likely to have the widest impact on human welfare were neglected.[7]

Indeed, Brazil has devoted considerable resources to social security (7.8 percent of GDP in 1990) and housing (1.4 percent of GDP), expenditures that almost exclusively benefit employed, urban dwellers. In contrast, the government only spent 0.3 percent of GDP on food and nutrition in 1990—an area of greatest importance to the most destitute.[8]

THE CARDOSO ADMINISTRATION AND SOCIAL POLICY

The election of Fernando Henrique Cardoso in 1994 gave many a new sense of optimism that Brazil would finally begin to seriously address its manifold social problems. Indeed, during his inaugural address to the nation, Cardoso stressed the need to focus on solving the "social debt" that has plagued so many in Brazil for so long. Fortunately, Cardoso's background as a sociologist makes him well qualified—and respected—to carry out this formidable task. In a letter to the United Nations Human Development Report in 1996, Cardoso laid out clearly the obligations facing Brazil today:

Realism obliges us not to ignore efficiency. But for any development to be human, we must go beyond the logic of economics. If growth is an indispensable prerequisite, particularly in poor countries, human development will have to be sustained by values that show how economic gain acquires social meaning . . . constructing a "state that cares for the well-being of citizens" is a necessity. True for developed countries, this is even more true for developing countries, which are far from a welfare state.[9]

To date, Cardoso's greatest contribution to poverty alleviation has been the dramatic reduction in inflation due to the highly successful Real Plan. Since the poor almost always lack access to banks, rampant inflation would cruelly eat away at their already meager purchasing power, as their money was "under the mattress" instead of in a bank earning interest to keep up with inflation. Since 1994, inflation in Brazil has averaged well under double digits, which has finally allowed the poor a fighting chance to survive. This example from a Rio de Janeiro *favela* vividly captures the effect that lower inflation has on the lives of the poor:

From Babylonia, a hillside slum that looks over Rio de Janeiro's beachfront, glass and steel towers glint below like beads on a long necklace. So splendid is this view that "Black Orpheus," a glamorous movie about Rio's famous Carnival, was filmed here. But life on the spot is another matter. Ask Percilia da Silva Pereira, mother of 13 and vice-president of the resident's association. She has plenty of troubles to see to in the slum, from the street crime that sucks in its children to tropical rains that wash away its houses of clapboard and crude brick. For years, she has lived, like many other Brazilians, on the fringe of opulence in plain view and forever out of reach.

In July 1994 when the *real* was launched, Mrs. Pereira was unmoved. Over the years, she had seen many a promise and programme come blowing in from Brasília, only to die away like an Atlantic breeze. Currencies too—five in eight years. Babylonia, like much of Brazil, only grew poorer. And, after all, on the eve of the *real's* arrival, prices had shot up "to the moon." Yet, even then, she recalls, there was something to be said for change. Those few months ago, with the old currency worth 2,800 to the dollar, confusion reigned. "All those zeros!" Mrs. Pereira shakes her head. "Prices went up every day, and no one knew what anything really cost any more. At least I know I can go to the market today and afford the same things as yesterday."

It is thin praise, but for Brazilians, after nearly a decade of boom and bust, roaring prices and (temporary) freezes, stability is a blessing. According to Gustavo Franco, an economist at the Central Bank, "If I were the devil and wanted to invent a tax on the poor, none would be crueller than inflation. Inflation corrodes money, and it is poor people who carry money around." The rest of Brazil—the part that dealt in dollars, gold and high-interest bank accounts—was protected from the devil's levy by the world's most advanced system of indexation.[10]

Yet while lower inflation has been good to the poor, there is still much that needs to be done—especially in health and education—to improve Brazil's still dire social conditions. Indeed, there were about 1 million more poor people in the early 1990s than in 1980. Also, during just the first half of the 1990s, the share of informal workers (who neither pay taxes nor receive most social services) rose from 40 percent to 50 percent.[11]

The question for the Cardoso administration is not whether to raise spending on social services (the government already spends around US$90 billion, or 20 percent of GDP) but rather how to spend the money more effectively. Cardoso's plan is to target services toward the "poorest of the poor" instead of the "nonpoor," who currently receive the lion's share of social spending. *Comunidade Solidária* is a R$4 billion a year government program that is using innovative techniques (e.g., highly decentralized) to cut through the red tape of the bureaucracy and to provide relief to those who most need it.

Yet this path will not be easy. With a disturbingly large budget deficit still yet to be reined in, many in Congress feel that social spending should be cut. Thus Cardoso has before him the formidable task of reducing the budget deficit while increasing the reach and efficacy of Brazil's social services.

HEALTH

Given Brazil's immense wealth, its health indicators are especially shocking. While it boasts the world's tenth largest economy, the general health of Brazilians is similar to those in Africa and the poorer countries of Latin America: 15.4 percent of all children under five years of age are physically stunted, and this number increases to 25 percent in Northeast Brazil; Brazil's infant mortality rate (52 per 1000 births) is greater than Malaysia's (16), Thailand's (27), and Colombia's (37).[12] Life expectancy in Brazil is six years shorter than in Uruguay and Venezuela, and nine years shorter than in Chile. The public health sector provides a good example of how the patrimonial regime has prioritized public spending in the social area:

When Brazil's government only spent 1 percent of GDP on health in 1950, almost all of that expenditure flowed through a preventive-medicine, public-health program. Since that time an individual, curative health sub-system financed through a federal payroll tax has grown up separate from, and independent of, the public-health program of the Ministry of Health and state secretariats of health. Over the past 40 years, the collective-preventive sub-system has lagged increasingly behind the individual-durative sub-system. ... The clear trend has been the progressive marginalization of the Ministry of Health, whose budgetary allocation actually declined in real terms of the period 1965–75 and again in the early 1980s.[13]

In essence, the government has opted to subsidize the private health care system used mostly by middle-class and wealthy Brazilians. This has happened instead

of, rather than in addition to, providing care through public facilities. As William
Paul McGreevey and his colleagues note, "The use of . . . high technology services in private hospitals at public expense diverts health-care resources to a tiny
fraction of the population, instead of serving a potentially larger group with
basic health care."[14]

By most estimates, the prioritization of public funds in this manner flies in
the face of a rational human development program, one in which public resources are used to benefit the largest number of the most needy in the population. As the United Nations Development Programme put it:

In health, preventive programmes—such as immunization, prenatal care and vector-borne
disease control—are estimated to be about five times more cost-effective than curative
programmes in reducing mortality. But [in Brazil] an estimated 78 percent of all public
spending on health goes to largely curative, high-cost hospital care, mainly in urban areas
and especially in the urban South. This is in sharp contrast with the 87 percent of public
health expenditures that Brazil allocated to preventive care in 1949, a share that fell
steadily to 41 percent in 1961 and to a low of 15 percent in 1982 before rising to 22
percent in 1986.[15]

According to McGreevey and others, the administrative structure of the public
health system in Brazil—especially the pricing of medical services—provides
incentives for physicians to devote themselves to providing high-cost services.
Unless and until the government revamps the public health care system in a
way that gives priority to basic health services through a rational pricing and
reimbursement scheme, the fortunate few will continue to enjoy specialized
health care at the expense of basic care for the masses.[16]

EDUCATION

In 1997, net primary enrollment in Brazilian schools (88 percent) was well
behind Mexico (98 percent) and Indonesia (100 percent). Adult illiteracy in
Brazil was 19 percent, while it was 7 percent in Chile, 13 percent in Colombia,
and less than 5 percent in South Korea.[17] It is within this context that a similar
case can be made for the way in which the patrimonial regime has chosen to
allocate resources for the education of Brazilians. Despite relatively high levels
of public investment, returns for Brazil's most needy are dismal. Primary education, which should be at least as strong as any other component of a national
education system, is woefully inadequate (see Table 7.2). As Cláudio de Moura
Castro observed:

Recent evidence suggests that a generation currently receives something in excess of 7.5
years of primary education. However, due to high rates of repetition that eventually arrest
progress through the system, recently educated generations complete only four *grades*
of instruction. Students remain in the primary school system for many years, but progress

Table 7.2
Education Levels, Selected Countries

Country	Pupils Reaching Grade 4 (Percent of Cohort)
Singapore	100
Korea	100
Malaysia	98
Uruguay	97
Chile	96
Indonesia	90
Thailand	85
Mexico	78
Ecuador	74
Colombia	73
Bolivia	59
Brazil	**50**

Source: The World Bank, *Brazil: A Poverty Assessment* (Vol. II, 1995), p. 58.

through the grade sequence at a very slow rate. Only 58 percent of those who complete the first grade go beyond the fourth grade, and only 16 percent of the same group go on to secondary education.[18]

Not surprisingly, the largest growth in enrollments in the Brazilian educational system has been traditionally at the university level. The student movement of the late 1960s and early 1970s helped catalyze the demands of university attendees during a period in which the Brazilian economy was best equipped to invest more in education and helped them gain the financial backing necessary to stimulate Brazilian university education.

But even in less prosperous times, the patrimonial regime has favored university over primary and secondary education, since "those who politically demand education are overwhelmingly members of an educated elite."[19] Indeed, the tragic reality is that the government spends nine times as much on the average university student (US$6,507) than on a student attending public secondary schools.[20] Thus most wealthy Brazilians attend private secondary schools, which then prepares them extremely well for the entrance examinations for the highly prestigious—and highly subsidized—public universities. Those Brazilians of lesser means are relegated to the underfunded public secondary schools, thus they have a much lesser chance of passing the exams. Recently, the Cardoso administration has begun to address this issue, as manifested by a 1996 constitutional amendment that earmarks more money from the education budget for primary and secondary schools.[21] But this is only the first step in a long process, which will be especially rough as the middle and upper classes will fight hard to preserve the subsidies for public universities.

THE NORTHEAST

Nowhere in Brazil is the legacy of disregard of the poor more evident than in the Brazilian Northeast. That region was viewed as a development problem during the Empire and Old Republic. The Northeast, from time immemorial, has been subjected to devastating droughts every decade or so. After one of the severest in 1877–1879, the Imperial government appointed a National Committee of Inquiry. Nothing came of its recommendations. In 1909, an Inspectorate of Works Against the Droughts was created, a predecessor of the infamous National Department of Works Against the Droughts (DNOCS). While the Northeast congressional delegation was successful in funding DNOCS, none of the funds went to alleviating poverty. Monies were spent on roads and irrigation projects for the large landowners and their acolytes. In response to a terrible drought in 1953, the Vargas government created the Bank of the Northeast (BNB) in 1952; it quickly became a marginal think tank with little impact on policy other than to provide short-term credit to big farmers. Other commissions and committees were formed from time to time, without any impact on the poverty of the region.

A breakthrough came during the developmentalist government of Juscelino Kubitschek in the late 1950s. The Roman Catholic Church had begun to develop a special interest in the Northeast. President Kubitschek agreed to appoint a Working Group for the Development of the Northeast (GTDN) in 1956 in response to a set of new suggestions from within the government and from a series of meetings with the Catholic bishops of the region. A drought in 1958 strengthened the resolve of the authorities to deepen their commitment to regional development, and plans were drawn up for the organization of the Superintendency for the Development of the Northeast (SUDENE). Under the leadership of Celso Furtado, a young economist and planner, the agency opened its doors in 1959—despite opposition from the elites in Congress from the Northeast. They feared that the mandate of SUDENE might actually accomplish some of the goals set forth over the decades to alleviate poverty.

SUDENE encountered a number of serious impediments to its success. It ran into the increasingly polarized politics of the pre-1964 military takeover. Among the conservative elites in the Northeast, it was a factor for change, which was not in the interests of the elite. Furtado was branded a leftist, as were his principal collaborators for wanting to upset the existing social and economic order. As the Goulart regime radicalized and finally collapsed in March 1964, SUDENE was gutted, and it became one more bureaucratic vestige of well-meaning Southern interest in the Northeast. Once again, the regional elites had won.

The interest of the military regime in introducing social change into the Northeast was nonexistent. The political elites that supported the government between

1964–1985 were principally from the region; they were the most fervent defenders of the status quo. The military regime increased the power of those elites by creating new states in the North and Northwest; the congressional delegations joined their Northeastern brethren in defending the patrimonial order. The regime's efforts at development in the area were aimed at opening the zone to large-scale foreign investment and export-oriented enterprises. It also was concerned with developing the region for national security purposes—to preclude unoccupied lands from being taken over by neighbors on the continent or by subversives. One response, which failed, was the construction of the Transamazon Highway. The road began in the Northeast, ran north, and then turned westward, north of the Amazon River. A spectacular undertaking for the period, it too was a failure.

The object of opening the Amazon, in part, was to draw off surplus population from the Northeast, which basically occurred, but without adequate infrastructure in the area, many destitute Northeasterners migrated only to find themselves "slash-and-burn" itinerants on the new Brazilian frontier. And they were soon joined by tens of thousands of farmers and peasants from the states in the South, also driven from small plots of land by the growth of agro-industry. Coming together, these groups of disposed and landless constituted the raw material for the emergence of the MST in the 1980s and the rapid escalation of violence in the North and Northwest in the 1990s.

In 1998, the Northeast was again hit by a serious drought. And, again, the response of the local and national authorities was handouts and temporary palliatives. Today, about 25 percent of the national population live in the area, but it produces only 10 percent of the country's GNP. It is estimated that every seventh adult is unemployed, although given hidden unemployment, that figure is probably closer to one-fifth. More than one-third of the population live on an income of less than one dollar a day.[22]

Earlier in the chapter, we looked at social data for Brazil, which is poor by international standards. The numbers for the Northeast are worse. At 50 deaths per 1,000 newborns for all Brazil, the infant mortality rate is frightening (the equivalent figure in Central Europe is five), and at 87 deaths per 100,000 births in the Northeast, the death rate at childbirth is still nine times the level established by the World Health Organization (WHO) as a desirable limit. One factor is that 36 percent of the population still lack sanitary drinking water, and only 28 percent are connected to a sewer system.[23]

Many of the children in the Northeast must work and, therefore, a large number must attend school at night or drop out early. Only 40 percent of students in the last year of secondary school were able to correctly solve simple math problems, only 28 percent were capable of extracting concrete information from texts, and only 1 percent had mastered the basics of Portuguese grammar. Table 7.3 summarizes the social degradation that characterizes the Northeast in relation to the other regions of Brazil.

Who is responsible for this appalling poverty and backwardness? Certainly

Table 7.3
A Statistical Profile of Brazil's Regions

	NE	SE	S	N	CW	Brazil
Area (%)	18.3	11	7	45	19	100
Population (%, 1991)	29	42	15	7	6	100
Life Expectancy (1990)	64	65	69	67	68	66
Infant Mortality (per 1,000 live births)	88	30	27	53	33	50
Literacy (% of persons over age 7, 1990)	62	88	90	75	84	80
Poverty Index (% of economically active population, 1990 making less than twice minimum wage)	84	63	68	68	68	71

NE = Northeast (Maranhão, Piauí, Ceará, Rio Grande do Norte, Paraíba, Pernambuco, Alagoas, Sergipe, Bahia); SE = Southeast (Minas Gerais, Espírito Santo, Rio de Janeiro, São Paulo); S = South (Paraná, Santa Catarina, Rio Grande do Sul); N = North (Rondônia, Acre, Amazonas, Roraima, Pará, Amapá, Tocantins); CW = Center-West (Mato Grosso do Sul, Mato Grosso, Goiás, Distrito Federal).
Source: Anuário estatístico do Brasil, 1995 (Rio de Janeiro: IBGE, 1996).

not the poor themselves. Successive national governments, civilian and military, have for decades been unable or unwilling to confront the local political elites and force them to support social development programs of even a minimal nature. In part, it represents a long tradition in the Northeast of neglect and even contempt for the poor, who often are black or of color. It also signifies the indifference of generations of self-perpetuating oligarchs of the patrimonial order that can ignore the poor with impunity. If malnutrition and ignorance are insufficient to hold down the population, violence is a real option that is used with increasing frequency.

The numbers speak for themselves. Centuries of neglect and decades of marginalization have produced one of the most intractable social problems in Brazil—the Northeast. This is compounded by the mendacity of local elites, the self-serving actions of congressional delegations from the region, and the appalling ineptitude of the central government in finding ways to deal with the stalemate in the region.

And it is in the Northeast that the conservative segment of the Cardoso government—the PFL—is strongest. While strongly in favor of market-oriented economic reform, the party has been notable in its unwillingness to support progressive reform programs for the region. It is easier to "vote" the people at election time, winning them over with handouts, free food, and small amounts of money. The dependency syndrome is now generations old and difficult to break without a massive effort by both the central and regional authorities. To say that the Northeast is one of the critical challenges of the Cardoso government is to strongly understate the case.

CONCLUSION

As we have seen throughout this book, the entrenched interests of the patrimonial regime do not yield easily, if ever, to major political and economic change. As the current discussion confirms, the axiom can be extended to the social sphere as well. The question for the next century is whether the patrimonial order currently values a civilian democratic government sufficiently to sustain the social change necessary to preserve it. For nothing less than the integrity of the patrimonial order is at stake as we consider the social agenda— the persistent need for a more equitable distribution of income and better social services for the lower classes—for the next several decades. Despite years of economic growth and industrialization, by the late 1990s Brazil still faces continued and growing challenges to its social cohesiveness and stability. As Hélio Jaguaribe and his colleagues note:

In Brazil there exists an unviable dichotomy between the minority of the population— which operates a modern industrial society and lives well within it, with a productive, technological and administrative capacity equal to or superior to many European countries—and the majority, urban as well as rural dwellers, which drifts along in miserable and extremely poor conditions, at the margin of the benefits of the industrial society. This dichotomy is incompatible with the preservation of a stable democracy.[24]

Clearly, during the next century the patrimonial order will have to reckon with a scandalously inefficient and inequitable social sector. Without greater attention to the basic needs of Brazil's poor, the fabric of democracy in the New Republic faces formidable challenges to its integrity. It is still too soon to measure the extent to which Fernando Henrique Cardoso has been able to break up the patrimonial system in order to better the lives of the marginalized sectors of society. The task is obviously quite difficult, but the fact that Cardoso is attempting to address this issue is something Brazil has never before seen. And, indeed, his success or failure could help determine the course of the Brazilian political and social system well into the next century.

NOTES

1. See Eugene Robinson, "Rio's Carnival of Carnage," *Washington Post*, October 27, 1991, p. F1.

2. See Ronald Schneider, *Order and Progress: A Political History of Brazil* (Boulder, Colo.: Westview Press, 1991), p. 372.

3. Phillip Musgrove, ed., *Economic Crisis and Health: The Experience of Five Latin American Countries in the 1980s* (Washington, D.C.: Pan American Health Organization, 1989), ch. 7, p. 7.

4. Hélio Jaguaribe, Wanderley Guilherme dos Santos, Marcelo de Paiva Abreu, Winston Fritsch, and Fernando Bastos de Avila, *Brasil, 2000: Para um novo pacto social* (Rio de Janeiro: Paz e Terra, 1986), p. 187.

5. Fernando Collor de Mello, *Brazil: Um projeto de reconstrução nacional* (Brasília: Secretaria de Imprensa da Presidencia da República, 1991), p. 79.

6. Musgrove, *Economic Crisis and Health*, ch. 7, p. 7.

7. See United Nations Development Programme, *Human Development Report 1990* (New York: Oxford University Press, 1990), pp. 56–57.

8. See the World Bank, *Brazil: A Poverty Assessment* (Vol. II, June 27, 1995), p. 62.

9. See United Nations Development Programme, *Human Development Report 1990* (New York: Oxford University Press, 1990), p. 44.

10. *The Economist*, October 1, 1994, p. 51.

11. World Bank, *Brazil: A Poverty Assessment* (Vol. II), p. xii.

12. See United Nations Development Programme, *Human Development Report 1997* (New York: Oxford University Press, 1997).

13. William Paul McGreevey, Sérgio Piola, and Solon Magalhães Vianna, "Health and Health Care Since the 1940s," in Edmar L. Bacha and Herbert S. Klein, eds., *Social Change in Brazil 1945–1985: The Incomplete Transition* (Albuquerque: University of New Mexico Press, 1989), p. 313.

14. Ibid., p. 334.

15. United Nations Development Programme, *Human Development Report 1990*, p. 58.

16. McGreevey et al., "Health and Health Care," p. 335.

17. World Bank, *Brazil: A Poverty Assessment* (Vol. II) p. 19.

18. Cláudio de Moura Castro, "What Is Happening in Brazilian Education?", in Edmar L. Bacha and Herbert S. Klein, eds., *Social Change in Brazil, 1945–1985: The Incomplete Transition* (Albuquerque: University of New Mexico Press, 1989), p. 267.

19. Ibid., p. 268.

20. *Brazil: A Poverty Assessment* (Vol. II), p. 70.

21. See Amaury de Souza, "Redressing Inequalities: Brazil's Social Agenda at Century's End," in Riordan Roett and Susan Kaufman Purcell, eds., *Brazil Under Cardoso* (Boulder, Colo.: Lynne Rienner, 1997), p. 76.

22. "Progress in Brazil's Poorhouse," *Swiss Review of Foreign Affairs*, April 1, 1997.

23. Ibid.

24. Jaguaribe et al., *Brasil, 2000*, p. 187.

Appendix A

Facts on Brazil

Land and People

Land Area	3,286,470 square miles
Population	170 million
Population Density	52 persons/square mile
Ethnic Groups	white (55%), mixed black and white (38%), black (7%)

Economy

Gross Domestic Product	US$1.022 trillion (1996 est.)
Per Capita GDP	US$6,300
Inflation	6.9 percent (1997)

Health and Education

Life Expectancy	59.4 years (male), 69.6 years (female)
Infant Mortality	50/1,000 live births
Physicians	1/681 persons
Literacy	83 percent

Brazilian States by Region

North	Acre, Amazonas, Pará, Rondônia, Roraima, Amapá, Tocantins
Northeast	Maranhão, Piauí, Ceará, Rio Grande do Norte, Paraíba, Pernambuco, Alagoas, Sergipe, Bahia
Southeast	Minas Gerais, Espírito Santo, Rio de Janeiro, São Paulo
South	Paraná, Santa Catarina, Rio Grande do Sul
Center-West	Mato Grosso, Mato Grosso do Sul, Goiás, Federal District

Principal Political Parties of Brazil and Composition of the Federal Congress at Century's End

Congressional Representation by Party after the October 4, 1998 Election	Chamber of Deputies	Senate
PC do B Communist Party of Brazil (Partido Comunista do Brasil, also PCB)	7	—
PDT Democratic Labor Party (Partido Democrático Trabalhista)	23	3
PFL Liberal Front Party (Partido da Frente Liberal)	111	20
PL Liberal Party (Partido Liberal)	9	—
PMDB Party of the Brazilian Democratic Movement (Partido do Movimento Democrático Brasileiro)	102	25
PMN Party of National Mobilization (Partido da Mobilização Nacional)	1	—
PPB Brazilian Progressive Party (Partido Progressista Brasileiro)	49	3
PPS Popular Socialist Party (Partido Popular Socialista)	6	1
PSB Brazilian Socialist Party (Partido Socialista Brasileiro)	14	3
PSD Social Democratic Party (Partido Social-Democrata)	1	—
PSDB Brazilian Social Democratic Party (Partido da Social Democracia Brasileira)	102	16
PSL Social Liberal Party (Partido Social Liberal)	1	—
PST Social Labor Party (Partido Social Trabalhista)	5	—
PT Workers Party (Partido dos Trabalhadores)	60	7
PTB Brazilian Labor Party (Partido Trabalhista Brasileiro)	21	1

Congressional Representation by Party after the October 4, 1998 Election	Chamber of Deputies	Senate
PV Green Party (Partido Verde)	1	—
Other congressional representatives (non-registered or independent)	—	2
Total	***513***	***81***

Note: In addition to the above-mentioned parties, Brazil has several dozen other parties, all of which are small. Further complicating the political scenario, many of the parties are continuously evolving, often times changing names or joining other parties, while some disappear and new ones appear.

Source: Official databases of the Brazilian Federal Chamber of Deputies and the Federal Senate.

Selected Bibliography

Baer, Werner. *The Brazilian Economy: Growth and Development*. 5th ed. Westport, Conn.: Praeger, 1999.

Eakin, Marshall C. *Brazil: The Once and Future Country*. New York: St. Martin's Press, 1997.

Hecht, Tobias. *At Home in the Street: Street Children of Northeast Brazil*. Cambridge: Cambridge University Press, 1998.

Jaguaribe, Hélio, Nelson do Valle e Silva, Marcelo de Paiva Abreu, Fernando Bastos de Ávila, and Winston Fritsch. *Brasil: Reforma ou caos*. 5th ed. Rio de Janeiro: Editora Paz e Terra, 1990.

Lamounier, Bolivar. "Brazil: Inequality Against Democracy." In Larry Diamond, Juan J. Linz, and Seymour Martin Lipset, eds., *Democracy in Developing Countries*. Vol. 4. Boulder, Colo.: Lynne Rienner, 1989.

Levine, Robert M. *Father of the Poor? Vargas and His Era*. Cambridge: Cambridge University Press, 1998.

Mainwaring, Scott. "Brazil: Weak Parties, Feckless Democracy." In Scott Mainwaring and Timothy R. Scully, eds., *Building Democratic Institutions: Political Party Systems in Latin America*. Stanford, Calif.: Stanford University Press, 1995.

Marx, Anthony W. *Making Race and Nation: A Comparison of the United States, South Africa, and Brazil*. Cambridge: Cambridge University Press, 1998.

Maybury-Lewis, Biorn. *The Politics of the Possible: The Brazilian Rural Workers Trade Union Movement, 1964–1985*. Philadelphia: Temple University Press, 1994.

Page, Joseph A. *The Brazilians*. Reading, Mass.: Addison-Wesley, 1995.

Schneider, Ronald M. *Brazil: Culture and Politics in a New Industrial Powerhouse*. Boulder, Colo.: Westview Press, 1996.

Skidmore, Thomas E. *The Politics of Military Rule in Brazil, 1964–85*. New York: Oxford University Press, 1988.

Souza, Amaury de. "Redressing Inequalities: Brazil's Social Agenda at Century's End."

In Riordan Roett and Susan Kaufman Purcell, eds., *Brazil Under Cardoso*. Boulder, Colo.: Lynne Rienner, 1997.

Von Mettenheim, Kurt. *The Brazilian Voter: Mass Politics in Democratic Transition, 1974–1986*. Pittsburgh: University of Pittsburgh Press, 1995.

Index

About the Author

RIORDAN ROETT is the Sarita and Don Johnston Professor and Director of the Western Hemisphere Program at the Paul H. Nitze School of Advanced International Studies at The Johns Hopkins University. He has authored or edited numerous works on Brazil's political development, including *The Politics of Foreign Aid in the Brazilian Northeast, Brazil in the Seventies*, and four previous editions of *Brazil: Politics in a Patrimonial Society* (Praeger).

ISBN 0-275-95899-X

90000>

HARDCOVER BAR CODE